Hebel, Joy, and the Fear of God

Hebel, Joy, and the Fear of God

Qoheleth's Design and Message

RYAN BALL

◆PICKWICK *Publications* · Eugene, Oregon

HEBEL, JOY, AND THE FEAR OF GOD
Qoheleth's Design and Message

Copyright © 2025 Ryan Ball. All rights reserved. Except for brief quotations in critical publications or reviews, no part of this book may be reproduced in any manner without prior written permission from the publisher. Write: Permissions, Wipf and Stock Publishers, 199 W. 8th Ave., Suite 3, Eugene, OR 97401.

Pickwick Publications
An Imprint of Wipf and Stock Publishers
199 W. 8th Ave., Suite 3
Eugene, OR 97401

www.wipfandstock.com

PAPERBACK ISBN: 979-8-3852-2815-7
HARDCOVER ISBN: 979-8-3852-2816-4
EBOOK ISBN: 979-8-3852-2817-1

Cataloguing-in-Publication data:

Names: Ball, Ryan, author.

Title: *Hebel*, joy, and the fear of God : Qoheleth's design and message / Ryan Ball.

Description: Eugene, OR: Pickwick Publications, 2025. | Includes bibliographical references and index.

Identifiers: ISBN 979-8-3852-2815-7 (paperback). | ISBN 979-8-3852-2816-4 (hardcover). | ISBN 979-8-3852-2817-1 (ebook).

Subjects: LCSH: Bible. Ecclesiastes—Criticism, interpretation, etc.

Classification: BS1475.52 B15 2025. | BS1475.52 (epub).

04/07/25

Scripture quotations are from the ESV® Bible (The Holy Bible, English Standard Version®), © 2001 by Crossway, a publishing ministry of Good News Publishers. Used by permission. All rights reserved. The ESV text may not be quoted in any publication made available to the public by a Creative Commons license. The ESV may not be translated in whole or in part into any other language.

Contents

Figures vii

Acknowledgments ix

Abbreviations xi

Introduction xv

1 The State of Scholarship 1

2 The Context of Qoheleth 25

3 The Design of Qoheleth 73

4 The Message of Qoheleth 118

Conclusion 167

Bibliography 171

Author Index 181

Scripture Index 185

Figures

2.1 The Prologue of Proverbs and the Epilogue of Ecclesiastes   35
2.2 Wealth and Poverty in Proverbs   42
2.3 Proverbs 22:17–18 and Amenemope   64

Acknowledgments

THIS BOOK IS A slightly revised version of my PhD dissertation presented to Wycliffe College and the University of Toronto in 2022.

I would like to thank my supervisor Christopher Seitz and the other members of my doctoral committee, J. Glen Taylor and Brian Irwin, along with the rest of the examination committee, Robert D. Holmstedt and Mark J. Boda.

I would also like to thank my wife, Sarah, for her ongoing support, encouragement, and belief in me, as well as my three children, Zoe, Linden, and Braelyn—you bring so much joy to my life.

Abbreviations

AB	Anchor Bible
AEL	Miriam Lichtheim, *Ancient Egyptian Literature*. 3 vols. 2nd ed. Berkeley: University of California Press, 2006
AIL	Ancient Israel and Its Literature
AMP	Amplified Bible
AnBib	Analecta Biblica
ANE	ancient Near East
ApOTC	Apollos Old Testament Commentary
ASV	American Standard Version
AUSS	*Andrews University Seminary Studies*
BBC	Blackwell Bible Commentaries
BCOTWP	Baker Commentary on the Old Testament Wisdom and Psalms
BDAG	Walter Bauer, *A Greek-English Lexicon of the New Testament and Other Early Christian Literature*. 3rd ed. Revised and edited by Frederick W. Danker. Chicago: University of Chicago Press, 2000
BHQ	*Biblia Hebraica Quinta*. Stuttgart: Deutsche Bibelgesellschaft, 2004–
BHS	Karl Elliger and Wilhelm Rudolph, eds. *Biblia Hebraica Stuttgartensia*. Stuttgart: Deutsche Bibelgesellschaft, 2006

Bib	*Biblica*
BibSem	Bible Seminar
BKAT	Biblischer Kommentar, Altes Testament
BTB	*Biblical Theology Bulletin*
BWL	W. G. Lambert, *Babylonian Wisdom Literature*. 1960. Reprint, Winona Lake, IN: Eisenbrauns, 1996
BZAW	Beihefte zur Zeitschrift für die alttestamentliche Wissenschaft
CBQ	*Catholic Biblical Quarterly*
CBR	*Currents in Biblical Research*
CEB	Common English Bible
ConcC	Concordia Commentary
COS	William W. Hallo, ed., *The Context of Scripture*. 4 vols. Leiden: Brill, 1997–2017
CSB	Christian Standard Bible
ERT	*Evangelical Review of Theology*
ESV	English Standard Version
GKC	Wilhelm Gesenius, *Gesenius' Hebrew Grammar*. Edited by E. Kautzsch and A. E. Cowley. 1910. Reprint, Oxford: Clarendon, 1966
HALOT	Ludwig Koehler, Walter Baumgartner, and Johann Jakob Stamm, eds., *The Hebrew and Aramaic Lexicon of the Old Testament*. Translated and edited under the supervision of M. E. J. Richardson. 5 vols. Leiden: Brill, 1994–2000
HCOT	Historical Commentary on the Old Testament
HS	*Hebrew Studies*
HTR	*Harvard Theological Review*
HUCA	*Hebrew Union College Annual*
IBHS	Bruce K. Waltke and M. O'Connor, *An Introduction to Biblical Hebrew Syntax*. Winona Lake, IN: Eisenbrauns, 1990
ITQ	*Irish Theological Quaterly*
JBL	*Journal of Biblical Literature*

JHebS	*Journal of Hebrew Scriptures*
JSJSup	Journal for the Study of Judaism Supplement Series
JSOT	*Journal for the Study of the Old Testament*
JSOTSup	Journal for the Study of the Old Testament Supplements
JTISup	Journal for Theological Interpretation Supplements
LHBOTS	The Library of Hebrew Bible/Old Testament Studies
LXX	Septuagint
OT	Old Testament
OTL	Old Testament Library
MT	Masoretic Text
NASB	New American Standard Bible
NCBC	New Century Bible Commentary
NET	New English Translation
NIBCOT	New International Bible Commentary on the Old Testament
NICOT	New International Commentary on the Old Testament
NIV	New International Version
NIVAC	NIV Application Commentary
NJPS	New Jewish Publication Society
NKJV	New King James Version
NLT	New Living Translation
NRSV	New Revised Standard Version
NSBT	New Studies in Biblical Theology
RTR	*Reformed Theological Review*
SBL	Society of Biblical Literature
SBLDS	Society of Biblical Literature Dissertation Series
SBT	Studies in Biblical Theology
SJT	*Scottish Journal of Theology*
SOTSMS	Society for Old Testament Studies Monograph Series
Syr.	Syriac

TDOT	G. Johannes Botterweck, Helmer Ringgren, and Heinz-Josef Fabry, eds., *Theological Dictionary of the Old Testament*. Translated by John T. Willis et al. 17 vols. Grand Rapids: Eerdmans, 1974–2021
THOTC	Two Horizons Old Testament Commentary
TOTC	Tyndale Old Testament Commentaries
TLOT	Ernst Jenni and Claus Westermann, eds., *Theological Lexicon of the Old Testament*. Translated by Mark E. Biddle. 3 vols. Peabody, MA: Hendrickson, 1997
TynBul	Tyndale Bulletin
VT	Vetus Testamentum
VTSup	Vetus Testamentum Supplements
Vulg.	Vulgate
WBC	Word Biblical Commentary
ZTK	*Zeitschrift für Theologie und Kirche*

Introduction

When it comes to the book of Ecclesiastes, matters as central as Qoheleth's basic message elude scholarly consensus with interpretations ranging from skeptical and pessimistic to pious and orthodox with seemingly everything in between.[1] Within this disparity, most scholars identify Qoheleth's message in some way with one or more of the key motifs found in Qoheleth's address; namely, *hebel*, joy, and the fear of God. Some scholars elevate one theme over the rest, while others seek to hold them together in various complementary or contradictory ways. It is within this lack of consensus surrounding Qoheleth's message that this work seeks to make a contribution. This book argues that the narrative of Qoheleth's address progresses to a conclusion in 11:7–12:7, in which Qoheleth brings together the primary motifs, makes clear their interrelation, and conveys his central message. And while *hebel* describes the findings of his failed quest and becomes the context from which he instructs and commends joy, Qoheleth ultimately upholds an orthodox position as he presents the fear of God as the foundation for wisdom.

While the majority of this project consists of a close reading of the text in conversation with the most significant secondary literature, behind it stands a canonical approach.[2] This means, first, that this study

---

1. This book uses "Ecclesiastes" to refer to the canonical book and "Qoheleth" to refer to the book's primary speaker, differentiated from the narrator. Further, all Scripture quotations are from the ESV unless otherwise stated; however, in place of the traditional translation of "vanity," this book will transliterate הבל as *hebel*, and in place of "Preacher," קהלת will be transliterated as Qoheleth.

2. Soulen and Soulen, *Handbook of Biblical Criticism*, 33–34. Note especially the close association of this approach with the work of Childs; see Childs, *Introduction to the Old Testament as Scripture*; and Childs, *Biblical Theology of the Old and New Testaments*.

will examine the book of Ecclesiastes in its final form as found in the MT. Thus, holding to the text's literary unity, Qoheleth's address is received in the context of a narrative frame. Second, this approach seeks a theological interpretation of Qoheleth's message within its more immediate and larger canonical context. Accordingly, particular attention will be given to the book's connections with Proverbs as well as other parts of the OT, such as the Law. This project will also make use of the insights from various other methods, such as narrative and literary criticism.

Chapter 1 addresses the state of scholarship. This will illustrate how most scholars identify Qoheleth's central message with one or more of his three primary motifs and understand that message largely through a reading of their interrelation.

Chapter 2 examines the context of Qoheleth on three levels: first, Qoheleth's address within the book of Ecclesiastes; second, Qoheleth/Ecclesiastes within Israel's wisdom tradition, particularly in relation to Proverbs; and third, Israel's wisdom books within the OT. And as it concerns the foundation of Israel's wisdom, this chapter will also speak on the relation of Israel's wisdom with that of the ANE as well as with the theme of creation.

Chapter 3 considers the design of Qoheleth and argues for reading it as a narrative, one that progresses to and culminates in Qoheleth's final section such that it can be read as a conclusion. Additionally, this chapter will consider Qoheleth's most prominent motifs and the role they play within this narrative arc.

Chapter 4 examines the message of Qoheleth by taking a detailed look at the conclusion of his address found in 11:7—12:7, in which he brings together the primary motifs and makes clear his understanding of their interrelation. This final chapter will also consider the narrator's evaluation of Qoheleth and his message and compare their respective conclusions.

1

The State of Scholarship

1.1 INTRODUCTION

THE SHEER BREADTH OF interpretations is a noteworthy fact of Ecclesiastes research in the modern period. The degree to which scholars arrive at opposite conclusions as to the basic message of Qoheleth's address is striking. This chapter briefly outlines the state of contemporary scholarship on the message of Qoheleth.[1] In sketching the landscape, this chapter illustrates how most scholars identify one or more of Qoheleth's key motifs as comprising his core message. Not only does this process reveal which motif(s) scholars take to be the most important but it also reveals their various understandings of the interrelation of the primary motifs.

In order to organize the many interpretive positions, this chapter utilizes three primary and broad categories based on the elevation of different key motifs and, in general, the identification of the particular motif with Qoheleth's primary message. The first category comprises those who elevate the *hebel* motif; the second, those who elevate the joy motif; and the third, those who elevate the fear of God motif. A fourth category will note the most prominent scholarship that does not fit this framework and that appeals to alternative themes.

Let me be the first to acknowledge the limitations of the proposed categorization. By no means can the breadth of scholarship be folded

---

1. That is, the concern is Qoheleth's message as distinct from the final message of the book of Ecclesiastes, which incorporates the view of the frame-narrator. While for some interpreters the perspectives put forward by Qoheleth and the frame narrator are similar, for others, they are starkly disparate.

into a few compartments. Rather than simply representing a single position, each of these categories represents a spectrum of interpretations. Scholars will differ at many significant points: the interpretation of what a particular motif means; the degree to which that motif is elevated above the rest; and the nature of the relation of that motif to the others. And as a spectrum implies, there are many mediating positions that fall between categories. Such positions often attempt to hold various motifs together in complementary or contradictory ways. While all attempts at categorization will encounter this difficulty, there is nevertheless benefit in brushing with such broad strokes. Each subsection of this chapter will begin with the scholars that most exemplify its position, after which the more mediating positions will be surveyed.

1.2 THE ELEVATION OF HEBEL

The most characteristic motif in the book is *hebel*. And it should come as no surprise that many scholars identify *hebel* as conveying Qoheleth's core message. While there is a significant variety of scholarly interpretations of *hebel*, those who elevate *hebel* to the highest position customarily understand *hebel* in predominantly negative terms. Additionally, those in this category tend to view the enjoyment motif as a resignation or concession. Longman and Crenshaw are, perhaps, most exemplary of this position.

Longman interprets *hebel* wholly negatively as "meaningless," elevates this motif above the rest, and sums up Qoheleth's message as "everything is meaningless."[2] To put it another way, "Life is full of trouble and then you die."[3] Corresponding to this elevation of *hebel* is the downplaying of the joy refrains, which Longman argues are not positive commendations but are rather concessions or resignations in light of the meaninglessness of life.[4] "In the darkness of a life that has no ultimate meaning, enjoy the temporal pleasures that lighten the burden."[5] While it is true that enjoyment does, in fact, come from God, it is shallow, temporary, restricted to the few, and only specified as the areas of eating,

---

2. Longman, *Ecclesiastes*, 32, 61–64.
3. Longman, *Ecclesiastes*, 34.
4. Longman, *Ecclesiastes*, 34.
5. Longman, *Ecclesiastes*, 35.

drinking, and working.[6] This superficial enjoyment that Qoheleth describes is nothing more than "a narcotic that numbs the recipient to the true nature of reality."[7]

Longman's interpretation of *hebel* also corresponds with a low view of Qoheleth's God, who is portrayed as "distant, occasionally indifferent, and sometimes cruel."[8] God has a plan but will not reveal it and while this sovereign God will judge, one should not expect to find justice; he "just does not seem to care much about earthly concerns."[9] Accordingly, passages speaking of the fear of God should not be interpreted as commending respect or awe but rather "fright before a powerful and dangerous being."[10]

Qoheleth's thoroughly pessimistic message is nothing more than a foil for the narrator, who rejects and corrects these unorthodox and dangerous words as he instructs his son.[11] Longman views Eccl 1:2 and 12:8 as the narrator's summary of Qoheleth's message and argues that other "positive" readings are straining to fit the book into preconceived notions of its message and purpose.[12]

In his commentary, Crenshaw's opening words unashamedly announce his strong, negative position: "Life is profitless; totally absurd. This oppressive message lies at the heart of the Bible's strangest book. Enjoy life if you can, advises the author, for old age will soon overtake you. And even as you enjoy, know that the world is meaningless. Virtue does not bring reward. The deity stands distant, abandoning humanity to chance and death."[13] Crenshaw's Qoheleth betrays an intellectual crisis as he mounts an unrelenting attack on traditional wisdom and its mechanical view of retribution.[14] In this environment, *hebel* (futile) is the final word on every aspect of existence. All that is left is to enjoy the

---

6. Longman, *Ecclesiastes*, 34.
7. Longman, *Ecclesiastes*, 35.
8. Longman, *Ecclesiastes*, 35.
9. Longman, *Ecclesiastes*, 36.
10. Longman, *Ecclesiastes*, 36.
11. Longman, *Ecclesiastes*, 38.
12. Longman, *Ecclesiastes*, 37–39.
13. Crenshaw, *Ecclesiastes*, 23. Crenshaw's position is very similar to that of Longman; both see Qoheleth as a skeptic. However, one important difference is that Crenshaw does not make the distinction between the body of the book and the epilogue and thus, takes the message of Qoheleth as the final message of the book; see Longman, *Ecclesiastes*, 36.
14. Crenshaw, *Ecclesiastes*, 28.

little pleasures. But, such enjoyment is nothing more than resignation in a meaningless life because death ultimately cancels everything.[15]

In his later book *The Ironic Wink*, Crenshaw reveals in more detail his handling of Qoheleth's recurrent commendations of joy. He argues that the contexts in which Qoheleth praised joy suggest irony.[16] His words of enjoyment "were spoken against a backdrop of serious questions about the meaning of everything. They did not grow out of belief in divine goodness."[17] Enjoyment was "outside one's control, was limited to royalty, and had nothing to do with the way people conduct their lives."[18] As ironic, they may be simply dismissed.

Qoheleth wrote in an absurd fashion to highlight his thesis that everything is *hebel*. The contradictions are a rhetorical strategy that illustrates the futility of all things.[19] "Because everything is *hebel*, according to Qoheleth, all his ideas partake of this quality, even the judgment that all is futile, transient, or mist. As such, they go up in smoke, every concept deconstructing its opposite."[20] This is different than the "yes . . . but . . ." interpretation for both the yes and the but are unreliable because everything is *hebel*.[21] The "ironic" in Qoheleth's address challenges the reader to consider the contradiction and the "wink" suggests that the reader knows the correct answer.[22]

Where does God fit in with Crenshaw's Qoheleth? God is uninvolved, unconcerned, his activity is ominous, and there is no moral order or justice.[23] The passages that speak of God's judgment "seem remarkably out of place" and represent later moralistic glosses.[24] In short, Qoheleth represents an intellectual crisis and an attack on traditional wisdom. Crenshaw elevates the *hebel* motif as preeminent, dismisses the commendations of joy as ironic, and ignores the calls to fear God as glosses.

---

15. Crenshaw, *Ecclesiastes*, 25. See also Crenshaw, *Old Testament Wisdom*, 142, 144.
16. Crenshaw, *The Ironic Wink*, 5–8, 116.
17. Crenshaw, *The Ironic Wink*, 114.
18. Crenshaw, *The Ironic Wink*, 83.
19. Crenshaw, *The Ironic Wink*, 30.
20. Crenshaw, *The Ironic Wink*, 116.
21. Crenshaw, *The Ironic Wink*, 31.
22. Crenshaw, *The Ironic Wink*, 7.
23. Crenshaw, *Ecclesiastes*, 23–24.
24. Crenshaw, *Ecclesiastes*, 27, 55, 84, 102, 184. Crenshaw suggests that the later added mention of divine judgment found in the second epilogue may have inspired subsequent additions throughout Qoheleth's address; namely, Eccl 3:17a; 8:12–13; 11:9b; see Crenshaw, *Ecclesiastes*, 24.

THE STATE OF SCHOLARSHIP

Longman and Crenshaw are by no means the only ones to find in Qoheleth a rather grim take on life. Indeed, they have no shortage of company. For Murphy, Qoheleth is a sage who thinks and writes from within the wisdom tradition. On the one hand, Qoheleth condemns folly, but he also rejects the wisdom tradition for the security it offered; that is, Qoheleth accepts traditional wisdom but modifies it in the direction of pessimism.[25] In the end, Murphy's Qoheleth succumbs to *hebel* (vanity) and puts forward a pessimistic message void of any substantial answer.

Murphy argues that the joy passages are not positive commendations but are rather concessions as Qoheleth is just offering a way to try to live in this troubling world—this advice does nothing to ameliorate the fundamental problem of *hebel*.[26] Murphy argues that those who see enjoyment as a positive affirmation and as the main theme interpret selectively with sweeping strokes and fail to respect Qoheleth's complex views.[27]

The passages that speak of the fear of God in Qoheleth's address do not play a significant role. While Murphy pushes for an interpretation of reverential fear stemming from Qoheleth's inability to comprehend God's ways, he still sees such words by Qoheleth as completely different from the view of fearing God found in the epilogue.[28] Qoheleth "recognized God as judge but nowhere does he attempt to explain this, much less to motivate human action on the basis of divine judgment. For him the judgment of God is a total mystery."[29] Thus, God should be reverentially feared, but this has little to no effect on one's life.

In sum, Murphy reads a sage who struggles to uphold his tradition in a troubling world. Qoheleth sees problems but has no answer. He searches but comes up empty. "For Qoheleth the road of the wise led nowhere, but it was the only one he could walk."[30]

---

25. Murphy, *Ecclesiastes*, xxxiv, lxii–lxiii. The pessimism detected by Murphy is not as pointed as that of Longman and Crenshaw mentioned above. For them, Qoheleth is speaking against and rejecting the wisdom tradition. Murphy, on the other hand, sees Qoheleth as remaining in, dialoguing with, and modifying the tradition.

26. Murphy, *Ecclesiastes*, lix–lx. In support, Murphy notes that four of the joy passages occur in the "nothing better than" form. He further points out that God arbitrarily grants or withholds enjoyment, showing that it is "at best a precarious possibility"; see Murphy, *Ecclesiastes*, lx.

27. Murphy, *Ecclesiastes*, lx–lxi. Specifically, Murphy calls out Gordis, Ogden, and Whybray.

28. Murphy, *Ecclesiastes*, lxv–lxvi, 126.

29. Murphy, *Ecclesiastes*, 126.

30. Murphy, *Ecclesiastes*, lxiv.

Noting a clear distinction between Qoheleth and the narrator, Enns interprets a Qoheleth who elevates *hebel* and offers a bleak message with no real answer.[31] His message reads, "Our labors are ultimately in vain, there is no payoff for anything we do, we all die, wisdom is only a temporary help at best, and this is God's doing. Hence everything is *hebel*."[32] In light of the complete absurdity of life, one should, if able, live life to the full. As such, the joy passages are not positives meant to cancel or counteract the negative declarations of *hebel*; they "are not a cause for celebration, but an act of resignation" and further confirmation of the total absurdity of life.[33] Qoheleth's stance is aptly captured by his climatic statements in 3:13, 5:18 [ET 19], and 7:2, where enjoyment and death are כל־האדם.[34]

For Shields, the unorthodox Qoheleth was no aberration but a true sage, even preeminent, and fully representative of the wisdom movement.[35] Qoheleth wholeheartedly embraced the tradition and rather than dishing out lies like others, he followed its wisdom with unwavering honesty to its logical conclusion and revealed its complete futility.[36] His message is thoroughly negative as it elevates *hebel*, understood as "senseless," as the final conclusion.[37] God is guilty of evil and the one who made things irrevocably corrupt.[38] And enjoyment, though advised, is no

---

31. Enns, *Ecclesiastes*, 31. Enns leans on Fox's translation of *hebel* as "absurd" with an understanding of "an affront to reason"; see Fox, *Time to Tear Down*, 31.

32. Enns, *Ecclesiastes*, 128. Qoheleth has a very critical view toward God, who is seen as the source of injustice and unpredictability and is the one responsible for Qoheleth's troubles; see Enns, *Ecclesiastes*, 123–24.

33. Enns, *Ecclesiastes*, 132.

34. Enns, *Ecclesiastes*, 14–16. Enns supports his interpretation of these verses as Qoheleth's climactic statements through the parallel he sees in the epilogue. While the epilogist affirms Qoheleth and his message and does not try to sanitize it, the epilogist offers a "mild corrective" and takes a step further by arguing that fearing God and keeping his commandments is truly כל־האדם; see Enns, *Ecclesiastes*, 5, 13, 16.

35. Shields, *End of Wisdom*, 6, 68–69.

36. Shields, *End of Wisdom*, 68–69, 236–37.

37. Shields, *End of Wisdom*, 112–21. In Eccl 1:2 and 12:8, *hebel* "is presented as a consistent and accurate summary of all of Qoheleth's words" (Shields, *End of Wisdom*, 122).

38. Shields, *End of Wisdom*, 236. Shields comments, "Although there is insufficient data upon which to build a comprehensive understanding of Qoheleth's concept of the fear of God, his must ultimately differ from the epilogist's (and, indeed, the concept in the remainder of the Hebrew Bible), for Qoheleth fears a distant, unknown God, whereas the epilogist fears a God who has revealed his will in his commands to his people" (Shields, *End of Wisdom*, 97).

solution.³⁹ Indeed, Qoheleth has no answer for this utterly senseless life. And following Qoheleth, the epilogist mounts an attack against the failed wisdom movement and offers a way forward with true wisdom: fear God and keep his commands.⁴⁰ Hereafter, the wisdom movement took a turn and thus, so to speak, Qoheleth marks the "end of wisdom."

Thus far, the discussion has focused on those who elevate the *hebel* motif to the highest position, dominating Qoheleth's message. There are, however, many who seek more mediating positions and attempt to hold *hebel* and joy together in tension and/or see them interacting in an intentional manner. As such, enjoyment is typically viewed not as a mere resignation or concession in a meaningless existence but as something positive to be commended and affirmed.

Fox is noteworthy for his view that the contradictions in the book, of which the tension between *hebel* and joy is foremost, are intentional and "the starting point of interpretation."⁴¹ It is not as much that Qoheleth is contradicting himself but more that he is reporting contradictions that he has observed.⁴² These contradictions are not to be eliminated but recognized for the role they play in tearing down meaning in order that Qoheleth might build up anew; hence the title to Fox's commentary, *A Time to Tear Down and A Time to Build Up*.⁴³ Fox writes, "The book of Qoheleth is about meaning. What unites all of Qoheleth's complaints is the collapse of meaning. What unites all of his counsels and affirmations

---

39. Shields, *End of Wisdom*, 204. He comments, "The only two pieces of advice Qoheleth can offer are entirely self-serving: enjoy yourself whenever you can, and experience whatever you can. This advice makes no reference to any overarching moral order in which some deeds can be said to be right and some said to be wrong. Qoheleth's conclusions are diametrically opposed to the religious ideal espoused throughout the remainder of the Hebrew Bible" (Shields, *End of Wisdom*, 204).

40. Shields, *End of Wisdom*, 236–37. While Qoheleth is unorthodox and incompatible with the rest of Scripture, it is through the epilogist's rejection of Qoheleth's errant wisdom and the offering of an appropriate alternative (12:13–14) that the book can stand with mainstream biblical thought and find a place in the canon; see Shields, *End of Wisdom*, 7.

41. Fox, *Time to Tear Down*, 3. See also his older book, Fox, *Qohelet and his Contradictions*. Fox does not interpret joy as merely a response to the pervasiveness of *hebel*, as many interpreters do. He sees the two contradictory motifs as intentionally standing next to each other as a literary technique. For his discussion and critique of various approaches dealing with Qoheleth's contradictions, which include harmonization, subtracting later additions, discovering quotations, hearing dialogue, detecting dialectic, and appeals to a fragmented psyche, see Fox, *Time to Tear Down*, 14–26.

42. Fox, *Time to Tear Down*, 3.

43. Fox, *Time to Tear Down*, 138–40.

is the attempt to reconstruct meanings."[44] These are the two movements in Qoheleth's address and while they are not two sequential phases, toward the end the emphasis is increasingly on the constructive.[45]

Fox argues that Qoheleth held to a mechanical view of retribution; that is, appropriate consequences to a particular action (or non-action) should be immediate, individual, recognizable, consistent, and final.[46] However, this is not what Qoheleth observed. Qoheleth saw a world that does not work in the way he expected, and so Qoheleth repeatedly made the declaration of *hebel*, which, taking influence from Camus's *The Myth of Sisyphus*, Fox translates as absurd and means irrational and an affront to reason.[47] The discrepancy between Qoheleth's rationality and the experienced world results in the deconstruction of meaning. Yet, according to Fox, this failure of reason is what God intended because he wants people to fear him.[48] But "this is not the end of the matter, for God allows us to build small meanings from the shards of reason."[49] To this end, Qoheleth's address is sprinkled with advice speaking to positive aspects of pleasure, work, wisdom, and life.[50] The building up that Fox speaks of is the acceptance and enjoyment, if given the opportunity, of various little things; they may not necessarily be good, but they may be better than an alternative.[51] However, Fox describes the meaning that Qoheleth "builds up" and "reconstructs" in rather unflattering terms. Qoheleth is simply "suggesting how we can make the best of the bad deal that is life."[52] Rather than reconstructing meaning, Fox says that "the best Qohelet can offer is some ephemeral, local tactics for coping with the vacuum" and "a distraction from painful reality."[53] Fox confesses that "these are not solutions but

---

44. Fox, *Time to Tear Down*, 133. Fox largely agrees with Murphy's interpretation but has two main points of disagreement: first, "Murphy does not recognize the decisive role of contradiction"; and second, he "does not identify the collapse of meaning as the central crisis that Qohelet confronts"; see Fox, *Time to Tear Down*, xi.

45. Fox, *Time to Tear Down*, 140.
46. Fox, *Time to Tear Down*, 138–39.
47. Fox, *Time to Tear Down*, 30–32.
48. Fox, *Time to Tear Down*, 49.
49. Fox, *Time to Tear Down*, 49.
50. Fox, *Time to Tear Down*, 140–44.
51. Fox, *Time to Tear Down*, 141.
52. Fox, *Time to Tear Down*, 140.
53. Fox, *Time to Tear Down*, 140, 240, 287. Fox further describes Qoheleth's calls to enjoyment as "almost a counsel of despair" and likens them to the "gesticulations of a lunatic"; see Fox, *Time to Tear Down*, 129, 130.

accommodations. The answers come down to embracing the very activities that elsewhere he calls senseless."[54] Fox concedes that the recovery of meaning is only partial.[55]

In sum, Fox sees Qoheleth's address as consisting of two foundational movements: tearing down meaning and building it back up anew. He says the contradictions should not be eliminated but allowed to speak and serve their role in breaking down meaning. And while Fox's interpretation largely holds tensions in balance and successfully tears down, it fails to build anything of substance back up. Thus, in the end, *hebel* is once again elevated as an inescapable problem and joy is, at best, a slight plus.

As this section demonstrates, many scholars interpret *hebel* as the most prominent motif and identify it as representing the core of Qoheleth's message. Correspondingly, the joy motif tends to be minimized.

1.3 THE ELEVATION OF JOY

Not everyone elevates *hebel*. For many, *hebel*, in one way or another, marks the situations that Qoheleth came up against and is not to be confused with Qoheleth's response to them. The most prominent alternative to a message of *hebel* is the elevation of enjoyment as constituting Qoheleth's primary advice.

When it comes to the elevation of joy, many turn first to Whybray, who identifies the positive commendations of joy as *the* dominant motif and labels Qoheleth as a preacher of joy.[56] Seven times throughout his address Qoheleth exhorts the reader to enjoyment, and it is these pronouncements that communicate Qoheleth's message.[57] These key passages steadily increase in emphasis, building like a crescendo, "and the last, the most elaborate of them all, directly addressed to the reader, introduces and dominates the concluding section of the book in which Qoheleth presents his final thoughts on how life should be lived and why."[58] Each of the seven joy passages is connected with a particular section and theme/problem in the book.[59] And the context of each gives the reasons for

---

54. Fox, *Time to Tear Down*, 140.

55. Fox, *Time to Tear Down*, 3.

56. Whybray, "Preacher of Joy," 87–98. See also, Whybray, *Ecclesiastes*.

57. The seven joy passages are as follows: 2:24a; 3:12; 3:22a; 5:17 [18]; 8:15a; 9:7–9a; 11:7–12:1a.

58. Whybray, "Preacher of Joy," 87–88.

59. Whybray, "Preacher of Joy," 88, 91. See Whybray, "Preacher of Joy," 91–92,

enjoyment: 1) the gift is from God; 2) the necessity to accept one's lot; 3) the brevity of life; and 4) one's ignorance of the future.[60] But more than mere advice, Whybray argues, enjoyment is a command, obedience to God's will, and the way one is to "remember your Creator."[61] In the end, the joy passages are "incapable of reconciliation with a fundamentally pessimistic standpoint."[62] And so, *hebel*, though recognized for its strong negative connotations, is the background against which Qoheleth proclaims joy.[63] Vanity is the problem; joy is the advice.

Ogden also advocates for a positive reading. He interprets the book as governed by a three-fold framework of question, answer, and response.[64] The book opens with its programmatic question in 1:3; namely, that of advantage.[65] It is this question that drives Qoheleth's search and address. As Qoheleth's efforts progress and he explores many facets of life, time and again he comes to the negative answer of *hebel*, which

---

where he outlines the seven problems and sections as follows:

1. The vanity of toil and human effort (1:12–2:26)
2. The vanity of man's ignorance of the future (3:1–15)
3. The vanity of the presence of injustice in the world (3:16–22)
4. The vanity of the pursuit of wealth (5:9–19)
5. The vanity of unpunished wickedness (8:10–15)
6. The vanity of the fact that all men share a common fate (9:1–10)
7. The vanity of the brevity of human life (11:7–12:7)

Whybray's point here is to argue for joy as central to Qoheleth's message and not to offer a comprehensive theory about the structure of the book; however, he notes that it may be possible; see Qoheleth, "Preacher of Joy," 95–96n8. The texts that many claim to express a pessimistic view, Whybray argues, do no such thing when considered in context. For example, when Qoheleth declared that he hated life (2:17), Whybray argues that this is "an expression not of Qoheleth's own teaching but of the thoughts of the supposed Solomon, reflecting the disillusionment which he felt before he came to make the more mature reflections which culminate in the positive conclusion of 2:24–26"; see Whybray, "Preacher of Joy," 92.

60. Whybray, "Preacher of Joy," 88.

61. Whybray, "Preacher of Joy," 91–92. See Eccl 12:1. Whybray notes, "The world, then, is as God made it, and nothing can alter it. The best thing for men to do is to accept this and to enjoy to the full what good things God has given; and indeed this is what God *requires* of them"; Whybray, *Ecclesiastes*, 28; emphasis original.

62. Whybray, "Preacher of Joy," 92.

63. Whybray, "Preacher of Joy," 93–94.

64. Ogden, *Qoheleth*, 16.

65. Ogden interprets יִתְרוֹן as follows: "It is the special term for the positive advantage here and in the future which the wise might expect from living according to the instructions of the wisdom tradition"; Ogden, *Qoheleth*, 17; see also 27–30.

Ogden takes as "enigmatic."⁶⁶ There is no overarching explanation for the account of things and there is no advantage under the sun. Qoheleth does, at many points, put forward *hebel* as a conclusion. However, Ogden argues, these *hebel* statements should not be mistaken as Qoheleth's thesis; these conclusions are the answer to the book's programmatic question of advantage (1:3) and not his advice and message in light of his findings.⁶⁷ While Qoheleth's answer to the programmatic question is negative, his response is positive and found in the structurally climactic passages commending enjoyment.⁶⁸ One is to enjoy life as a good gift from God and know that God will even judge one according to how one has done so.⁶⁹ In sum, Ogden argues for a framework of question (advantage), answer (*hebel*), and response (joy). In this way, joy alone is elevated as the true message of Qoheleth.

For Krüger, joy is presented as the highest good. Qoheleth's hedonism and eudaemonist ethic, an alternative ethic to the retribution of traditional wisdom, hold that one should seize every possibility without postponing.⁷⁰ This interpretation is supported by Qoheleth's criticism of other assumptions of what is good; by the description of enjoyment as a gift from God; and by the fleetingness and futility of human life.⁷¹ This does not mean that life is meaningless. "Rather, the meaning of human life consists in affording oneself and others the enjoyment of good things within the context of the possibilities and limits set by God."⁷² As such, Qoheleth's hedonism is not to be egocentric but more communal.⁷³ Time, fate, chance, and death represent the judgment of God over humanity, a judgment that all people receive because none are innocent.⁷⁴ And while God's judgment is against all, it will be more severe against

---

66. Ogden, *Qoheleth*, 17, 21–26.

67. Ogden, *Qoheleth*, 17.

68. Ogden, *Qoheleth*, 17.

69. Ogden, *Qoheleth*, 17, 210–11. Ogden describes the joy passages as "theological statements of faith" in God; Ogden, *Qoheleth*, 26. Although Ogden expresses the calls to enjoyment as commands and gives a nod to future judgment, his presentation is not as strong as that of Whybray's above.

70. Krüger, *Qoheleth*, 1, 172.

71. Krüger, *Qoheleth*, 1–3.

72. Krüger, *Qoheleth*, 206.

73. Krüger, *Qoheleth*, 1.

74. Krüger, *Qoheleth*, 2. Yet, God is ambivalent in the gift of enjoyment and the distribution of judgment; see Krüger, *Qoheleth*, 3.

those who fail to enjoy what was given them.[75] The acceptance of this reality, described as fearing God, frees and enables one to fully embrace and enjoy all that comes.

Loader explores the phenomenon of polarization and argues that polar structures are not only found in almost every unit of the text but are *the* characteristic of the book.[76] By "polar structures," Loader means, "patterns of tension created by the counterposition of two elements to one another."[77] Both poles are valid, yet cannot both be true; thus, the poles create an unresolved tension, which is expressed negatively through the *hebel* statements.[78] Rising as a contra-pole to this tension (*hebel*), Qoheleth puts forward his final advice and conclusion; namely, carpe diem.[79]

For Weeks, Qoheleth is less of a king and more of a businessman.[80] He demands a profit in life (1:3) but instead he finds that "what humans achieve beneath the sun is *hebel*, and that it constitutes not a profit, but an incalculable loss."[81] He writes, "what confronts humans is *hebel* because it is misleading or illusory, but what they typically do in response to it is also *hebel* because it is misguided or deluded."[82] Further, nothing in life is really one's own except at the level of feeling and so enjoyment is the best one can achieve for oneself.[83] Indeed, "the need to take pleasure in life is the principal conclusion which Qohelet draws from his discussion

---

75. Krüger, *Qoheleth*, 197.

76. Loader, *Polar Structures*, 1. This polarity is not in Qoheleth's own thinking, per se, but in the received literary product; Loader, *Polar Structures*, 1. Note the similarities with Fox's intentional contradictions outlined above; see Fox, *Time to Tear Down*, 1–26. Additionally, the ground for Qoheleth's polarity is that he accepts God, but God is far off; accordingly, the book is not accounted for by the influence of Greek philosophy, though there are points of contact; see Loader, *Polar Structures*, 129.

77. Loader, *Polar Structures*, 1. Loader identifies many polar structures: life and death, the worth and worthlessness of wisdom, risk and assurance, political power and powerlessness, talk and silence, the value and uselessness of wealth, labor without product, the inhuman human, the lack of retribution, and toil and joy; see Loader, *Polar Structures*, 29–110.

78. Loader, *Polar Structures*, 65–66.

79. Loader, *Polar Structures*, 111.

80. Weeks, *Ecclesiastes and Scepticism*, 33–43. See also, Weeks, "Solomon and Qoheleth," 80–95, where Weeks also seeks to make a sharp disconnect between Qoheleth and Solomon.

81. Weeks, *Ecclesiastes and Scepticism*, 58.

82. Weeks, *Ecclesiastes and Scepticism*, 119. Thus, *hebel* speaks to "a misapprehension of the world, and their place in it, by humans"; Weeks, *Ecclesiastes and Scepticism*, 119.

83. Weeks, *Ecclesiastes and Scepticism*, 1.

as a whole."[84] More than a simple caricature of skepticism or pessimism, Qoheleth thinks that "humans are missing the point."[85] There is no profit in life so settle for a portion; that is, enjoyment.

Christianson puts forward a detailed argument for reading Qoheleth as a narrative, pointing to aspects such as first-person narration, framing, and characterization.[86] He sees an older Qoheleth writing about his past experiences, failures, and excesses so readers can learn from and avoid his mistakes. Qoheleth's quest is mostly found in the first seven chapters and afterward, he focuses more on his present concern of instruction.[87] As such, Qoheleth's pessimism reflects his regret of the past and his own failures, but this pessimism is his own and is not to be shared by the reader for as Qoheleth moves from quest to expression and instruction, he lifts his head to the reader, so to speak, and commends joy.[88] Through his follies, Qoheleth is able to offer hard-earned wisdom to guide the reader on how to live in the absurd, and so he puts forward enjoyment and satisfaction as obtainable objects.[89] For Qoheleth, this time of remembering and telling is also an act of redemption; that is, through his recounting and instruction he has made his past experiences meaningful and so transcends the absurd.[90]

Johnston seeks a more mediating position as he offers a theological interpretation with the aim of challenging critics who reduce Qoheleth to simply cynicism or pessimism.[91] While Qoheleth's occasion and purpose for writing is a "discussion of man's inability to discover the key to

---

84. Weeks, *Ecclesiastes and Scepticism*, 79. However, Weeks argues that this is not hedonism nor the "Preacher of joy" put forward by Whybray; see Weeks, *Ecclesiastes and Scepticism*, 79n2, 84. He writes, "we are not supposed to be undertaking a search for pleasure, but finding pleasure in what we undertake"; Weeks, *Ecclesiastes and Scepticism*, 84.

85. Weeks, *Ecclesiastes and Scepticism*, 169.

86. Christianson, *Time to Tell*, 19–50.

87. Christianson, *Time to Tell*, 243.

88. Christianson, *Time to Tell*, 242–54.

89. Christianson, *Time to Tell*, 247–50. Here, Christianson points to similarities with Fox and his discussion of the reconstruction of "little meanings"; compare Fox, *Time to Tear Down*, 140–44. In many respects, Christianson and Fox share similar views. Yet, Fox is placed in the *hebel* category because of his failure to build up new meaning(s) and his rather unappealing portrait of enjoyment. For Christianson, on the other hand, Qoheleth is able to transcend the absurd, make something meaningful, and put forward enjoyment as a positive and attainable object; see Christianson, *Time to Tell*, 251.

90. Christianson, *Time to Tell*, 250–51.

91. Johnston, "Confessions," 14.

life's meaning," his underlying mindset comes out in the admonitions to enjoy life.[92] Thus, "Qoheleth is skeptical in his intent, but affirmative in his intentionality."[93] Qoheleth is not an outlier of the wisdom tradition but rather seeks to push the tradition back to the heart of Israel's wisdom, which Johnston takes to be the enjoyment of the life that God gives.[94] This wisdom is not about the misguided endeavor of mastering life but rather is the "art of steering" or navigating life.[95]

Johnston argues that Qoheleth writes with a recurring three-pronged framework: first, he gives a lengthy discussion on some negative aspect of life; second, he counters the negative with a positive call to enjoyment; and third, he quickly qualifies the positive commendation with another negative.[96] In this way, the two themes of *hebel* and joy actively work together. The negative statements serve as qualifiers denoting the rightful limits of enjoyment and not as retractions of it and in doing so, they serve to guard against misunderstanding and the false apotheosizing of joy.[97] In the end, Johnston upholds joy but one qualified by *hebel*.

For Seow, Qoheleth focuses his attention on the human condition and continually concludes that people are not in control; that is, everything is *hebel*.[98] "What is *hebel* cannot be grasped—neither physically nor intellectually."[99] It does not speak to what is meaningless but to that which is "beyond human apprehension and comprehension."[100] Qoheleth's main advice in response to the inability to control is to find joy.[101] Enjoyment is not just the "best-option" in light of the state of the world but is a gift from God, who decides who has the possibility for joy and he will call one to account for not enjoying.[102] Seow writes,

92. Johnston, "Confessions," 14.
93. Johnston, "Confessions," 14.
94. Johnston, "Confessions," 14–15.
95. Johnston, "Confessions," 15.
96. Johnston, "Confessions," 24. Following Wright's structural analysis, Johnston argues that this three-pronged, dialectical approach is found in each section of the first half of the book and constitutes both sections of the second half of the book. For his structural analysis, see Wright, "Riddle," 313–34.
97. Johnston, "Confessions," 24–25.
98. Seow, *Ecclesiastes*, 59–60.
99. Seow, *Ecclesiastes*, 102.
100. Seow, *Ecclesiastes*, 59.
101. Seow, *Ecclesiastes*, 57.
102. Seow, *Ecclesiastes*, 48, 58.

> One should enjoy whenever there is the opportunity, because this is the "portion" that God has assigned to humanity. It is, as it were, an antidote given by God to counter life's miseries . . . The point is not that one must go through life looking for joy everywhere. Nowhere in the book does the author say one should seek pleasure or pursue joy. The issue is, rather, acceptance of the fact that human beings have no control over what will happen. So when the possibility of joy presents itself, one must not fail to be in it, see it, and experience it.[103]

For Seow, fearing God means recognizing the distance between God and humanity and the limitations he has put in place—God made things the way they are, and humans have no control.[104] "God has given humanity the possibility of each moment. Hence people must accept what happens, whether good or bad. They must respond spontaneously to life, even in the midst of uncertainties, and accept both the possibilities and limitations of their being human."[105] In sum, Seow interprets a message about the acceptance of reality and the embrace, with joy, of all that comes.

Lee argues that enjoyment and the fear of God are not only both integral to Qoheleth's address but are paired motifs.[106] In addition to the eight joy passages, Lee also notes other expressions explicating a similar viewpoint.[107] The result is that this message of enjoyment is found in almost every unit of the book and increases as it progresses.[108] Enjoyment is not to be understood as merely pleasure, happiness, or bliss but more broadly as "an authentic experience of the world that recognizes both its tragic limitations and its joyous possibilities of good" and has to do with "living life to the full."[109] As a paired motif with the fear of God, enjoyment is seen as a religious duty and a command, and 11:9 informs the reader that "those who fail to enjoy have refused to accept the will of God,

---

103. Seow, *Ecclesiastes*, 57.
104. Seow, *Ecclesiastes*, 59, 69.
105. Seow, *Ecclesiastes*, 59–60.
106. Lee, *Vitality of Enjoyment*, 1–10.
107. Lee, *Vitality of Enjoyment*, 33; for example, "look into good" (2:1); "see good" (2:24); "do good" (3:12); "be in good" (7:14); "see life" (9:9). While Whybray and most scholars view seven joy passage, Lee adds 7:14 as the eighth; cf. Whybray, "Qoheleth, Preacher of Joy," 87.
108. Lee, *Vitality of Enjoyment*, 33, 81.
109. Lee, *Vitality of Enjoyment*, 33. Lee notes affinities with Johnston's view of wisdom and its focus on life; compare, Johnston, "Confessions," 14–15.

and will be called to account."¹¹⁰ Indeed, failure to keep this command results in cosmic chaos, which accounts for the various societal troubles witnessed in Qoheleth's address.¹¹¹

Lee holds that in Ecclesiastes, fearing God does not mean the same thing as found in the rest of the OT, which Lee describes as "obedience, service, conformity to God's moral command, avoidance of sin, honest conduct, etc."¹¹² Qoheleth's unique view primarily and most emphatically associates fearing God with enjoyment.¹¹³ The essence of fearing God is recognizing his otherness and humanity's place before him and this manifests through the religious duty of enjoyment, living life to the full. Since Lee views joy and the fear of God as paired motifs, Lee represents a more mediating position and could arguable be placed in the category of those who elevate the fear of God motif. However, since Lee interprets the fear of God fundamentally as enjoyment, this position finds a better fit here among those that elevate joy as the central message of Qoheleth's address.

Lohfink interprets Qoheleth as a peripatetic philosopher.¹¹⁴ "The book of Qoheleth can only be understood as an attempt to profit as much as possible from the Greek understanding of the world, without forcing Israel's wisdom to give up its status."¹¹⁵ This mediated entry into Greek

---

110. Lee, *Vitality of Enjoyment*, 49. Lee writes, "enjoyment is not only a divine gift but also a divine imperative with ultimate implications" (Lee, *Vitality of Enjoyment*, 72).

111. Lee, *Vitality of Enjoyment*, 49–50. For Lee, proper enjoyment carries a strong sense of social responsibility; see Lee, *Vitality of Enjoyment*, 129–35. Lee writes, "For Qohelet, the moral life is grounded in the responsible practice of enjoyment, that is, enjoyment that promotes not only the flourishing of the individual, but also the life of the larger human community"; Lee, *Vitality of Enjoyment*, 10. Note the affinities with Krüger's view of Qoheleth's more communal and less egocentric hedonism; see Krüger, *Qoheleth*, 1.

112. Lee, *Vitality of Enjoyment*, 85. While earlier positions tended to greatly downplay or dismiss the fear of God motif, such as by viewing those passages as later editorial glosses or as citations of orthodox wisdom for the purpose of refutation, Lee notes that these are less common now as many recognize the evidence for the integrity of the book. However, Lee notes that most who take the fear of God motif to be integral filter it through a pessimistic view of the book such that the result is an interpretation of fear simply as terror before a God who is distant, arbitrary, and even dangerous. Lee argues that the optimistic alternative is no better and that its view that this motif is identical with the view of fearing God in the rest of the Old Testament is sweeping, unhelpful, and fails to reveal Qoheleth's distinct contributions. See Lee, *Vitality of Enjoyment*, 84–85.

113. Lee, *Vitality of Enjoyment*, 121. Lee does note various aspects of piety as part of fearing God, but argues that for Qoheleth, the principal connection with fear is enjoyment; see Lee, *Vitality of Enjoyment*, 121–22.

114. Lohfink, *Qoheleth*, viii, 10–11.

115. Lohfink, *Qoheleth*, 6.

thinking provides a model of enculturation.[116] One can hold on to one's heritage and identity while still being modern and realistic.[117]

In his broad address, Qoheleth discusses cosmology (1:4–11), anthropology (1:12—3:15), and after offering a social critique (3:16—6:10) and a deconstruction of traditional wisdom (6:11—9:6), he offers his ethic (9:7—12:7), which carries the framing advice of the enjoyment of life.[118] Indeed, one should constantly seek enjoyment and embrace it with all one's being whenever it presents itself because it is from God.[119] Yet, at the center of Lohfink's chiastic structure is Qoheleth's religious critique (4:17—5:6 [5:1–7]) of a busy religiosity, against which he puts forward the fear of God.[120] This true fear of God will guide one as to when to follow traditional wisdom and when to reject it.[121] And so, one is to fully live in and embrace each moment and accept from God whatever he gives, whether good or evil; indeed, everything that happens is an act of God.[122] While the final message is one of enjoyment, it attempts to retain some semblance of the fear of God.

Just as with the elevation of *hebel*, many scholars elevate the joy motif as comprising Qoheleth's central message. While this category represents a broad range, there are some common trends. Rather than constituting a conclusion, *hebel* is commonly understood as the situation or problem against which Qoheleth gives his advice. And there is in these interpretations the beginnings of a move toward interpreting *hebel* in more neutral

---

116. Lohfink, *Qoheleth*, 6, 13. Lohfink argues that Ecclesiastes became a textbook for temple schools in Jerusalem, which were under pressure to modernize; further, this inclusion as part of the library of good texts for schools led to its inclusion in the canon; Lohfink, *Qoheleth*, 11–12.

117. Lohfink, *Qoheleth*, 9.

118. Lohfink, *Qoheleth*, 1–3. In Qoheleth's critique of classical wisdom, ten major themes are cited and refuted; however, the overriding issue at hand is that of retribution and Lohfink's interpretation thus carries the idea of Qoheleth as representing a sort of wisdom crisis. Lohfink writes, "the old philosophy of life, as expressed in the book of Proverbs, for example, was no longer helpful"; Lohfink, *Qoheleth*, 6.

119. Lohfink, *Qoheleth*, 120.

120. Lohfink, *Qoheleth*, 3, 8. The central position of this religious critique is highly significant for Lohfink's view of Qoheleth seeking to fuse Greek and Jewish thinking. He writes, "It reveals a supreme art in the use of literary form, and also a settled refusal, amid total openness to Greek, to give up one's own heritage. What is true of form is equally true of message"; Lohfink, *Qoheleth*, 8.

121. Lohfink writes, "This fear of God is not limited to special religious activities, or able to be expressed through them alone. Rather, when life is freed from inauthenticity, it is the hidden essence of each moment of normal living"; Lohfink, *Qoheleth*, 75.

122. Lohfink, *Qoheleth*, 2–3, 9.

and less exclusively negative terms. Additionally, the joy motif, as Qoheleth's message, is commonly elevated to the position of a divine command or to the softer position of a positive commendation or affirmation.

1.4 THE ELEVATION OF THE FEAR OF GOD

As the previous sections have illustrated, many scholars elevate either the motif of *hebel* or joy as Qoheleth's central message. There are some scholars, albeit a small minority, who seek to elevate to varying degrees the fear of God motif.[123] This section will first consider the work of Bartholomew as exemplifying this position, after which other mediating positions will be charted.

Bartholomew seeks to avoid what he sees as the trap that scholars continually fall into; that is, the trap of leaning too far toward either the *hebel* pole or the carpe diem pole and elevating one above its rightful place and consequently leveling Qoheleth's message to one side.[124] Bartholomew argues that the *hebel* conclusions and the joy passages are diametrically opposed and the tension created from their deliberate juxtaposition should not be resolved.[125] The resulting tension opens a gap, in which Qoheleth puts forward the fear of God as the proper foundation for life.[126]

The methodology of Qoheleth's pursuits is his autonomous epistemology; that is, he relies only on his own experience, observations, and reason.[127] This methodology leads him time and again to the conclusion

---

123. There is a broad consensus that to whomever wrote the final words of the book (that is, 12:13–14), the fear of God was unmistakably foundational. But as it concerns Qoheleth's position on this motif, any type of consensus is still a long way off.

124. Bartholomew, *Ecclesiastes*, 93.

125. Bartholomew, *Ecclesiastes*, 81–82. Bartholomew is similar to Fox with respect to the recognition of purposeful contradictions; however, they differ greatly in their interpretation of that purpose. For his discussion of contradictions, see Fox, *Time to Tear Down*, 1–4, 14–26. Additionally, Bartholomew's interpretation of two poles in contradiction differs from others like Johnston, who sees *hebel* and joy as qualifying each other and working together in a positive way; see Johnston, "Confessions," 24–25.

126. Bartholomew, *Ecclesiastes*, 93–95, 353–58. Note the similarities with Loader's polar structures; see Loader, *Polar Structures*, 1. However, Loader interprets many polar structures and the tension between these various poles results in *hebel*, to which Qoheleth presents joy as a counterpole. In contrast, Bartholomew understands a primary polarity between *hebel* and joy that results in tension and a gap, in which Qoheleth puts forward the fear of God.

127. Bartholomew, *Ecclesiastes*, 93. Bartholomew argues that Qoheleth is adopting Greek thinking and taking it to its logical conclusion to show that it leads to *hebel* rather than truth; see Bartholomew, *Ecclesiastes*, 94–95. This is contrary to, for example,

of *hebel* as he is confronted with the way the world is.¹²⁸ In contrast, the joy passages represent Qoheleth's vision of shalom, which stems from his view of Eden in Gen 2 and from the good land promised to Israel (Deut 6:10–11; 30:9).¹²⁹ It is the contradictory juxtaposition between this shalomic vision and Qoheleth's picture of reality that his autonomous epistemology has produced that creates tension in the address and this tension opens up a gap.¹³⁰ "The book is precisely about how to resolve the tension."¹³¹ The reader is invited to ponder this gap.

Throughout the address, there is a growing intensity both in the joy passages as well as in the joy-*hebel* tension.¹³² The tension increases until 11:7, where it finally breaks and there is a switch.¹³³ In the gap opened by the joy-*hebel* tension, Qoheleth puts forward the call to remember one's Creator, which Bartholomew takes as equivalent to fear God, as Qoheleth's main message and the answer around which one is to reorient one's life and the foundation from which one can approach life and all

---

Lohfink, who argues that Qoheleth encourages the incorporation of Greek philosophy into Hebrew wisdom; see Lohfink, *Qoheleth*, 13.

128. Against readings of meaningless and absurd, Bartholomew understands *hebel* as "enigmatic"; see Bartholomew, *Ecclesiastes*, 93–94, 104–07. While he acknowledges the strong negative connotations of this key word, he seeks a more neutral option because it ultimately leaves open the possibility of meaning. Additionally, Bartholomew argues that Qoheleth's early epistemology and wisdom are ironized as they lead him into *hebel*; this is made particularly clear in Eccl 7:23–29, where Qoheleth confesses the failure of his quest and his entrapment by folly; see Bartholomew, *Ecclesiastes*, 94.

129. Bartholomew, *Ecclesiastes*, 152.

130. Bartholomew, *Ecclesiastes*, 81–82. Here, there is an interesting point of departure from the majority of literature. Many scholars see Qoheleth's presentation of joy specifically as a response to *hebel* and understand joy as a meaningless resignation or as a more positive commendation. But for Bartholomew, joy is *not* a response to *hebel* but rather a diametrically opposite vision; see Bartholomew, *Ecclesiastes*, 152.

131. Bartholomew, *Ecclesiastes*, 81.

132. Bartholomew, *Ecclesiastes*, 81. Bartholomew quotes and agrees with Whybray about the increasing emphasis of joy and of the great significance of the final joy passage but disagrees with Whybray about the nature of the role that the joy passages play; see Bartholomew, *Ecclesiastes*, 355; cf. Whybray, "Qoheleth, Preacher of joy," 87–88.

133. Ecclesiastes 11:8–12:7 continues and explains how the switch happened; see Bartholomew, *Ecclesiastes*, 354–58. In the end, Qoheleth does affirm joy but with right thinking and not cheap joy; Bartholomew, *Ecclesiastes*, 95. For Bartholomew, this affirmation of joy is only in the final joy passage—which is not contributing to the tension rising from the juxtaposition of joy and *hebel*— in which Qoheleth presents an affirmation of joy in the right context. Bartholomew roots this view of joy in the final section on its mention of joy before *hebel* instead of the other way around; see Bartholomew, *Ecclesiastes*, 353–54.

its *hebel*.[134] In this way, remembering God as the Creator (fearing God) undermines Qoheleth's autonomous epistemology, relieves the joy-*hebel* tension, and fills the gap.[135]

Fuhr seeks a balanced approach in his analysis of the most prominent motifs in the book and makes an argument for their inter-dependency.[136] He identifies as prominent the following seven motifs: *hebel*; under the sun; wisdom; divine determinacy and the imposition of limitations on humanity; the inevitability of death; the enjoyment of life; and the fear of God.[137] Most significantly, he argues that it is the final two motifs that function on the level of a conclusion.[138] First, life's unpredictability, life's fleetingness, and death's inevitability lead the wise to enjoy life as a given responsibility.[139] Second, life's fleetingness, death's inevitability, God's enigmatic ways, and a future judgment lead the wise to fear God and keep his commandments.[140] The result is a two-fold, practical, wisdom-based paradigm with which the wise, living under the sun, can approach life in a *hebel* world.[141] Instead of each motif being a vital aspect of the other, Fuhr argues that the two conclusory motifs exist in equal balance with the other.[142]

This section illustrates the interpretations of some who elevate the fear of God motif. And to this category one could add the works of Lee and Lohfink (discussed above), since they seek to elevate the fear of God motif; however, their final messages lean toward joy. Some endeavor to hold the fear of God and joy in equal balance. And some elevate the fear of God to the central position of comprising Qoheleth's message.

---

134. Bartholomew, *Ecclesiastes*, 93–95. Bartholomew notes that 12:1 is important for this view, but it is finally 12:13–14 that makes this viewpoint definitive and supports his reading of 12:1; see Bartholomew, *Ecclesiastes*, 356.

135. Bartholomew, *Ecclesiastes*, 354, 358. For another scholar who holds a near-identical view to that of Bartholomew's, see Beldman, "Framed! Structures in Ecclesiastes," 137–61.

136. Fuhr, *Inter-Dependency*, xiii, 9–10. Fuhr acknowledges the subjectivity of which motifs he deems to be "prominent" and which are not as well as in his decisions about the categorization of the motifs; see Fuhr, *Inter-Dependency*, 22–23.

137. Fuhr, *Inter-Dependency*, 22–26.

138. Fuhr, *Inter-Dependency*, 26.

139. Fuhr, *Inter-Dependency*, 27, 191.

140. Fuhr, *Inter-Dependency*, 27, 191.

141. Fuhr, *Inter-Dependency*, 27.

142. Fuhr, *Inter-Dependency*, 27, 179, 185–86. Despite their similarities, Fuhr disagrees with Lee's view that enjoyment and the fear of God overlap in essence and fulfillment; see Fuhr, *Inter-Dependency*, 178–79. Fuhr also speaks against those who root enjoyment *in* the fear of God; see Fuhr, *Inter-Dependency*, 177–78.

1.5 ALTERNATE FOCI

More recently, some have put forward interpretations that differ more considerably from the rest of scholarship and do not identify Qoheleth's message as closely with the key motifs of *hebel*, joy, or the fear of God. This section is, in part, an acknowledgement of the limitations of the above threefold categorization and a recognition of scholars who read Ecclesiastes in a different light. The two most noteworthy contributions here are by Barbour and Bundvad, which will be discussed in turn.

While many scholars have taken Ecclesiastes, and Wisdom Literature in general, as being distinct from and unconcerned with Israel's history, Barbour argues that Qoheleth is much more connected with that history and closer to the deuteronomistic theological mainstream than often supposed.[143] She suggests that the book is haunted by Israel's history, particularly the exile, and is Israel's account to itself of its past, forming a sort of post-exilic penitential.[144] Barbour sees Qoheleth as a composite king built on Solomon as the base pastiche and representative of all the past kings of Israel.[145] Various stories and accounts in the book, such as 4:13–16 and 4:17–5:6 [5:1–7], are understood through the lens of cultural memory and interpreted as being about the follies and failings of past kings, on whom all the blame is squarely placed for the current situation and troubles.[146] Echoes of the exile sound through Qoheleth's address, as in 5:12–16 [13–17] and 6:1–6, while 9:11–18 speaks of its deferral.[147] And the closing poem of 12:1–7 is understood as a city lament over the fall of Jerusalem at the hands of the Babylonians in 586 BC.[148] Further, this closing poem forms a bracket with the opening account of Solomon's building projects and splendor in Eccl 2 such that the reader is invited to read the material found between these two brackets as a

---

143. Barbour, *The Story of Israel*, 1–3.

144. Barbour, *The Story of Israel*, 3, 35.

145. Barbour, *The Story of Israel*, 10, 30. The very use of the name "Qoheleth" is a backing away from a strict correspondence to Solomon and the inclusions and omissions found in the description of the so-called royal experiment of Eccl 2 were guided by an attempt to make the character and account more re-applicable; see Barbour, *The Story of Israel*, 10, 17.

146. Barbour, *The Story of Israel*, 77–105.

147. Barbour, *The Story of Israel*, 106–37. Barbour sees 9:11–18 as specifically referring to the siege of Jerusalem by Sennacherib in 701 BC and its subsequent deliverance.

148. Barbour, *The Story of Israel*, 139.

meditation on Israel's demise and downfall from the opening scene of prosperity to the closing scene of ruin.[149]

For Barbour, *hebel* is, in part, a historical judgment and speaks about the distance between historical events and the records of them for posterity.[150] Barbour admits that her focus has been on the "darker side" of the book, much to the neglect of the recurrent joy passages; nevertheless, she holds that the particular strand of Qoheleth's pessimism that she presents still leaves the door open for some readings of joy.[151]

Bundvad explores the theme of time in Ecclesiastes and argues that it is the main theme that holds the book together.[152] Most poignantly through the framing poems of 1:4–11 and 12:1–7, the book presents a fundamental and inescapable conflict between the cyclicality of created order and the linearity of human experience.[153] The reality of time hinders human cognition; humans are unable to understand the temporal reality in which they live, proving "highly problematic for human attempts to fashion a meaningful existence."[154] The effect of the inaccessibility of the two temporal horizons of past and future is that the present is rendered ultimately meaningless.[155] In an attempt to challenge his conclusion regarding the inaccessibility of the past, Qoheleth uses three stories (1:12–2:20; 4:13–16; 9:13–15) but he ends up demonstrating the transient nature of all human undertakings and upholding the very conclusion he tried to escape: "the inevitability of oblivion."[156]

With the loss of the temporal horizons, Qoheleth does, at times, put forward enjoyment as a "positive alternative" to the view that the present is meaningless; however, this advice is downplayed and overshadowed by

---

149. Barbour, *The Story of Israel*, 164–65.

150. Barbour, *The Story of Israel*, 46. Barbour believes there is room for this position within a multifaceted understanding of *hebel* and that, in particular, it is naturally connected with a view of *hebel* as transience; see Barbour, *The Story of Israel*, 46–47.

151. Barbour, *The Story of Israel*, 171. However, she elsewhere demonstrates an interpretation of joy as a resignation as she notes that Qoheleth offers enjoyment as the only means of possible escape; see Barbour, *The Story of Israel*, 70.

152. Bundvad, *Time*, 1.

153. Bundvad, *Time*, 46, 72–73.

154. Bundvad, *Time*, 1, 60.

155. Bundvad, *Time*, 1–3, 45–46, 72–74.

156. Bundvad, *Time*, 184–85. In contrast to Bundavd's interpretation of the inaccessibility of the past and the author's use of anonymity to obscure the past, Barbour sees the book as pointing to something reasonably concrete, such that the tale of Eccl 9:13–15 points specifically to the siege of Jerusalem in 701 BC, even if its reference is more to the literary memory than to the actual event; see Barbour, *The Story of Israel*, 126.

Qoheleth's more poignant assertions.[157] In the end, Qoheleth is simply pessimistic. And this negative attitude also applies toward his view of God, who is to blame for the present state of affairs. "It is God who has established the temporal structures that hinder our cognitive engagement with the temporal process—and he maintains them so as to keep us in the dark. Not only would it seem that God is aligned with the oppressors in human society, he is also the original oppressor."[158] Bundvad takes the closing poem, with its description of God as the giver, as Qoheleth's final sarcastic sting—the first being 1:13, where God is mentioned as the one who gave humanity an evil task—against the deity and could be paraphrased as follows: remember your Creator; this is all his fault.[159]

1.6 SUMMARY

This chapter has briefly surveyed and outlined the current state of scholarship with respect to the message of Qoheleth. A large number of scholars argue that *hebel* represents the core of Qoheleth's message. Typically, these proponents understand *hebel* in primarily negative terms and interpret the commendations of joy as merely resignations and concessions. An additional cohort of no small size argues that the main message is found not in *hebel* but in the recurrent joy passages. Scholars in this category commonly view *hebel* not as a conclusion but more as the situation or difficulty that Qoheleth faced. And joy is usually interpreted as either a positive commendation or more strongly as a divine command. A smaller number of scholars seek to give greater weight to the fear of God motif and root Qoheleth's message in this traditional dictum. Of course, there are a myriad of mediating positions that hold various motifs together in various ways. Some see *hebel* and joy actively interacting (as opposed to the latter simply being a response to the former) in either complementary or contradictory ways. Some hold joy and the fear of God together as paired motifs comprising an essential part of the other or as two separate motifs in equal balance.

While admittingly selective, this portrait of the landscape reveals the propensity of scholars to associate Qoheleth's core message with one

---

157. Bundvad, *Time*, 150. For example, Bundvad argues that the commendation of joy in the final joy passage (11:9) is pushed into the background by the final poem; Bundvad, *Time*, 73.

158. Bundvad, *Time*, 113.

159. Bundvad, *Time*, 70, 113.

or more of the primary motifs of either *hebel*, joy, or the fear of God. Further, scholars tend to understand Qoheleth's message in terms of the interrelation of the key motifs. It is within, or more appropriately, building upon, this varied landscape that this project aims to make a contribution.

The thesis of this project bears a few similarities with the field. Of note, there are similarities with Christianson and Fox in terms of a narrative understanding of Qoheleth's address—Qoheleth is recounting his past experiences and offering subsequent advice. With respect to the elevation of certain motifs and Qoheleth's message, this project sits squarely within the third group; that is, those who elevate the fear of God. And the closest scholar to the thesis of this project is, perhaps, Bartholomew.

For all the similarities, there are many differences. While Lee argues that joy and the fear of God are paired motifs and interprets joy as a religious duty, this project does not see joy as a command but more as a positive commendation. Further, the fear of God does not carry a primary understanding of enjoyment but is closer to the understanding found in Proverbs and the rest of the OT. While Fuhr sees joy and the fear of God as two motifs in equal balance and as a two-fold model for life in a *hebel*-world, this project sees the fear of God motif as foundational, one which is to qualify all of one's actions, including one's enjoyment. Bartholomew sees a primary contradictory juxtaposition between *hebel* and joy, the tension of which forms a gap in which Qoheleth puts forward the fear of God. This project, however, does not see the fear of God rising from such a gap and views the intensifying joy passages as part of Qoheleth's positive advice. Additionally, this project does not view tension building until the breaking point at 11:7 but sees the first half of Qoheleth's address as largely conveying his quest and then the second half focusing more on instruction with an acknowledgment of the limitations of human wisdom; however, this is not a strictly linear progression, as Qoheleth's instruction is sprinkled throughout. But of course, the many similarities and differences will become much clearer and be explored in greater detail in the ensuing chapters.

2

The Context of Qoheleth

2.1 INTRODUCTION

THE PREVIOUS CHAPTER SURVEYED the breadth of scholarship on Qoheleth's address and demonstrated the great range of interpretations. One's interpretation of Qoheleth is affected by one's view of the text's context. Does the book belong to a category of Israelite wisdom literature or is it, perhaps, more at home in the various wisdom traditions of the ANE? Should it belong to a Solomonic corpus, or is it more settled in the Megilloth? Maybe these categories say too much, and the book should be left to speak by itself as one of the many texts found in the Writings or even as an independent and unrelated work in the OT?

This chapter examines the context of Qoheleth's address.[1] Specifically, three contextual levels will be considered, moving from the most proximate and progressing outward; namely, 1) the context of Qoheleth within the book of Ecclesiastes, 2) the context of Qoheleth/Ecclesiastes within Israel's wisdom tradition, particularly in relation to Proverbs, and 3) the context of Israel's wisdom books within the OT. As it concerns the foundation of Israel's wisdom, this chapter will also touch on wisdom's relation to the traditions of the ANE as well as to creation. In considering the various levels of context, this chapter argues that Qoheleth's

---

1. The interpretive context in question gives primary focus to the literary and theological rather than the historical. The majority of scholars attribute Ecclesiastes to the Hellenistic period, that is, the third century BC (Longman, *Ecclesiastes*, 9–11; Bartholomew, *Ecclesiastes*, 46; Krüger, *Qoheleth*, 19), with some arguing for the slightly earlier Persian context of the late fifth to early fourth century BC (Seow, *Ecclesiastes*, 21–36; Enns, *Ecclesiastes*, 21).

address should be interpreted in the context of and thus, informed by, 1) the frame narrator of Ecclesiastes, 2) in a complementary relationship with Proverbs, rather than an antithetical one representing a wisdom crisis, and 3) as rooted in Israel's covenantal relationship with God and thus, complementary to what is found in the rest of the OT. This understanding of the context provides an important foundation for examining Qoheleth's address in the following chapters. Each of the three contextual levels will be addressed in turn.

2.2 THE WISDOM OF QOHELETH AND THE BOOK OF ECCLESIASTES

The present discussion of the context of Qoheleth's address begins with its immediate proximity; namely, the book of Ecclesiastes. The purpose of this section is twofold: first, to demarcate the boundaries of Qoheleth's address; and second, to situate his address within the context of the book.

Upon an initial reading of Ecclesiastes, the reader will quickly discern that the book presents two distinct voices. The most prevalent of the two is the voice of Qoheleth. This voice first appears in 1:12 with a self-introduction: "I [Qoheleth] have been king over Israel in Jerusalem." This voice is responsible for the book's first-person narration and his address covers the majority of the book. Qoheleth tells the reader, "And I applied my heart to seek and to search out..." (1:13); "I have seen everything that is done under the sun..." (1:14); "So I became great..." (2:9); "I hated all my toil..." (2:18); "Again I saw..." (4:1); "In my vain life I have seen..." (7:15); "Then I saw..." (8:10); "But all this I laid to heart..." (9:1); "I have seen..." (10:7); *passim*. Qoheleth's address is markedly autobiographical in nature.

In contrast to Qoheleth's presentation, there are a few occasions on which a second voice is clearly discernable. This voice reveals itself most plainly in six verses as it speaks about Qoheleth in the third-person:

> The words of [Qoheleth], the son of David, king in Jerusalem. (1:1)
>
> Vanity of vanities, says [Qoheleth], vanity of vanities! All is vanity. (1:2)
>
> Behold, this is what I found, says [Qoheleth] . . . (7:27)
>
> Vanity of vanities, says [Qoheleth]; all is vanity." (12:8)
>
> Besides being wise, [Qoheleth] also taught the people knowledge . . . (12:9)

[Qoheleth] sought to find words of delight, and uprightly he wrote words of truth. (12:10)

A consideration of these verses reveals not only the voice of a narrator but also a voice that is found in three textual locations: beginning, middle, and end. First, the narrator opens the book and introduces Qoheleth as the primary speaker. The narrator also closes the book with some final thoughts after Qoheleth has concluded. Lastly, and more subtly, the narrator makes a passing appearance in the middle of Qoheleth's address.[2]

As this project is foremost concerned with the message of Qoheleth, the boundaries of his address must be identified and differentiated from that of the narrator. Taking into consideration the evidence and location of the narrator's voice, Qoheleth's address may be identified as 1:12–12:7, apart from the momentary intrusion by the narrator in 7:27. The result is a basic structure of the book as follows:

Superscription (1:1)
Frame A: Prologue (1:2–11)
  Qoheleth's Address (1:12—12:7)
Frame B: Epilogue (12:8–14)

Not everyone accepts this basic division. And the most contentious real estate continues to be the leading question and opening poem of 1:3–11 and the issue of its ascription to the narrator or Qoheleth.[3] The primary argument for attributing the opening poem to Qoheleth is the presence of the literary *inclusio* of 1:2 and 12:8, which is thought to mark the *immediate* bounds of Qoheleth's address; that is, 1:3—12:7.[4] The most significant evidence for narratorial ascription is that Qoheleth's self-introduction does not come until 1:12. And this is further supported by comparable ANE texts.[5] Though scholarly consensus is unreached, there

---

2. For a discussion of the role and significance of this midpoint self-revelation, see chapter 3.

3. A second point of contention concerns the *inclusio* comprised of 1:2 and 12:8, though, it is the latter half that is more disputed. However, the clear presence of the narrator's voice, as evidenced by the third-person reference to Qoheleth, makes their attribution to the narrator quite convincing.

4. Christianson, *Time to Tell*, 98, describes an *inclusio* as "a kind of framing, a formal mark of structure with an emphatic rhetorical function. The inclusion serves to mark off a specified section of text . . . [like] two identical doors at either end of the same room . . . or perhaps the ornate covers of a book." See also Longman, "Inclusio," 323–25.

5. One notable proponent of viewing 1:12 as the beginning of Qoheleth's address

is considerably more evidence, in the opinion of this writer, for attributing the opening poem to the narrator.[6] And so, this project works with the position that Qoheleth's address begins in 1:12 and concludes in 12:7.

Considering this basic structure, the result can properly be described as a frame narrative. A frame narrative "is a text in which an external narrator narrates an inner story at its beginning and end, thereby framing (highlighting, privileging, delimiting, etc.) the story that it narrates."[7] A few observations may be drawn: 1) the narrator introduces and presents Qoheleth; 2) after Qoheleth's address, the narrator provides an epilogue, in which he evaluates Qoheleth and offers his own conclusion; 3) the frame narrative is an integral part of the book; 4) the narrator is the implied author of the book; 5) the narrator is the one who gives Qoheleth room to speak and does so for his own reasons; 6) the narrator, through the frame with its introduction and conclusion, guides the reader's approach to Qoheleth; and 7) The narrator has the final word, both sequentially and authoritatively. To say this another way, Qoheleth's address is set within the context of the narrator's frame.

The recognition of this structure leads to an important question: what is the frame narrator trying to communicate or highlight to the reader by framing Qoheleth's address?[8] That is, what is the nature of

---

is Longman, who argues that 1:12–12:7 (and not the prologue or epilogue) bears great structural similarities with fictional autobiographies from the ANE; see Longman, *Fictional Akkadian Autobiography*; and Longman, *Ecclesiastes*, 8, 15–20, 58–59. See also Shields, "Qohelet and Royal Autobiography," 117–36. For an assessment of Longman's Akkadian connection and application to Ecclesiastes, see Koh, *Royal Autobiography*, 106–12; and Weeks, "Wisdom, Form and Genre," 168–71.

6. For further discussion on the opening poem, see Beldman, "Framed! Structure in Ecclesiastes," 150–51; Bartholomew, *Ecclesiastes*, 109–12; Fox, *Time to Tear Down*, 163–69; and Seow, *Ecclesiastes*, 111–17. While the opening poem's prefatory function is relatively unchanged by its attribution to either the narrator or Qoheleth, one implication is that the leading question of יתרון in 1:3 is posed by the narrator rather than Qoheleth, who presents his own question, of sorts, as he introduces his quest. This is, for example, contra Ogden, who sees 1:3 as the first of three prongs—question (יתרון); answer (*hebel*); and response (joy)—that form the basic structure for Qoheleth's address; see, Ogden, *Qoheleth*, 16–18.

7. Christianson, *Time to Tell*, 57; see 52–72 for his larger discussion. Fox notes that many ANE wisdom texts were framed by a third-person introduction and/or conclusion around first-person autobiography and points to the following: The Instructions of Kagemeni; The Prophecy of Neferti; The Admonitions of Ipuwer; Onchsheshonqy; Deuteronomy; Tobit; and, as an example from modern literature, *Uncle Remus* (Fox, "Frame Narrative," 92–96).

8. While many scholars recognize the presence and importance of the frame, there are varying opinions on its function. For discussion, see the following: Fox, "Frame

the relationship between Qoheleth and the narrator? Are the theologies they espouse identical, complementary, diverging, or antithetical? The question of their relationship is no small matter; however, it is one that must be put on hold for the time being. The subsequent chapters will examine Qoheleth's message, after which the latter part of chapter 4 will resume this question and consider the epilogue with its assessment, warning, and concluding message.

In sum, this section has identified two voices in Ecclesiastes and demarcated the scope of Qoheleth's address as 1:12—12:7. Further, in the final form of the book, Qoheleth's address is presented within the context of the frame provided by the narrator. An interpretation of Qoheleth's message must account for this context.

2.3 QOHELETH AND ISRAEL'S WISDOM TRADITION

2.3.1 Introduction

This section takes a second step back and considers the next level of context for Qoheleth's wisdom. Not only is his teaching set within the context of the frame narrator but the book of Ecclesiastes is also set within the context of Israel's wisdom literature.[9] Ecclesiastes is not simply an isolated

---

Narrative," 83–106; Christianson, *Time to Tell*, 52–125; Enns, *Ecclesiastes*, 4–16; Provan, *Ecclesiastes*, 26–31; Longman, *Ecclesiastes*, 37–39; Beldman, "Framed! Structure in Ecclesiastes," 150–54; Shields, *End of Wisdom*, 47–49; and Bartholomew, *Ecclesiastes*, 63–79.

9. The designation "wisdom literature," commonly referring to the books of Job, Proverbs, and Ecclesiastes, has become quite contested. The traditional paradigm of wisdom literature, stemming largely from Gunkel's work in the early twentieth century on form-criticism, connected the *Sitz im Leben* of wisdom literature with the sages, who were distinct from the prophets and priests in their worldview (see Gunkel, "The Literature of Ancient Israel," 69–70). Further, this wisdom was understood as originally secular in character, with origins going back to Egypt. The result of the paradigm was a strong disconnect, even incompatibility, between biblical wisdom and the rest of the OT. Though some would uphold this traditional paradigm, such as Crenshaw, who sees the wisdom corpus as an alien group within the OT and an "alternative to Yahwism" (Crenshaw, *Old Testament Wisdom*, 24–25), there is general agreement that it is faulty in its rigid categorization and segregation. Various modern theories of genre are being employed as many scholars seek to either reform the category of wisdom or move on from it entirely. While rejecting the traditional paradigm, as the present chapter will make clear, this project still uses the term "wisdom literature" as it carries utility. For discussions on the history and state of scholarship and for various approaches and proposals, see the following: Kynes, *An Obituary for "Wisdom Literature"*; Longman, *Fear of the Lord*, 276–82; Sneed, "Is the 'Wisdom Tradition' a Tradition?" 50–71; and Sneed, *Was There a Wisdom Tradition?*, which includes chapters on the subject by Sneed, Weeks, Dell, Fox, Kynes, and others.

book; it exists within a tradition. But how does it fit within and relate to its inherited tradition?

There is general acceptance that Proverbs represents the wisdom tradition of Israel in which Ecclesiastes later comes into being. And most scholars readily affirm some connection between these two works—either with Proverbs directly or to the tradition more generally that Proverbs represents. However, views of the nature of their relationship vary considerably. For some, Ecclesiastes is operating within and upholding the tradition. For others, the book is critiquing and reforming the tradition. And for others still, the book is exposing the folly of the tradition and rejecting it wholesale. And of course, there a several nuanced positions surrounding these.

This section argues that Ecclesiastes occurs in the context of and thus, is to be read in connection with Israel's wisdom tradition in general and with Proverbs in particular. Moreover, this section argues that Ecclesiastes and Proverbs are fully compatible and complementary, expressing the same basic theology and understanding of wisdom and that Qoheleth does not represent what has come to be known as a "wisdom crisis." To this end, this section will consider first, the evidence for the relationship between Proverbs and Ecclesiastes and second, the nature of their relationship.

2.3.2 The Evidence for the Ecclesiastes-Proverbs Relationship

There is much evidence to suggest that Proverbs and Ecclesiastes share a similar context and that the latter is meant to be read with the former.[10] The first and most obvious line of evidence is that the books of Proverbs and Ecclesiastes share considerable similarities with respect to form and content.[11] And the level of similarity is of a higher degree than between either of these books and any other OT book.[12] These books contain many

---

10. By context, what is meant is a canonical context. This is not a claim that these two books were written at the same time nor does it deny the lengthy, complicated, and mysterious process of the formation of these texts.

11. Fox writes, "To understand the course and significance of Qohelet's ideas we must set them within the context of his intellectual background. For this we look primarily (but not exclusively) to didactic Wisdom Literature, because the book of Qohelet is closest to this genre in form, subject matter, and, to a large extent, ideology" (Fox, *Time to Tear Down*, 5).

12. The next closest OT book in terms of shared form and content is Job. Similarities are also found with the apocryphal works Ben Sira and the Wisdom of Solomon; however, since these texts were written after Ecclesiastes, they will not be discussed

sayings of various kinds, admonitions, poems, reflections, etc.[13] And at their core, both address the subject of wisdom and contrast the wise person and the fool. One would be hard-pressed to find a commentary on Ecclesiastes that does not compare it with Proverbs on some level.

The second point of evidence concerns the book's superscription, along with its Solomonic association. Ecclesiastes opens with the superscription, "The words of [Qoheleth], son of David, king in Jerusalem" (1:1; see also 1:12). While such superscriptions are a common feature in Hebrew literature, this opening sounds particularly reminiscent of the one found in Proverbs, which begins, "The Proverbs of Solomon, son of David, king of Israel" (Prov 1:1). Additionally, Proverbs contains several superscriptions introducing various collections:[14]

> The Proverbs of Solomon. (Prov 10:1a)
> Incline your ear to hear the words of the wise . . . (Prov 22:17a)
> These also are sayings of the wise . . . (Prov 24:23a)[15]
> These also are proverbs of Solomon . . . (Prov 25:1a)
> The words of Agur son of Jakeh . . . (Prov 30:1a)
> The words of King Lemuel . . . (Prov 31:1a)

The dominant scholarly position is that the writer of Ecclesiastes simply appealed to Solomon in an effort to imbue his address with credibility and weight.[16] Wilson, however, pushes for a stronger connection between the superscriptions of the two books and argues that their similarities create a dual effect: first, Qoheleth is associated with Solomon,

---

here. For a discussion of the wisdom of Ben Sira and the Wisdom of Solomon, see Murphy, *The Tree of Life*, 65–96; Crenshaw, *Old Testament Wisdom*, 155–87; McLaughlin, *Israel's Wisdom Tradition*, 112–40. Additionally, Proverbs and Ecclesiastes share significant similarities with numerous ANE texts; these will be addressed below.

13. For a discussion of literary forms, see Waltke, *Proverbs 1–15*, 38–50; Murphy, *Proverbs*, xxii–xxv.

14. While some superscriptions speak of words/sayings (דבר) or proverbs (משל)—note also "saying" (מליצה) and "riddles" (חידת) in Prov 1:6—Wilson argues that there is "no appreciable difference in the contents of these collections that can be correlated with the terminology" (Wilson, "Words of the Wise," 179). And, observing דברים as more general, he concludes that Proverbs can be viewed as a collection of "words of the wise[men]" (Wilson, "Words of the Wise," 179).

15. The Hebrew does not include "sayings": גַּם־אֵלֶּה לַחֲכָמִים. Wilson argues that this superscription is more generic and indicates that the authors that follow also belong to the wise; see Wilson, "Words of the Wise," 179.

16. Additionally, the view holds that after the initial royal experiment, the writer discards the façade. For various examples, see the following: Crenshaw, *Ecclesiastes*, 70–71; Enns, *Ecclesiastes*, 16–22; Seow, *Ecclesiastes*, 37, 48; Longman, *Ecclesiastes*, 6–7; and Bartholomew, *Ecclesiastes*, 47.

binding the two books together under a single wisdom figure; and second, Qoheleth's address is viewed as a collection similar to those found in Proverbs, either as another in succession to the various collections in Proverbs or as a second work to the first.[17]

But of course, Ecclesiastes' superscription is not its only Solomonic connection. Qoheleth's self-introduction in 1:12 echoes the book's superscription and his opening royal experiment alludes to the historical account of Solomon found in Kings and Chronicles. Qoheleth is described as the son of David (1:1, 12), king in Jerusalem/Israel (1:1, 12), he possessed incredible wealth and possessions (2:7–8), he conducted great building projects (2:4–6), and he was greater than all before him in Jerusalem (1:16; 2:9). These additional Solomonic connotations serve to bolster the connection between the superscription and the book and Proverbs.

An important note concerning the superscription, and the book, is that Solomon is not explicitly named. In place of Solomon, the speaker is identified as Qoheleth seven times (1:1, 2, 12; 7:27; 12:8, 9, 10). Stemming from the root קהל, Qoheleth translates roughly as "the assembler." Some find in this name a specific reference to Solomon, or at least to an aspect of his character.[18] Though, some argue for a broader or more distanced association.[19] Much could be said about the connection between Qoheleth and Solomon and its implications, but that is not the purpose here.[20] While there is disagreement concerning the extent, nature, and

---

17. Wilson, "Words of the Wise," 179. Others who see a more substantial purpose behind the superscription include Lohfink, who argues that the title was added to make Ecclesiastes a Solomonic book so as to join the book, as a textbook, to other official Jewish books (more specifically, other Solomonic books) to be used in temple/synagogue schools; see Lohfink, *Qoheleth*, 11–12. Schultz holds that the Solomonic ascription suggests not only a connection with Proverbs but also a basic harmony between them; see Schultz, "Unity or Diversity," 279–81.

18. For example, Seitz argues that the name/title "Qoheleth" is not so much a direct reference to the historical Solomon, per se, but an evocation of an aspect of Solomon's kingship as it focuses on the particular juncture of 1 Kings 8, where King Solomon assembles—the root קהל occurs six times in the chapter—prays for, and blesses Israel; see Seitz, "A Canonical Reading of Ecclesiastes," 105–06.

19. Barbour connects such allusions less specifically to Solomon, though he is the base pastiche, but more generally to all of Israel's kings; see Barbour, *The Story of Israel*, 10, 17, 30. Bundvad sees the name Qoheleth as a stylistic choice reflective of intentional distancing from Solomon, for the past is forgotten and inaccessible; see Bundvad, *Time*, 172–73.

20. For further discussion on wisdom's Solomonic connection, see Bartholomew, *Ecclesiastes*, 43–54; Seow, *Ecclesiastes*, 36–38; Longman, *Ecclesiastes*, 2–11; Provan, *Ecclesiastes*, 26–31; and Jackson, "Solomon," 733–37.

purpose of Solomonic association in Ecclesiastes, the combined evidence unmistakably makes a connection.

In sum, the superscription, bolstered by other Solomonic allusions and echoes, including the name Qoheleth, suggests a shared context.

Third, a connection between Ecclesiastes and Proverbs is supported by the larger view expressed in the epilogue of Ecclesiastes. The opening verses of the epilogue present some sort of evaluation of Qoheleth and his address (12:9–10), after which the epilogist appears to shift focus. Ecclesiastes 12:11 begins, דִּבְרֵי חֲכָמִים, "The words of the wise." The move from the singular Qoheleth to a plurality of wise men indicates the epilogist's shift of focus. No longer commenting solely on this single sage, the larger tradition comes into view.[21] To be sure, Qoheleth is included—he was just allowed to speak at great length (1:12—12:7) and was evaluated in a positive manner by the epilogist (12:9–10)—but he cannot alone fill the enlarged referent. Wilson notes that the phrase "words of the wise" occurs only four times in the MT (Prov 1:6; 22:17; Eccl 9:17; 12:11), all of which, he argues, refer to a knowable body of knowledge, which was for meditating, understanding, and personal benefit.[22] The next verse of the epilogue continues the plurality: וְיֹתֵר מֵהֵמָּה, "Beyond these" (12:12).[23] Wilson argues that this verse represents a canonical statement of limitation, one that would place the wisdom of Qoheleth in a group with other wise men.[24] The point here, for now, is that the epilogue of Ecclesiastes has in view and speaks on more than just Qoheleth. And this leads to the next point.

The fourth line of evidence for a connection between the two wisdom books comes in the form of similarities between the epilogue of Ecclesiastes and the prologue of Proverbs. The argument is that the writer of the epilogue intentionally alluded to the prologue so as to tie the two wisdom books together. Wilson argues that the prologue and epilogue display "correspondences of theme, structure, and function."[25] First, both serve a hermeneutical function. The prologue of Proverbs (Prov 1:2–7) introduces the book and sets the purpose, while in the epilogue

---

21. Childs, *Introduction*, 585.

22. Wilson, "Words of the Wise," 176, 179–80. Additionally, that the only occurrences are found in Proverbs and Ecclesiastes may suggest that these two books comprise the larger view in mind.

23. There is much debate about the referent of "these" as well as the warning that follows. For discussion, see chapter 4.

24. Wilson, "Words of the Wise," 177, 179–80.

25. Wilson, "Words of the Wise," 180.

of Ecclesiastes, the narrator evaluates Qoheleth, guides the reader's response, and provides the book's final message.[26] Second, both present the fear of the Lord/God as the basic wisdom principle. This claim is both the pinnacle of Proverb's prologue (Prov 1:7) and the final, climactic exhortation of Ecclesiastes' epilogue (12:13). Third, both mention the "words of the wise" (Prov 1:6; Eccl 12:11). Moreover, both indicate that the words of the wise are to be the object of meditation and source of direction.[27] Fourth, the description of Qoheleth in 12:9–10 is illustrative of the outcome anticipated in the prologue.[28] Qoheleth is wise, able to teach others, has understanding, and communicates truth. Fifth, the prologue states that the fear of the Lord is the *beginning* of wisdom, and the epilogue declares that the *end* of the matter, one's whole duty, is to fear God and keep his commands. Sixth, Prov 1:3 urges the pursuit of right conduct (צֶדֶק וּמִשְׁפָּט וּמֵישָׁרִים) and, correspondingly, Eccl 12:14 speaks of the judgment to come over every deed.[29] See figure 2.1, which illustrates the many similarities, arranged according to their occurrence in the epilogue.

Some of the prologue-epilogue connections are stronger than others—the image of a father instructing his son is, after all, a common wisdom trope. One may argue that the similarities in vocabulary and thought merely reflect a common wisdom milieu and are thus, coincidental rather than indicative of an intentional correlation.[30] However, when combined,

---

26. Wilson, "Words of the Wise," 180.

27. Wilson, "Words of the Wise," 180.

28. Wilson writes, "It is not impossible that the epilogist has purposely cast his description of Qohelet in light of the exhortation of Proverbs" (Wilson, "Words of the Wise," 181).

29. Wilson, "Words of the Wise," 181–82.

30. In particular, note the dissenting voice of Sheppard. While he, like Wilson, picks up the idea of canon-consciousness from Childs, he turns not to Proverbs but rather goes in the opposite direction to Sirach; see Sheppard, "Epilogue," 186–87. Sheppard wishes to temper connections between Proverbs and Ecclesiastes and rejects the view of intentional association as extreme (Sheppard, "Epilogue," 184). For another voice in agreement with Sheppard, see Murphy, *Ecclesiastes*, 126; cf. Childs, *Introduction*, 586. Sheppard's position is largely based on Eccl 12:13–14 and the dissimilarities he finds between it and Proverbs and the similarities he finds between it and Sirach. He notes that while Proverbs speaks of the LORD (יהוה), Ecclesiastes refers to God (אלהים), and while Ecclesiastes speaks of God's commands (12:13), Proverbs only speaks of a father's commands to his son; thus, Ecclesiastes greatly exceeds in its understanding (Sheppard, "Epilogue," 184–85). As such, Sheppard argues that the specific phrase found in Eccl 12:13, "Fear God and keep his commandments," does not occur in Proverbs and is alien to that book; moreover, "only Sirach has exactly the same ideology" (Sheppard, "Epilogue," 184–85, 187; see Sir 1; 2:15; 15:1; 19:20; 43:27). And concerning the "words of the wise" in Prov 1:6 and Eccl 12:11, Sheppard sees these as vague, general terms

the accumulative effect persuasively suggests a correspondence that cannot so casually be dismissed.

	The Prologue of Proverbs		The Epilogue of Ecclesiastes
1:2	To know wisdom	12:9	Qoheleth was wise
1:4	To give knowledge	12:9	Qoheleth taught the people knowledge
1:5	Let the wise hear	12:9	Qoheleth weighed/heard[31]
1:3	To receive instruction in uprightness	12:10	Uprightly wrote words of truth
1:6	The words of the wise	12:11	The words of the wise
1:5	That one may obtain guidance[32]	12:11	The words of the wise are like goads
1:4	The youth	12:12	My son
1:7	The fear of the Lord is the beginning	12:13	The end of the matter ... fear God
1:3	Instruction in righteousness, justice, and equity	12:14	God will judge every deed, whether good or evil

Figure 2.1. The Prologue of Proverbs and the Epilogue of Ecclesiastes

without any intentional link (Sheppard, "Epilogue," 184).

Wilson considers Sheppard's conclusion based on the different names for the divine exaggerated and argues that the terms are practically equivalent; further, "fears God" is found in Job 1:1, 8; 2:3, suggesting at least some interchangeability of the terms (Wilson, "Words of the Wise," 181n14). Further, Wilson writes, "The contention of some that Qoh 12:9–14 finds its closest parallels with Sirach since both are concerned with the 'commandments of God/YHWH' while Proverbs is not, is not ultimately persuasive due to the implicit connection of *miṣwôtāy* in Proverbs 1–9 with YHWH's commandments. Rather it would seem likely that Qoh 12:9–14 occupies a mediating position between the implicit connections of Proverbs and the emphatic professions of Sirach" (Wilson, "Words of the Wise," 190).

31. While the Hebrew verb אָזַן is often thought to represent אזן II, "to weigh," and possibly relate to the Aramaic cognate noun "scales," Longman argues that it stems from the root אזן I, "to hear, listen to," an understanding which makes logical sense and carries strong textual support; see Longman, *Ecclesiastes*, 275n62.

32. The word תַּחְבֻּלוֹת, "guidance," is likely a nautical term connoting a helmsman steering a ship (*HALOT*, תַּחְבֻּלוֹת, IV:1716; see also Waltke, *Proverbs 1–15*, 96). This word also occurs in Job 37:12, where God guides the clouds to accomplish that which he has commanded them (see also Prov 11:14; 12:5; 20:18; 24:6). While the specific vocabulary is absent from the epilogue, a similar picture is presented in Eccl 12:11, where the words of the wise are likened to a shepherd's goad that guides the flock along a certain path and toward an intended outcome.

A fifth and final line of evidence for the connection of Ecclesiastes with Proverbs concerns the canonical ordering of the books. Wilson notes that while the Writings enjoyed much variety, from Baba Batra 14b (c. second century BC, the earliest extant ordering) to the Council of Laodicea (c. AD 400), Proverbs and Ecclesiastes were always located together and in that order.[33] He writes, "while order does not in itself prove connection, its persistence in the face of the general variety of Hagiographic arrangement is consistent with the recognition of a close relationship between the two books."[34] As such, the early canonical ordering offers a measure of support.[35]

In sum, there are several lines of evidence suggesting a significant and intentional connection between Ecclesiastes and Proverbs. This is not to claim that they are or ever were a single book but that they are to be read together in a shared context. While some of the evidence in the section is stronger than others, the overarching picture establishes a strong case.

2.3.3 The Nature of the Ecclesiastes-Proverbs Relationship

To say that Ecclesiastes and Proverbs should be interpreted in a similar context and in conversation is only part of the matter. Indeed, most scholars hold that Ecclesiastes stands in relation to Proverbs, although they see wildly different purposes at play. Thus, the more significant question is that of the nature of their relationship. To what extent does Ecclesiastes put forward the same theology as Proverbs? Conversely, to what extent are they divergent? Is it more appropriate to speak of Ecclesiastes as upholding, reforming, criticizing, or even rejecting the earlier wisdom represented in Proverbs?

The most dominant scholarly position of the past couple generations has understood Qoheleth in an adverse relationship with Proverbs, in which Qoheleth is redirecting, correcting, or rejecting the tradition in

---

33. Wilson, "Words of the Wise," 190–91. He holds that the ordering in the LXX and MT, which do not continue this early tradition, reflect later movements that aimed to group together the Megilloth; however, in the early formative years of the canon, Proverb-Qoheleth was the rule; see Wilson, "Words of the Wise," 191.

34. Wilson, "Words of the Wise," 191. In response to the ordering of Baba Batra 14b, Sheppard notes that "one could perhaps conceive of this ordering as an early constant" (Sheppard, "Epilogue," 183).

35. For further discussion on the ordering of the books, see Steinberg, "The Place of Wisdom Literature," 147–73. See also the other essays in the volume.

some way. And this general position is often described as a sort of wisdom crisis. To understand the wisdom crisis theory, one can look back to some of the presuppositions that led to its ascent.

The rise and dominance of historical criticism, in its various manifestations, significantly affected wisdom scholarship. Gunkel's form-criticism saw wisdom as overly separate from the rest of the OT.[36] Shifts included the dissociation of Ecclesiastes from Solomon, a developmental view of wisdom from secular to religious, and the dissection of the books in novel ways at the hands of source and redaction-critical theories.[37] Wisdom was seen as more universal than particular and foreign to Israel's faith, and the god of wisdom was no longer Yahweh but an *Urhebergott*, a god of origins.[38] This god established order in creation and the sage's job was to discover, apply, teach, and live according to this order.[39] This was often coupled with an understanding of early Egyptian views of a deterministic *ma'at* order.[40] The result is that the wisdom enterprise was understood as the search for order.[41] And one of the basic orders was retribution.

In 1955, Koch presented a paper arguing that there is an act-consequence connection in Proverbs and elsewhere in the OT.[42] That is, certain actions led to certain consequences. Wise and good actions led to good results and foolish and evil actions led to bad results. The correspondence

---

36. Gunkel, "The Literature of Ancient Israel," 69–70. Although he saw a strong distinction between early wisdom and Israel's faith, Gunkel's work did greatly contribute to the increase of scholarly attention on wisdom.

37. For an overview, see Bartholomew, "Old Testament Wisdom Today," 7–13. Here, he provides an overview of wisdom scholarship through the helpful framework of a series of scholarly "turns"; namely, the historical, literary, postmodern, and theological turn; see Bartholomew, "Old Testament Wisdom Today," 3–36.

38. Murphy, *Ecclesiastes*, lxi; Murphy, *Proverbs*, 289.

39. Murphy, *Ecclesiastes*, lxi.

40. Murphy, *Tree of Life*, 115–18. *Ma'at*, the foundation of Egyptian wisdom, roughly means "truth," "justice," or "order" and came to be divinized as a goddess and was thought to serve as the base for lady wisdom; see Murphy, *Tree of Life*, 115, 161–62; Murphy, *Proverbs*, 289. For a brief survey of other proposed prototypes for Lady Wisdom, see Lucas, "The Book of Proverbs," 44–48. The study of ANE wisdom has often led to the superimposing of Egyptian ideas and worldview on Israel in what Murphy calls the *ma'atizing* of Israel's wisdom; see Murphy, *Tree of Life*, 115–18, 161–62; and Murphy, *Proverbs*, 289.

41. This is reflected in the view that Israel's wisdom tradition is rooted in creation and in the subsuming of wisdom under creation, or even natural, theology. For example, see Zimmerli, "The Place and Limit of the Wisdom," 146–58.

42. Koch, "Gibt es ein Vergeltungsdogma im Alten Testament," 1–42.

was mechanical; actions essentially had *built-in* consequences. Moreover, God did not actively reward or punish; his involvement was like a midwife who assists at birth—she facilitates that which is already set in motion.[43] Some argue that the idea of act-consequence is less precise and that character-consequence provides a more apt description for a couple of reasons: first, Proverbs is not just about actions but about one's character; and second, it is more reflective of the book's long-term perspective.[44] This mechanical act/character-consequence nexus was thought to be foundational to early Israelite wisdom and was associated with Proverbs.

Then real life happened, so to speak. Job, the righteous sufferer, was thought to call this nexus into question. And Ecclesiastes was seen as representing pessimism and skepticism, showing the complete failure of the nexus and humanity's inability to control outcomes in life. Thus, these latter two works represented a "wisdom crisis." Subsequently, a later, orthodox editor was thought to have appended an epilogue to Qoheleth's address. He not only criticized Qoheleth's message—whether severely as outright rejection and correction or more mildly as a redirection of emphasis—he also paved a new way forward for the tradition by connecting wisdom/fear of the Lord with Torah obedience, a nascent movement that progressed to greater maturity, as evidenced in Sirach.[45]

While nearly ubiquitous for a time, the wisdom crisis no longer has the same stranglehold on scholarship that it once did—though scholarship has only begun to recover. As belief in a full-blown crisis has fallen, somewhat, out of favor, many scholars have proposed various emendations to the theory. These proposals vary in the nature and severity of the perceived crisis. As such, the scholarly positions represent a broad spectrum. For some, Qoheleth rests well within Israel's wisdom tradition. For others, he is drifting away. Still others hold that Qoheleth stands at the very edge of Israel's wisdom and though he may be radical and may criticize those who came before him, he remains, at the end of the day,

---

43. Koch, "Doctrine of Retribution," 42–56. This is an abbreviated, English version of Koch's original.

44. For example, see van Leeuwen, "Wealth and Poverty" 27; Bartholomew and O'Dowd, *Old Testament Wisdom Literature*, 270–75; and Boström, "Retribution and Wisdom Literature," 139.

45. Compare with Schultz, who describes what he sees as the three contributing factors to the crisis theory; namely, 1) the rise of historical criticism, 2) Job and Ecclesiastes were thought to parallel a wisdom crisis in ANE texts, and 3) quotations, that is, Qoheleth quoted traditional wisdom in order to refute it; see Schultz, "Unity or Diversity," 275–79.

under the tradition's large umbrella. Lastly, some see Qoheleth as decidedly rejecting and stepping outside the bounds of the wisdom tradition. The following considers a few such approaches.

Crenshaw takes a position near one end of the spectrum. First, he rejects Koch's theory of retribution as being too strong and affirms that there was always a level of tension.[46] While the sages discovered such an order embedded in creation, it was still subject to God, since he could overrule it; however, he did not veto this foundational order arbitrarily and so, one could pursue it with confidence.[47] Nevertheless, Qoheleth's search leads to the conclusion that wisdom cannot achieve its goal; the entire enterprise has become bankrupt.[48] Crenshaw writes, "Qoheleth thus struck at the heart of the tradition in which he had been nurtured. Between him and old wisdom stretched a great abyss that was too deep for either to cross."[49] While Crenshaw's take on retribution is a shade softer than that of Koch's, Crenshaw's crisis is as strong as they come.

For Shields, Proverbs represents the beginning of Israel's wisdom movement and its "terse nature readily permits a naïve, mechanistic, (mis)interpretation of the world."[50] Even God is not free but bound to this embedded order.[51] Although Job reacts against this wisdom, Qoheleth takes it much further as his words "present a view of the world that appears diametrically opposed to the theistic framework upon which the Scriptures stand."[52] For Shields, the crisis is not found in a rejection of the wisdom tradition by Qoheleth, for Qoheleth fully embraced the

46. Crenshaw, *Old Testament Wisdom*, 88n2.

47. Crenshaw, *Old Testament Wisdom*, 61.

48. Crenshaw, *Old Testament Wisdom*, 127.

49. Crenshaw, *Old Testament Wisdom*, 129. Note the view of Brueggemann, who speaks of a crisis in response to the uncritical and oppressive Solomonic wisdom of Proverbs. He argues that "the Solomonic wisdom instituted a theodic settlement that was in fact a rationalization for the present system of inequity and exploitation"; see Brueggemann, "Social Significance," 131. Also note Clines, who argues that Proverbs—the most stalwart defender of the doctrine of retribution besides Deuteronomy—is rigid in its understanding and lacks sophistication and realism, qualities that are finally introduced by Job and Ecclesiastes as they challenge the tenets of Proverbs; see Clines, *Job 1–20*, lxi.

50. Shields, *End of Wisdom*, 238–39.

51. Shields writes, "Furthermore, God, as portrayed in the Wisdom Literature, is not a free agent but appears to be bound by the rules of moral cause and effect that the sages supposed were foundational to the universe in which they lived. According to Proverbs 8, even God must operate within the confines dictated by the wisdom that orders creation" (Shields, *End of Wisdom*, 7).

52. Shields, *End of Wisdom*, 7.

movement and was its true representative. Rather, Qoheleth finds himself in a crisis as he honestly takes wisdom to its logical conclusion, and in so doing, reveals the complete futility of the tradition.[53]

To better understand Qoheleth's relationship with Proverbs, Whybray investigates Qoheleth's quotation and use of traditional wisdom (as represented by Prov 10–29). To identify such quotations, Whybray establishes fourfold criteria: 1) it is self-contained; 2) the form is close to that of Proverbs; 3) the theme is close to that of Proverbs; and 4) there is no late language.[54] While Whybray identifies some forty sayings that meet the first two criteria, only eight qualify on all four accounts (Prov 2:14a; 4:5, 6; 7:5, 6a; 9:17; 10:2, 12).[55] From an examination of these, he draws a few conclusions: 1) Qoheleth saw himself as a wisdom teacher; 2) he quoted because he accepted their truth; and 3) he reinterpreted traditional wisdom in that instead of seeing the optimistic call to pursue wisdom, he saw the pessimism that folly prevails, and so, life is meaningless.[56] Whybray tries to hold together the two wisdom books and argues against those who see Qoheleth as rejecting his inherited tradition; nevertheless, Whybray ends up in much the same place.

Murphy puts forward a softer approach as he finds Koch's view of retribution unsatisfactory. He writes, "It is certainly true that the verbal expression of many sayings allows one to infer a correspondence, even a mechanical correspondence, between a good/bad action and its good/bad result. But along with such statements is the view that directly connects good and bad results with the Lord who rewards and punishes."[57] Although Qoheleth was clearly in conflict with traditional wisdom, his quarrel does not represent a crisis or a bankruptcy, but something subtler.[58] While Qoheleth rejected his inherited tradition for its simplicity and false security, he nevertheless thought, wrote, and remained

---

53. Shields, *End of Wisdom*, 6–7, 68–69, 106–07, 236–37. Though Qoheleth does not criticize the tradition and is even praised for his honesty as a sage, it is the epilogist who subsequently attacks the wisdom movement and warns his son of its grave dangers; see Shields, *End of Wisdom*, 69–92.

54. Whybray, "Quotations in Ecclesiastes," 437.

55. Whybray, "Quotations in Ecclesiastes," 438.

56. Whybray, "Quotations in Ecclesiastes," 450.

57. Murphy, *Tree of Life*, 117. See also Murphy, *Proverbs*, 264–69; and Boström, "Retribution and Wisdom Literature," 137, who criticizes the mechanical nature of the nexus and argues that it is hard to get away from the clear fact in Scripture that God is *actively* involved.

58. Murphy, *Ecclesiastes*, lxi.

within his tradition.⁵⁹ "The work of Qoheleth can be seen as a veritable purification of the ongoing wisdom movement, a blow in favor of divine freedom."⁶⁰ Thus, Murphy's interpretation represents a sort of soft- or mild-crisis, so to speak.

For Dell, Ecclesiastes, like Job, is wisdom in revolt.⁶¹ While the book steps beyond Job toward realistic resignation, Qoheleth remains within the tradition.⁶² Dell writes, "Ecclesiastes stands at the end of the biblical wisdom tradition and from that context criticizes it. Therefore, Ecclesiastes, in my view, represents a protesting or skeptical strain which arises closely out of the wisdom exercise even if it is of a deeply questioning kind."⁶³ Whether Qoheleth has stepped outside of his tradition or remains barely within, the crisis remains.

Those who retain a wisdom crisis generally share a few common traits. First, Proverbs is interpreted somewhat dogmatically; that is, the book is taken to represent a simplistic, mechanical act/character-consequence correspondence. Second, Qoheleth is interpreted as pessimistic or skeptical of his inherited wisdom tradition and Qoheleth's primary message is typically seen as decrying the futility of life or resigning to enjoyment. Third, the epilogue of Ecclesiastes is usually seen as a later editorial addition appended in order to offer an orthodox message in contrast to Qoheleth. While many of these scholars would claim some distance from the traditional crisis theory with its unnecessary rigidity and opt instead for descriptors such as reformation, purification, protest, etc., the gist remains. While not exactly the crisis of old, it is a crisis nonetheless.

Though some interpreters cling to the past crisis, many scholars call the overarching framework into question. They claim that Proverbs has been gravely misunderstood and that the book betrays a much more nuanced understanding of reality. Once this foundation has been challenged, the distance between Proverbs and Qoheleth is no longer what it once was, and the crisis theory has no legs to stand on.

59. Murphy, *Ecclesiastes*, lxiii–lxiv.

60. Murphy, *Ecclesiastes*, lxix. While Murphy proposes what seems to be some sort of a wisdom reformation, he also notes that Qoheleth had no real answer for the troubles he encountered, only the resigned conclusion to accept any pleasure that might happen to come one's way; see Murphy, *Ecclesiastes*, lxiv.

61. Dell, "Reading Ecclesiastes with the Scholars," 97.

62. Dell, "Reading Ecclesiastes with the Scholars," 97.

63. Dell, "Reading Ecclesiastes with the Scholars," 97.

Lucas argues against the view that Proverbs presents a simplistic act-consequence nexus and points to many proverbs that reveal a more complex understanding. He identifies several categories: 1) contradictory proverbs, which reflect the fact that proverbs are contextual and partial sayings (e.g. Prov 26:4–5); 2) "better-than" proverbs (e.g. Prov 16:8, 16); 3) "not fitting/becoming" sayings, which recognize that the nexus does not always work out (e.g. Prov 19:10); 4) a recognition that the wicked prosper and innocent people suffer (e.g. Prov 11:16; 13:23); 5) a recognition of incalculables (e.g. Prov 14:12; 27:1); and 6) a recognition that God can do his own plans (e.g. Prov 19:21; 21:30).[64] The sages knew that the "nexus" was simply a rule-of-thumb and not binding; life was complex and full of exceptions.[65]

Van Leeuwen offers an insightful study revealing the inaccuracy of simplistic dogmatism about acts and consequences. He analyzes sayings in Proverbs about wealth and poverty in relation to righteousness and wickedness and shows that the book discloses systematic contradictions on the matter.[66] He identifies four relationships represented by four quadrants, as shown in figure 2.2.[67]

	Righteousness	Wickedness
Wealth	1	3
Poverty	2	4

Figure 2.2. Wealth and Poverty in Proverbs

It is true that many sayings assert a simple cause and effect relationship: righteousness leads to wealth and wickedness leads to poverty; that is, representing quadrants one and four. For example, consider Prov 13:25:

> The righteous has enough to satisfy his appetite,
> but the belly of the wicked suffers want.
> (See also Prov 3:7–10; 11:8; 20:20; 26:27)

But there are also many sayings that reveal that this is not always the case, acknowledging the existence of quadrants two and three:

---

64. Lucas, "Book of Proverbs," 43. See also Lucas, *Proverbs*.

65. Lucas, "Book of Proverbs," 43.

66. Van Leeuwen, "Wealth and Poverty," 25–36. While van Leeuwen focuses his attention on wealth and poverty in connection with righteousness and wickedness, his findings are illustrative of the inaccuracy of a dogmatic nexus and can carry over to other areas.

67. Van Leeuwen, "Wealth and Poverty," 28.

> A gracious woman gets honor,
> and violent men get riches. (Prov 11:16)

> The fallow ground of the poor would yield much food,
> but it is swept away through injustice.
> (Prov 13:23; see also 19:10; 28:15–16a; 30:14)

Moreover, Proverbs places greater weight/importance on the righteous-unrighteous aspect than on the wealth-poverty aspect.[68] Proverbs 16:8 states this well,

> Better is a little with righteousness
> than great revenues with injustice.
> (See also Prov 15:16–17; 16:16, 19; 17:1; 28:6)

Further, Proverbs holds that quadrants two and three will eventually be corrected and that in the future, God will bring justice.[69] Van Leeuwen writes, "The sages' stance is to maintain faith in God's justice, even when they personally cannot see it or touch it, even when the recorded past does not verify it. Here religion provides no escape from the pain or absurdities of existence. The book of Job was inevitable, not because Proverbs was too simplistic, but because life's inequities, as reflected in Proverbs, drive faith to argue with the Deity."[70] The sages held the proverbs to be generally true, but they were well aware of exceptions and that there were no guarantees; moreover, they sought first to teach the basics.[71] Van Leeuwen's close look reveals a complex world that has no room for a rigid character-consequence correspondence. Further, the world he finds in Proverbs recognizes much of the same difficulties that Qoheleth wrestles with.

Appealing to van Leeuwen's article, Bartholomew argues against the crisis view, noting that the retributive paradox is also found in Proverbs.[72] While there are many sayings that may be taken to convey a simplistic message, "taken as a whole, Proverbs by no means presents a mechanical, automatic character-consequence understanding of retribution."[73] Proverbs, by their nature, are partial utterances; they speak to a particular

---

68. Van Leeuwen, "Wealth and Poverty," 31.

69. Van Leeuwen, "Wealth and Poverty," 33. For example, see Prov 21:13; 22:16; 23:17–18; 24:20; 28:20.

70. Van Leeuwen, "Wealth and Poverty," 34.

71. Van Leeuwen, "Wealth and Poverty," 32, 35.

72. Bartholomew, "The Theology of Ecclesiastes," 376.

73. Bartholomew and O'Dowd, *Old Testament Wisdom Literature*, 271. See also, Bartholomew, *Ecclesiastes*, 84–87.

situation, and part of wisdom is knowing the right time and place.[74] A proper understanding of the wisdom of Proverbs must grasp the whole.

Longman argues that it is only an over-simplistic reading of Proverbs—through a misunderstanding of the nature and function of proverbial sayings—that one reaches a mechanical view of retribution.[75] In particular, Longman point to the generic nature of proverbs; that is, they do not make promises nor offer guarantees.[76] Additionally, he draws attention to better-than proverbs, which acknowledge that A is more valuable than B and hence, A is to be pursued over B, for one may have to choose between them.[77]

> Better is a little with the fear of the Lord
> than great treasure and trouble with it. (Prov 15:16)

> Better is a poor person who walks in his integrity
> than one who is crooked in speech and is a fool. (Prov 19:1)

While Job and Ecclesiastes may criticize the misappropriation of proverbs, they are fully in agreement with the book of Proverbs; the three books are not in contradiction and thus, there is no crisis.[78]

In his article, Schultz considers both the diversity and unity represented in Israel's wisdom tradition, and while there is certainly some diversity, he argues that there is a fundamental unity.[79] Schultz holds that Proverbs, Job, and Ecclesiastes are in agreement on a number of key points; namely, 1) the limitations of wisdom, 2) the affirmation of divine freedom and inscrutability, 3) the relative value of wisdom and righteousness, and 4) their view of the retribution dogma.[80] He writes,

> Therefore, though Proverbs and Job-Ecclesiastes represent distinct generic options for communicating wisdom, it is misleading to characterize these books as containing contradictory wisdom theologies. Though wisdom by no means presents a monolithic ideology, Proverbs is in basic agreement with Job and Ecclesiastes that justice is not always immediately served, that wisdom will not give us mastery over life, and that God is

---

74. Bartholomew and O'Dowd, *Old Testament Wisdom Literature*, 270–75.
75. Longman, *The Fear of the Lord*, 179–90.
76. Longman, *The Fear of the Lord*, 185–86.
77. Longman, *The Fear of the Lord*, 185.
78. Longman, *The Fear of the Lord*, 188–90. See also Provan, *Ecclesiastes*, 34–36.
79. Schultz, "Unity or Diversity," 271–306.
80. Schultz, "Unity or Diversity," 281–89.

not bound to reward or punish, to shelter or afflict, in response to human actions, expectations, or demands. Furthermore, Ecclesiastes and Job are in basic agreement with Proverbs that righteousness and wisdom are beneficial and that God does reward good and punish evil.[81]

Thus, Schultz concludes, Job and Ecclesiastes do not present a rejection of the wisdom tradition.[82]

Hatton investigates how the influential position that Proverbs primarily teaches a rigid view of retribution led to the marginalization of Proverbs, and he examines if such a view of retribution is justified.[83] Focusing on Prov 10–12, he argues against Koch's thesis (which focused on Prov 11) and shows that the book is far more complex.[84] Proverbs contains, according to Hatton, many provocative contradictions to "deliberately problematize" such a relationship, giving the book "the character of a lively debate."[85] Moreover, these contradictions were "part of a subtle and profound didactic strategy to awaken the critical faculties of the reader."[86]

In sum, many scholars have convincingly shown that the wisdom crisis view is inadequate and built on a misunderstanding of Proverbs and of the nature of Israelite wisdom. While Israel's wisdom books certainly represent a diversity, it is more a matter of degree than one of kind. Proverbs is well aware of the complexities of the world, and Qoheleth's questioning is not a rejection of but at home in Israel's wisdom tradition, and in the OT for that matter. The following chapters will examine Qoheleth's progression of thought and response to various difficulties. For now, it is sufficient to note that Proverbs does not endorse a rigid doctrine of retribution. For one, this shows that the distance between the theologies of Proverbs and Qoheleth is not as great as many have led to believe. And second, this reveals that the wisdom crisis theory was constructed on a faulty foundation and needs to be put to rest.

---

81. Schultz, "Unity or Diversity," 288–89.
82. Schultz, "Unity or Diversity," 288–89.
83. Hatton, *Contradiction in the Book of Proverbs*.
84. Hatton, *Contradiction*, 83–116.
85. Hatton, *Contradiction*, 83.
86. Hatton, *Contradiction*, 1.

2.3.4 Conclusion

This section considered the second contextual level of Qoheleth's address; namely, Israel's wisdom tradition. First, it considered the evidence suggesting a connection between the books of Ecclesiastes and Proverbs and concluded that Ecclesiastes intentionally connects with Proverbs and is meant to be read in a shared context. Indeed, most scholars readily accept as much, though to varying degrees. The second half of this section considered the more significant question of the nature of the relationship between these two books. The traditional view of a wisdom crisis has stood for some time, holding that Qoheleth represents a strong reaction against the mechanical act/character-consequence nexus purported by Proverbs. And while many scholars today aim to temper Koch's claims, they largely retain the theory's premise. However, a number of scholars have compellingly demonstrated that Proverbs does not uphold the simplistic view that the crisis model claims. Rather, it presents systematic contradictions, revealing an awareness of the complexities of reality. This would mean that Proverbs and Ecclesiastes are much closer, even holding unity, in their wisdom, and this strongly challenges any interpretation that claims a crisis and posits one book against the other. In conclusion, an interpretation of Qoheleth's message needs to take seriously its context within Israel's wisdom tradition in general, and with Proverbs in particular.

2.4 WISDOM AND THE OLD TESTAMENT

2.4.1 Introduction

With the first two levels of context behind, that is, Qoheleth in the context of a frame narrator and within a wisdom tradition, the third canonical context comes to the fore. Israel's wisdom tradition, as represented by the canonical books, occurs within the context of the OT. The wisdom books have often been considered quite disconnected from the rest of Scripture. Consider the following:

> Whether apart or together, the wisdom books cannot be shoehorned into Israel's ... covenantal traditions.[87]

---

87. Brown, *Wisdom's Wonder*, 3.

> [Wisdom] does not fit into the type of faith exhibited in the historical and prophetic books.[88]
>
> Within Proverbs, Job, and Ecclesiastes one looks in vain for the dominant themes of Yahwistic thought: the exodus from Egypt, election of Israel, the Davidic covenant, the Mosaic legislation, the patriarchs, the divine control of history and movement toward a glorious moment when right will triumph. Instead, the reader encounters in these three books a different world of thought, one that stands apart so impressively that some scholars have described that literary corpus as an alien body within the Bible.[89]
>
> Wisdom has no relation to the history between God and Israel.[90]

Such views have greatly influenced wisdom studies. But is wisdom really so detached from the rest of the OT? A closer look reveals that this is not the case.

The purpose of this section is to consider connections between wisdom and the OT so as to allow this larger context to inform an understanding of the wisdom books. This section will argue that Israel's wisdom is deeply connected with the law and presupposes Israel's covenantal relationship with the Lord. And while wisdom is divergent from much of the OT in form, there is a fundamental unity. Accordingly, wisdom functions as a complementary voice of instruction alongside the many found in Scripture. This section will first focus on wisdom's connection with the law. Afterward, the rest of the OT will receive attention.

2.4.2 Wisdom and the Law

Though long considered incompatible, even antithetical, the wisdom tradition reveals many points of connection with the law, particularly Deuteronomy. First, the wisdom books reveal a general cultic awareness. Proverbs mentions sacrifices, vows, and offerings (Prov 7:14; 14:9; see Lev 27:2–29; Num 30:3). It speaks of honoring God with one's firstfruits (Prov 3:9–10; see Exod 23:16; 34:26; Lev 2:14; Num 18:12; Deut 26:1–11). Job offers burnt offerings for his children (Job 1:5) and for his friends (Job 42:8). Ecclesiastes reveals an awareness of the temple and related activities, such as the offering of sacrifices and vows (4:17—5:6 [5:1–7];

---

88. Wright, *God Who Acts*, 103.
89. Crenshaw, *Old Testament Wisdom*, 24–25.
90. Zimmerli, "The Place and Limit of the Wisdom," 147.

see Deut 23:21–23 [22–24]). Further, Eccl 8:10 may refer to the temple and Eccl 9:2 speaks of various categories of cultic life: the righteous and the wicked; the clean and the unclean; the one who sacrifices and the one who does not; the good and the sinner; the one who swears an oath and the one who refrains. While perhaps not at the fore, a general cultic awareness is certainly present.

Second, wisdom employs much vocabulary that relates to the law. Bartholomew notes that Ecclesiastes contains many examples, such as judgment (3:17; 11:9), sinner/sin (2:26; 5:5 [6]; 7:26; 8:12), wicked and righteous (3:17; 7:25), and so on.[91] Longman sees connections in Proverbs as early as 1:3, which describes the book as instruction for righteousness, justice, and uprightness.[92] Longman also notes how Prov 2:16–17 mentions a covenant (ברית) with God and that the book contains a prevalence of ideas associated with the covenant, such as "covenant love and faithfulness" (חסד and אמת; see Prov 3:3; 14:22; 16:6; 20:28).[93] Schultz notes how in both Proverbs and Deuteronomy, sin is described as an abomination (תועבה; 17x in Deut; 21x in Prov) and authoritative instruction is called either torah (תורה; 22x in Deut; 13x in Prov) or commandments (מצות; 42x in Deut; 8x in Prov).[94] Further, wisdom makes a close association between the wise and the righteous and between the fool and the wicked (Prov 9:9; 10:21, 23; 23:24). Longman argues that wisdom and righteousness are interchangeable, so too are wickedness and folly.[95] Wisdom begins with the fear of the Lord (Prov 9:10) and the fear of the Lord is hatred of evil (Prov 8:13). Lady wisdom walks in the way of righteousness (Prov 8:20) and all her words are righteous (Prov 8:8). The father instructs his son to search out wisdom, for "then you will understand righteousness and justice and equity, every good path" (Prov 2:9). Without the background of the law, much of this vocabulary loses its value.

---

91. Bartholomew, *Ecclesiastes*, 88. Bartholomew notes that "the strong distinction between law and wisdom is a modern construct and that by the third century BC, wisdom and law would certainly not be considered separate paths to successful living in the minds of teachers and populace, since both relate to ordering life in all its dimensions" (Bartholomew, *Ecclesiastes*, 90). Compare Murphy's view of a "shared approach to reality"; see Murphy, "Wisdom—Theses and Hypotheses," 38.

92. Longman, *Fear of the Lord*, 10.

93. Longman, *Fear of the Lord*, 172.

94. Schultz, "Unity or Diversity," 297–98.

95. Longman, *Fear of the Lord*, 11. Schultz holds that they are not exactly synonymous but co-referential; see Schultz, "Unity or Diversity," 298.

Third, in addition to the odd passing reference to cultic practices and no small amount of general, shared vocabulary, many proverbs mirror laws. Schultz outlines many of the similarities and parallels between wisdom and the law.[96] Note the following: not moving landmarks;[97] not using false weights;[98] not taking bribes;[99] not practicing perjury;[100] not dishonoring parents;[101] but having impartial judgment;[102] and caring for the widow, the orphan, and the poor;[103] to name a few. Longman points out that all the ten commandments relating to other people, that is, commandments number five through ten (Exod 20:12–17), are all echoed in Proverbs: honor your father and mother (see Prov 1:8; 4:1, 10; 10:1; 13:1); do not murder (see Prov 1:10–12; 6:17); do not commit adultery (see Prov 2:16–19; 5:1–23; 6:20–35; 7:1–27); do not steal (see Prov 1:13–14; 11:1); do not bear false witness (see Prov 3:30; 6:18, 19; 10:18; 12:17, 19); and do not covet (see Prov 6:18).[104]

Further, Proverbs also states that "If one turns away his ear from hearing the law, even his prayer is an abomination" (Prov 28:9), and "blessed is he who keeps the law" (Prov 29:18). Noting the myriad of parallels, Schultz concludes that "there is no inherent reason not to assume that the sage derived his ethical standards from the covenantal law, if this already had been formulated."[105]

Fourth, the wisdom presentation in Proverbs echoes the law's presentation of the two ways and their outcomes. Both Proverbs and Deuteronomy see in life a fundamental tension between the two ways: one is the path that leads to life and the other is the path that leads to death (Deut 5:16; 11:26–28; 30:15–18; Prov 3:33–35; 4:10–19; 8:32–36).[106] And

---

96. Schultz, "Unity or Diversity," 296–97.

97. Prov 22:28; 23:10; see Deut 19:14; 27:17.

98. Prov 11:1; 16:11; 20:10, 23; see Lev 19:35–36; Deut 25:13–16.

99. Prov 15:27; 17:8, 23; 19:6; 21:14; see Exod 23:8; Deut 10:17; 16:18–20; 27:25.

100. Prov 6:19; 12:17, 19; 14:5, 25; 19:5, 9, 28; see Exod 20:16; 23:1; Deut 5:20; 19:15–21; 22:13–19.

101. Prov 13:1; 15:5; 19:26; 20:20; 28:24; see Deut 5:16; 21:18, 21; 27:16.

102. Prov 17:15, 26; 18:5; 24:23–25; see Exod 23:1–3; Deut 1:16–17; 27:25.

103. Prov 14:20–21, 31; 15:25; 17:5; 19:17; 21:13; 22:7, 9, 16; 23:10–11; see Deut 15:7–11; 24:11–12; 27:19.

104. Longman, *Fear of the Lord*, 11, 113–14.

105. Schultz, "Unity or Diversity," 296.

106. Wilson, "Words of the Wise," 186. See also Schultz, "Unity or Diversity," 299. The concept of the "two ways" is not only presented in Prov 1–9 as an introduction for the whole, but is also seen, for example, in the antithetical nature of the proverbs

both speak of the possession of the land as dependent on following the righteous path.

> So you will walk in the way of the good
> and keep to the paths of the righteous.
> For the upright will inhabit the land,
> and those with integrity will remain in it,
> but the wicked will be cut off from the land,
> and the treacherous will be rooted out of it.
> (Prov 2:20–22; see Deut 5:32–33)

In addition to these similarities, there are other signs of connection between wisdom and law. Deuteronomy is a covenant renewal book, structured after ANE suzerain-vassal treaties with their five-part structure: 1) introduction (Deut 1:1–5); historical review of the relationship between the parties (Deut 1:9—3:27); 3) law outlining obligations (Deut 4–26); 4) rewards and punishment for obedience and disobedience of the law/covenant stipulations (Deut 27–28); and 5) witnesses (Deut 30:19–20).[107] At the beginning of the main section, that is, the presentation of the covenant stipulations, Moses informs that he has given all the statutes and rules that God has commanded and says, "Keep them and do them, for that will be your wisdom and your understanding in the sight of the peoples, who, when they hear all these statutes, will say, 'Surely this great nation is a wise and understanding people'" (Deut 4:6). At this key point in the book, one finds an explicit connection between wisdom and covenantal obedience; wisdom is keeping the Lord's commands.[108]

It is also worth mentioning that in the wisdom books, one finds the name Yahweh (יהוה), the covenantal name of the Lord. The very presence of this name assumes a covenantal relationship between God and his people.[109] Schultz argues that the God of the sages is the same God as

---

that dominate Prov 10–15. While the forms may vary throughout the book, there is a consistent contrast and/or description of these fundamental two ways.

107. Longman, *Fear of the Lord*, 167–68. See also Walton and Walton, *The Lost World of the Torah*, 46–53, 104–11; Craigie, *The Book of Deuteronomy*, 20–24; and Weinfeld, *Deuteronomy 1–11*, 6–9.

108. Longman, *Fear of the Lord*, 65–66. See also Craigie, *Deuteronomy*, 131; Wilson, "Words of the Wise," 188–89; Weinfeld, *Deuteronomy 1–11*, 64.

109. While Proverbs predominantly uses "Yahweh" (87x) over "God" (6x), Job makes use of both "Yahweh" (32x) and "God" (112x), with the former found predominantly in the narrative frame and the latter dominating the cycles of speeches. Interestingly, Ecclesiastes uses only "God" (40x) and not the divine name. Note that one also finds "Holy One" (Job 6:10; Prov 9:10; 30:3), "Almighty" (31x in Job), "Maker" (Job

found in the rest of the OT and wisdom's use of the divine name cannot be a simple superimposition of the Lord's name upon that of another ANE deity; rather, the covenantal relationship is foundational to the wisdom it conveys.[110]

This leads the discussion to the characteristic wisdom phrase, "the fear of the Lord/God." Not only does this phrase capture the heart and foundation of Israel's wisdom, but it is also found in key, hermeneutically significant places in the wisdom texts, such as the prologue of Proverbs, the epilogue of Ecclesiastes, and the climax of the great wisdom poem in Job 28. Additionally, the call to fear the Lord/God is linked with keeping God's commands, and this connection is found in both the law and in the wisdom books (Deut 6:2; 8:6; 13:5 [4]; 17:19; Job 28:28; Prov 1–9; Eccl 12:13–14). Positively, fearing the Lord means serving, obeying, and trusting in the Lord, and in him alone. Expressed negatively, fearing the Lord means turning away from all evil and wickedness. This key wisdom phrase will be further discussed below.

In his article, Wilson focuses his attention on Prov 1–9 and outlines many insightful connections with Deuteronomy. In both, keeping commands not only prolongs one's life (Deut 4:40; 6:1–2; Prov 3:1–2), it is the necessary basis for life (Deut 4:1; 5:28–29; 8:1–2; Prov 4:4; 6:23; 7:1–2).[111] Both speak of keeping the commandments in one's heart and binding them to the body so that they would accompany one while walking, laying down, rising, and talking, and both reflect a responsibility placed on parents to instruct their children in the ways of the Lord (Deut 6:6–9; 11:18–19; Prov 6:20–23; 7:1–3).[112] While Deuteronomy *commands* parental instruction, wisdom *displays* this—a foundational image of Israel's wisdom tradition is that of a parent instructing a child (Prov 1:8; 2:1; 3:1; 4:1; 5:1; 6:1, 20; 7:1; Eccl 12:12). In wisdom, commands are adapted into short sayings that can easily be taught and memorized. "Consequently, the commandments of Proverbs would be assumed to proceed ultimately from YHWH himself (as did the teaching of Moses)

4:17, 32:22; 35:10; 36:3; Prov 14:31; 17:5; 22:2), and "Creator" (Eccl 12:1); clearly, there is a level of fluidity. On Proverbs' use of the divine name, Oswalt suggests that "Proverbs is at pains to assert that it is Yahweh, Israel's God, the God of the covenant, who is in fact the sole fount of wisdom in the earth. This would make sense if Solomon was indeed the originator of the collection" (Oswalt, "God," 250–51).

110. Schultz, "Unity or Diversity," 293.
111. Wilson, "Words of the Wise," 183–84.
112. Wilson, "Words of the Wise," 185–86.

whether voiced by father, mother, or sage."[113] Both use the language of a father disciplining his son with love to describe the Lord's dealings with his people (Deut 8:2–6; Prov 3:11–13). Both have a similar understanding of wisdom that is not rooted in human observation and experience but in divine revelation. In Proverbs, this is expressed in that the fear of the Lord is the source of wisdom (Prov 1:7; 2:1–8; 3:5–7; 9:10) and in Deuteronomy, wisdom is tied with God's revealed commandments (Deut 4:6).[114] The resulting effect of these abundant connections is the association of the wisdom commandments with those in Deuteronomy. Wilson concludes that Israel's wisdom is "inextricably bound up with the Torah of Israel's God, YHWH—*his* commandments—and cannot be read apart from them."[115]

Beyond theological and thematic similarities, and even echoed commands, there are a couple of wisdom passages that are believed to directly rely upon the text of Deuteronomy. Most scholars believe that Eccl 4:17—5:6 [5:1–7] quotes Deut 23:22–24 [21–23], at least in part. While scholars differ on their interpretation of Qoheleth's handling of and purpose for the quotation, a connection is widely accepted.[116] Another textual connection is proposed by Overland, who argues that Prov 3:1–12 displays intrabiblical exegesis of the Shema (Deut 6:4–9) and that "the product was a sapiential rendition of classic covenantal piety."[117]

Thus far, this section has presented many connections between wisdom and law. What should be made of the evidence? Two points are in order. First, it is clear that wisdom presupposes Israel's covenant with God. Cultic awareness, covenantal vocabulary, echoed commands, etc.—these make clear that there is a covenantal background informing the wisdom tradition in a significant way. Grant writes, "Covenantal ideas provide the backbone to the presuppositions of Israel's wisdom worldview, and the three books of the Wisdom Literature cannot be understood apart from covenant."[118] Wisdom comes in a covenantal context.

113. Wilson, "Words of the Wise," 186.

114. Wilson, "Words of the Wise," 188–89.

115. Wilson, "Words of the Wise," 192; emphasis original.

116. For a discussion of Qoheleth's connection here with Deuteronomy, see Schultz, "The Reuse of Deuteronomy's 'Law of the Vow,'" 120–32. For an alternative (though, ultimately unconvincing) interpretation of Qoheleth's adaptation of the Deuteronomic law, see Levinson, "Better That You Should Not Vow," 28–41.

117. Overland, "Did the Sage Draw from the Shema?" 440; see 424–40 for the larger discussion.

118. Grant, "Wisdom and Covenant," 862.; see also Bartholomew and O'Dowd, *Old*

The second point is that wisdom is instruction for how God's people were to live. The good life that wisdom promotes is not just a life in general but rather a particular life; that is, a righteous life in a faithful, covenantal relationship with the Lord. Built on the same covenantal foundation as the law, expressed by the fear of the Lord, wisdom provides continued instruction in order to shape one's character and to provide guidance so that one might walk uprightly and trust in the Lord. And echoing the law, wisdom largely communicates within the framework of the two ways: the way of the wise and the way of the fool; the way of the righteous and the way of the wicked; the way of life and the way of death. Wisdom speaks of the desires, actions, and character that lead one down each path, describes the one who is found walking on each path, and reveals the end of each path. As Kline put it, "the way of wisdom is the way of the covenant."[119]

In sum, wisdom is integrally connected with the law. Wisdom is built on a similar foundation, reiterates many of the same commands, and puts forward the same core teaching of a life of complete faithfulness in covenantal relationship with the Lord. In light of the copious connections that this section has only begun to outline, one should be wary of any interpretation that drives a wedge between wisdom and the law.

2.4.3 Wisdom, the Prophets, and the Writings

Thus far, the matter of wisdom's relation to the rest of the OT has focused on the Torah, especially Deuteronomy—and rightly so. However, it would be remiss not to mention, even if brief, a few points about wisdom's connection with the rest of the OT. The question here is not simply a matter of searching the OT for occurrences of the word "wise" or "wisdom" in order to discern the OT's attitude toward the tradition, as others have done.[120] In short, there are numerous examples of good and bad wisdom.[121] Neither is the question here a generic one. This is not

---

Testament Wisdom Literature, 283–88.

119. Kline, *The Structure of Biblical Authority*, 64.

120. See the following discussions: Firth, "Worrying about the wise," 155–73; McLaughlin, *An Introduction to Israel's Wisdom Traditions*, 141–70; and Klingbeil, "Wisdom and History," 863–76.

121. The prophets criticize the false wisdom of the nations (Isa 19:11; Jer 49:7; 50:35; Obad 8) and of Israel (Isa 44:24–25; Jer 8:8–9), making it clear that false wisdom is that which turns away from the Lord and rests on human understanding (Isa 5:21;

a matter of searching Scripture for wise sayings, parables, instructions, and various types of proverbs to discern which texts display wisdom influence—it was, after all, a form–critical approach that contributed to wisdom's segregation from the rest of the OT. The question here is rather one of similarities in topic and aim. This leaves open the possibility that Israel, through her history, made use of various forms to communicate, without assuming that different generic forms equate to opposing traditions and views. Concerning topic, many themes found in the wisdom books are not only parallel with the Torah, as discussed earlier, but are also raised by the Prophets and in the Writings. Moreover, it is at the level of wisdom's aim/goal that one finds significant similarities. There is a shared primary concern for instructing God's people to live righteous lives in covenantal faithfulness. The form of literature may differ, as do many particular emphases, but still, the similarities reveal a complementary character and an underlying unity to the whole.

The teaching offered through the wisdom books is often very similar to that found in the historical books. While the wisdom books communicate the difference between the wise and the fool or the righteous and the sinner through sayings and other forms, the historical books (and much of the Pentateuch, for that matter) commonly illustrate these same concepts through narratives. Joseph in Egypt and Daniel in Babylon—these two are often considered paragons of wisdom.[122] Pharaoh sought to deal shrewdly (חכם) with the Israelites (Exod 1:10), but the midwives feared God and did not listen to Pharaoh (Exod 1:17). Joshua was full of the spirit of wisdom (Deut 34:9). 1 Samuel 25 tells the story of Nabal (meaning "fool") and his wife Abigail, who models the wisdom her husband lacked. The narrative begins by describing Abigail's discernment (טוֹבַת־שֶׂכֶל) and Nabal's folly (קָשֶׁה וְרַע מַעֲלָלִים) and shows the outcomes of their actions.[123] In 2 Sam 13, Amon's friend, who was "very wise" (v. 3), assembled a plan, yet Tamar, and the narrative, decries his folly (v. 13). Another story tells of how a wise woman (2 Sam 20:16), who was faithful

---

29:13–14). In contrast, the Lord is wise (Isa 31:2; 33:5–6), and those who are truly wise are those who trust in the Lord and fear him (Jer 9:23–24). Surveying the good and bad examples of wisdom in Israel's narrative traditions, Firth concludes that "the true test of wisdom is whether or not its application promotes justice and faithfulness to Yahweh" (Firth, "Worrying about the Wise," 172–73).

122. Longman, *Fear of the Lord*, 78–93. For an examination of the presence and interplay of wisdom and covenant themes in the Joseph narrative, see Wilson, *Joseph Wise and Otherwise*.

123. Sneed, "Is the Wisdom Tradition a Tradition?" 70.

in Israel (v. 19), diverted violence and saved the city (v. 14–22). And of course, the strongest and most obvious connection between wisdom and the Deuteronomistic history is with King Solomon (1 Kings 3–11).[124] Other accounts may not contain such explicit wisdom connotations but still illustrate and teach the contrast between the righteous and the wicked, which is akin to the wise and the fool, inviting the reader to consider their character, choices, actions, and outcomes.[125] Sneed argues that a lot of wisdom literature does not make much sense apart from this larger canonical context. He writes, "words like wisdom and righteousness remain largely abstract concepts without the plethora of narratives in the Hebrew Bible that provide concrete examples of what these virtues mean."[126] And just as the various narratives do not stand in isolation but are presented within the larger Deuteronomistic history, that is, within the context of Israel's covenantal relationship with God, the wisdom literature also occurs in the same larger canonical context. Instruction about the righteous and the wicked, the wise and the fool, came through both proverbs and narratives.

The Psalms, which are closely connected with Israel's faith and worship, have significant overlap with wisdom to the extent that many scholars label a number of psalms as "wisdom psalms."[127] For example, Psalms 1, 37, 112, and 119 have parallels with Proverbs, and Psalms 39, 49, and 73 have similarities with Job and Ecclesiastes. Further, the Psalter opens with a presentation of the fundamental two ways, contrasting the

---

124. Scholars have nearly always agreed that there is a special connection between wisdom and Solomon, although, the extent of this connection and its purpose have been matters of much debate. For example, Barbour pushes against a universal, secularistic, non-Israelite, developmental theory of wisdom, and argues that Ecclesiastes is much closer tied to Israel's history as a post-exilic reflection on the failures of Israel's past kings (Barbour, *The Story of Israel*, 10–30). Contrast this with the view of a more distanced Solomonic connection (Bundvad, *Time*, 172–73) or a more specific evocation (Seitz, "A Canonical Reading of Ecclesiastes," 106). For further discussion on wisdom's Solomonic connections, see Bartholomew, *Ecclesiastes*, 43–54; Seow, *Ecclesiastes*, 36–38; Longman, *Ecclesiastes*, 2–11; and Jackson, "Solomon," 733–37.

125. Klingbeil argues that the wisdom tradition does have many references to people, places, and actions as well as numerous shared motifs, but suggests that connections are intentionally more general for applicability; see Klingbeil, "Wisdom and History," 873.

126. Sneed, "Grasping After the Wind," 56.

127. Still, there is much debate about which psalms qualify as wisdom, about what the qualifications for such a group should be, and even about the extent to which such a generic categorization is helpful or detrimental. For discussions about wisdom and the Psalms, see Jacobson, "Wisdom Language in the Psalms," 147–57; and Forti, "*Gattung* and *Sitz im Leben*," 205–20.

way of the righteous and the way of the wicked, and sets up the book as instruction to be meditated upon.[128]

Wisdom shares many of the same concerns found in the rest of the OT, such as the social justice called for by the prophets, including the care of widows, orphans, and sojourners (Isa 1; Jer 7; Mal 3; see Job 31:16–23; Prov 14:21, 31; Eccl 4:1–3; 5:7–8 [8–9]). But wisdom does not exclusively address practical matters; it has much to teach about God that is consonant with the rest of the OT. Waltke writes,

> Solomon ascribes the same attributes and actions to God as those ascribed to him by Moses and the prophets. According to all three, he is Creator of the cosmos (Deut 10:14; Prov 3:19–20; Prov [sic] 1:7) and of all humanity (Deut 4:32; Prov 14:31; 29:13; Isa 42:5). He is the same living God who will avenge wrong (Deut 32:35, 40–41; Prov 5:21–22; Nah 1:2) and the same spiritual Being who comforts people and knows their ways (Deut 23:14 [15]; Prov 5:21; 15:3; Jer 16:17). He is the Sovereign directing history (Deut 4:19; 29:4 [3], 26 [25]; Prov 16:1–9, 33; 19:21; 20:24; Isa 45:1–13) and yet present in it, withholding and giving rain (Deut 11:13–17; Prov 3:9–10; Hag 1:10–11), disciplining his children (Deut 8:5; Prov 3:11–12; Isa 1:4–6) and in his mercy answering their prayers (Deut 4:29–31; Prov 15:8, 29; Isa 56:7). He is merciful (Deut 4:31; Prov 28:13; Isa 63:7), delights in justice and hates iniquity (Deut 10:17; Prov 11:1; 17:15; Isa 1:16–17), and has aesthetic-ethical sensibilities (Deut 22:4–11; 23:10–14 [11–15]; Prov 3:32; 6:16–19; 11:20; 15:9; Jer 32:35).[129]

Long seen as a hallmark of wisdom literature (more Job and Ecclesiastes than Proverbs), the theme of theodicy and the question of retribution is really a broad theme found across the Psalms and prophetic traditions. Murphy points out that the confessions of Jeremiah and the psalms of lament are equally as strong as what is found in the wisdom texts.[130] The wisdom texts are not at odds with the Prophets and the Writings.

The conclusion of the many similarities between wisdom and the rest of the OT is not that one should classify various narratives or psalms

---

128. The introductory nature of Psalm 1 and the Psalter as instruction for meditation particularly come into focus in light of the book's final canonical shape. The following are select overviews and discussions of the shape of the Psalter: Wilson, *The Editing of the Hebrew Psalter*; Firth and Johnston, *Interpreting the Psalms*; deClaissé-Walford et al., *The Book of Psalms*, 21–38; and deClaissé-Walford, *The Shape and Shaping of the Book of Psalms*.

129. Waltke, *Proverbs 1–15*, 65.

130. Murphy, *Ecclesiastes*, lxvi.

as belonging to a wisdom genre—such a move would warrant the criticism put forward by Kynes in his warning of pan-sapientialism.[131] Rather, the conclusion is one of recognition of not only the immense overlap in themes but also of how the goal of wisdom is far closer together with that of the Prophets and the Writings than what much scholarship has led to believe—a goal of instructing God's people in the way they should go. While there are certainly many differences and each wisdom text has its unique focus and contributions to make, Estes argues that the great similarities between the wisdom books and the rest of the OT reveal "an underlying unity of thought."[132] He writes, "Even a casual reading of the wisdom books reveals that the actions and attitudes that are condemned as folly and wickedness are the same kind as those that are prohibited in the law and denounced by the prophets."[133] And in every case, it is clear that the one who is truly wise is the one who walks in the way of the Lord, trusting, obeying, and fearing him alone. While the medium may vary, the root message and purpose are largely the same.

2.4.4 Conclusion

This section has briefly considered connections between wisdom and the rest of the OT. The wisdom books cannot be simply dismissed as unrelated and unconcerned with the major themes of the OT. Rather, the wisdom material is built on a similar covenantal foundation, its teachings echo that found in much of the law and the prophets, and it works toward a shared goal of instructing one how to live faithfully before God, guiding one to walk in the way of the Lord.

---

131. Kynes, "Threat of Pan-Sapientialism," 11–38.
132. Estes, "Wisdom and Biblical Theology," 856.
133. Estes, "Wisdom and Biblical Theology," 855. Seitz writes, "Maybe the point of the book of Ecclesiastes is to push us and to expose our lurking predispositions by asking us to see if there is a wisdom genuinely linking texts like Genesis 1, Psalm 19, Psalm 104, the books of Proverbs, Job, 1 Kings 2–13, and Koheleth after all. Not by arguing for protest and opposition, but by seeing the maxims of the Preacher and the sentences of Proverbs and the commandments of the Pentateuch as equally 'sayings of the wise,' which like goads (12:11) demand of us a deeper wisdom, competent to guide in youth and in middle age and on the other side of excess and folly, at the portal of death itself" (Seitz, *The Elder Testament*, 236).

2.5 THE FOUNDATION OF ISRAEL'S WISDOM

2.5.1 Introduction

Wisdom's covenantal connection was introduced above. Yet, the question of wisdom's foundation needs further attention, particularly as the discussion here will address two primary counter-foundations commonly put forward in wisdom scholarship. The first argues that Israel's wisdom texts are more at home with the various wisdom traditions of the ANE and thus, they should be interpreted primarily in that context rather than in connection with Israel's faith. The second argues that the foundation of Israel's wisdom is creation and not covenant. This section will start by outlining the fear of the Lord as wisdom's foundation, after which the two primary counter contexts will be addressed.

2.5.2 The Fear of the Lord

"The fear of the Lord" is a common phrase in Israel's wisdom literature. In Proverbs, this phrase occurs fourteen times.[134] Additionally, the concept also recurs.[135] But much more than simply constituting *a* theme, this note is sounded at the most crucial points in the book. First, it is found marking the peak of Proverbs' introduction:

> The fear of the LORD is the beginning of knowledge;
> fools despise wisdom and instruction. (Prov 1:7)

What does it mean to fear the Lord? Waltke writes, "to fear him means essentially to submit to his revealed will, whether through Moses or Solomon."[136] Grant argues that Deut 10:12–13 provides, as it were, the dictionary definition as it asks the primary question, gives an initial answer, and provides a series of epexegetical statements:[137]

> And now, Israel, what does the LORD your God require of you, but to fear the LORD your God, to walk in all his ways, to love him, to serve the LORD your God with all your heart and with all your soul, and to keep the commandments and statutes of the

---

134. Prov 1:7, 29; 2:5; 8:13; 9:10; 10:27; 14:26, 27; 15:16, 33; 16:6; 19:23; 22:4; 23:17.
135. Prov 3:7; 14:2; 24:21; 31:30.
136. Waltke, *Proverbs 1–15*, 65. See also Longman, *The Fear of the Lord*, 12–14.
137. Grant, "Wisdom and Covenant," 861. See also Christensen, *Deuteronomy 1–21*, 135, 203–04.

Lord, which I am commanding you today for your good? (Deut 10:12–13; see Deut 6:2)

He also argues that while the term may have originated from a root meaning of terror, it came to be used as a short-hand expression for total commitment to God.[138]

And what is to be made of the presentation that the fear of the Lord is the *beginning* of wisdom? Longman argues that "beginning" may be taken temporally or foundationally; either way, it is clear regarding the centrality of one's relationship with Yahweh for wisdom.[139] To put this another way, without a proper relationship with the Lord, one cannot truly be wise. And this declaration foregrounds all of Israel's wisdom.

The opening of Proverbs is not the only significant location in which this phrase occurs. After coming in the words of the father to his son and by Lady Wisdom, it is found at the end of the description of the way of wisdom located at the end of the first collection (Prov 1–9):

> The Fear of the Lord is the beginning of wisdom,
>   and knowledge of the Holy One is insight. (Prov 9:10)

Presented at the beginning and end, this phrase comprises an *inclusio* around the first collection.[140] Additionally, this first collection serves as a prologue to the whole book, presenting the hermeneutic and providing the religious foundation for understanding all the wisdom that follows.[141] After continuing to appear throughout the subsequent collections, this concept is also found at the close of the book, where it represents the culminating and foundational trait of the woman in Proverbs 31.[142] Many take this final occurrence (Prov 31:30) to work with the first (Prov 1:7) to form an additional *inclusio* marking the book as a whole.[143]

---

138. Grant, "Wisdom and Covenant," 860–61.

139. Longman, *The Fear of the Lord*, 161. See also, Bartholomew and O'Dowd, *Old Testament Wisdom Literature*, 80; Fuhs, "מוֹרָה, יִרְאָה, יָרֵא, יָרֵא," *TDOT* 6:290–315.

140. Longman, *The Fear of the Lord*, 12; Schultz, "Unity or Diversity," 294; Childs, *Introduction*, 552–55; Grant, "Wisdom and Covenant," 859; Belcher, *Finding Favour*, 45.

141. Belcher, *Finding Favour*, 51.

142. Bartholomew and O'Dowd, *Old Testament Wisdom Literature*, 81, describe how the key refrain is placed at the main "seams" of the book. Waltke writes, "As part of the poem's climactic conclusion, this vertical virtue with Israel's covenant-keeping God provides the necessary theological base for her horizontal social virtues" (Waltke, *Proverbs 15–31*, 535).

143. Bartholomew and O'Dowd, *Old Testament Wisdom Literature*, 81; Waltke, *Proverbs 15–31*, 535–36; Belcher, *Finding Favour*, 61. Lucas, "Book of Proverbs," 50, sees

Grant writes, "This bracketing method informs the reader that the whole book should be read through the lens of the 'fear of the Lord.' The image engendered by enveloping the major sections and the complete book with 'fear of Yahweh' is one of true wisdom being inextricably linked to right relationship with the covenant God."[144] This is the proper context for understanding *all* of Proverbs' wisdom.

The book of Job presents a corresponding understanding. In the opening narrative frame, Job is emphatically portrayed as one who is blameless and upright, who feared God and turned from evil (Job 1:1, 8; 2:3). Though exemplifying the character that Proverbs proclaims, Job suffers great loss. Through the many rounds of speeches, there is one chapter in the middle of the book that particularly stands out. Job 28 presents a poem about the search for wisdom. After repeated refrains questioning where wisdom can be found (Job 28:12, 19), the poem concludes with God giving the answer:

> Behold, the fear of the Lord, that is wisdom,
> and to turn away from evil is understanding. (Job 28:28)

The poem plays an important part in the book as a whole and marks its first literary climax, declaring the answer to the search for true wisdom.[145]

When it comes to Ecclesiastes, the most noteworthy occurrence is found at the climax of the book's epilogue: "The end of the matter; all has been heard. Fear God and keep his commandments, for this is the whole duty of man" (Eccl 12:13). While this concluding declaration easily accords with the similar refrains found in Proverbs, it comes at the hand of the epilogist rather than Qoheleth. Qoheleth's use of the concept is greatly debated and will be discussed in the following chapters. Regardless of one's take on Qoheleth's attitude toward such matters, the final form of the book imbues the epilogue with a special hermeneutical function, where it presents the final message for the book as a whole. Lastly, the epilogue connects with the prologue of Proverbs, forming a frame around the two books. The frame declares that the beginning and end of wisdom is the fear of the Lord and that this is the foundation with which one is to approach and understand all of the wisdom contained therein.

---

additional bracketing between the woman of Prov 31 and Lady Wisdom of Prov 1–9.

144. Grant, "Wisdom and Covenant," 859.

145. See Lo, *Job 28 as Rhetoric*; Bartholomew and O'Dowd, *Old Testament Wisdom Literature*, 167–87; and Hartley, *The Book of Job*.

In sum, the fear of the Lord represents the foundation of Israel's wisdom and reflects a covenantal relationship. Proverbs, Job, and Ecclesiastes each make this clear. While the refrain does recur with some frequency, its positioning is particularly significant.[146] There is no wisdom apart from this foundation.

2.5.3 Wisdom and the Ancient Near East

One counter-foundation common in scholarship claims that wisdom belongs not in the context of Israel's covenant faith but in the context of the numerous wisdom traditions of the ANE.[147] This position is evidenced by many examples of Israel's interaction with and borrowing from the wisdom of other cultures. This view is further supported by the many differences between Israel's wisdom books and the rest of the OT. Accordingly, Israel's wisdom is taken to be secular and universal. Brown writes, "Ancient Israel's sages had no qualms incorporating the wisdom of other cultures. Biblical wisdom seeks *the common good along with the common God*. Wisdom's international, indeed universal appeal constitutes its canonical uniqueness. The Bible's wisdom corpus is the open door in an otherwise closed canon."[148] Could this be the case? Should Israel's wisdom be interpreted as secular and universal rather than theological and particular to Israel?

---

146. Schultz, "Unity or Diversity," 294.

147. Most scholars situate the historical context of Ecclesiastes in the third century BC and identify various points of Hellenistic influence, often noting Qoheleth's individuality, universal outlook, not to mention the strong linguistic connections. However, Qoheleth's Hellenistic connections are typically viewed as less direct and more the result of the general spirit of the times. Loader argues that while there are points of contact with Greek philosophy, this influence cannot account for the book as a whole (Loader, *Polar Structures*, 129). Bartholomew writes, "Any idea of strong Greek influence on the book tends to be rejected although broad connections with Greek thought are recognized. Generally, Qohelet is thought to be rooted in Hebraic thought and part of the wisdom movement in Israel" (Bartholomew, "Old Testament Wisdom Today," 13). The discussion here will focus on the theological difference between the wisdom of Israel and that of the ANE rather than its connections with Hellenism. For a study of Judaism's relation to Hellenism from the time of Alexander the Great (330 BC) to the Maccabean revolt (168 BC), see Hengel, *Judaism and Hellenism*. For a study of wisdom's ongoing relation with Hellenism after Qoheleth, see Collins, *Jewish Wisdom in the Hellenistic Age*.

148. Brown, *Wisdom's Wonder*, 3; emphasis added. See also, Brueggemann, *In Man We Trust*, 81–82; and Eichrodt, *Theology of the Old Testament*, 81.

To be sure, there are many similarities between Israel's wisdom books and numerous ANE wisdom texts.[149] Of note, Proverbs shares similarities with many Egyptian texts, such as the Instructions of Ptahhotep, Instructions of Any, Instructions of Amenemope, Instructions of Ankhsheshonq, and Papyrus Insinger, not to mention the Egyptian concept of *ma'at*. Job is similar to the Mesopotamian texts A Man and his God, I will Praise the Lord of Wisdom, and The Babylonian Theodicy—dealing with issues of righteous suffering, loss, divine healing, and restoration—as well as the Canaanite text The Epic of Kirta, in which a righteous sufferer loses his family but later received divine healing and new family. Ecclesiastes shares similarities with several texts. The Egyptian texts The Song of Intef and The Dialogue of a Man with his Soul talk about death, express skepticism about the afterlife, and endorse the enjoyment of life. The Mesopotamian text The Dialogue between a Master and his Slave displays oscillating perspectives and The Epic of Gilgamesh has similarities at several points. There are also Canaanite texts, such as Enlil and Namzitarra and The Ballad of Early Rulers, that speak of looming death and call for the enjoyment of life. Much more could be said; however, most books that address Israel's wisdom texts discuss various connections.[150]

Yet, for all the similarities, the differences are striking. Similarities of form, genre, and even content, do not equate to a shared message or purpose. Before addressing some of the key differences, the false secular-religious dichotomy needs to be dispelled. Bartholomew rightly pushes back against the developmental view of Israel's wisdom from early secular to later religious, pointing out that ancient wisdom was intrinsically religious and moral and that the religious-secular dualism of modernity

---

149. For ANE texts, see the following: Hallo, *The Context of Scripture*; Lambert, *Babylonian Wisdom Literature*; Lichtheim, *Ancient Egyptian Literature*; Matthews and Benjamin, *Old Testament Parallels*; and Pritchard, *The Ancient Near East*.

150. In his recent introduction, McLaughlin includes a chapter providing a good, concise survey of the international context of Israel's wisdom; however, his focus is on the many similarities to the point that the chapter neglects to mention any differences; see McLaughlin, *Israel's Wisdom Tradition*, 11–24. In contrast to the historical-critical approach, others, while noting the similarities with ANE wisdom, employ a more canonical-theological method and focus on the distinctiveness of Israel's wisdom; see Longman, *The Fear of the Lord is Wisdom*, 147–62; and Bartholomew and O'Dowd, *Old Testament Wisdom Literature*, 32–46. For other treatments, see Kidner, *The Wisdom of Proverbs, Job and Ecclesiastes*, 125–41; Murphy, *The Tree of Life*, 151–79; and Crenshaw, *Old Testament Wisdom*, 251–72.

was not present in ancient times.[151] All wisdom was religious and all wisdom presupposed various views of god(s), creation, order, and justice. And this is where many of the key differences between wisdom traditions are most conspicuous.

Bartholomew and O'Dowd discuss how behind different wisdom texts, there are wildly divergent worldviews.[152] While Israel held monotheism, other cultures held henotheism and pantheism. While Israel viewed God as set apart from all reality, others viewed consubstantialism and polytheistic naturalism. For Israel, the act of creation was ordered and purposeful rather than chaotic, violent, sexual, and purposeless. For Israel, the Lord instituted laws and wisdom began with fearing him, while in other cultures, wisdom often carried strong humanistic overtones. While there was assuredly an international aspect to Israel's wisdom, as the OT testifies,[153] the fundamental differences cannot be disregarded. That Israel learned from other wisdom traditions does not mean that Israel incorporated their beliefs and practices.[154] Common good? Possibly. Common God? No.

Consider what is, perhaps, the clearest evidence of Israel's wisdom tradition borrowing from her neighbors; that is, Prov 22:17—24:22 and its reliance on the Instructions of Amenemope.[155] In this text, Amenemope instructs his son Hor-em-maakher, and the text begins with a prologue indicating the purpose, followed by thirty chapters (see *Amen* XXVII.6). Proverbs 22:17—24:22 contains many similar sayings as those found in Amenemope. Moreover, it also begins with a prologue, which states its purpose and informs that it has provided thirty sayings (Prov 22:20).[156]

---

151. Bartholomew, *Ecclesiastes*, 89–90.

152. See Bartholomew and O'Dowd, *Old Testament Wisdom Literature*, 32–46; esp. 44. For a study on Israel's view of God, the divine counsel, the sons of God, and other spiritual beings, see Heiser, *The Unseen Realm*. See also van der Toorn et al., *Dictionary of Deities and Demons in the Bible*.

153. The chief example of cordial interaction is the visit of the Queen of Sheba, who came to test Solomon after hearing of his famed wisdom (1 Kings 10).

154. On this point, Longman notes the concept of "common grace," in which one could acknowledge and glean from the wisdom of other traditions, for all wisdom comes from God, while still holding to the particularity of God's special revelation; see Longman, *Fear of the Lord*, 116, 160–62.

155. There is widespread scholarly acceptance that Proverbs drew from Amenemope rather than the reverse. See Murphy, *Proverbs*, 291–94; McLaughlin, *Israel's Wisdom Traditions*, 15, 57–60.

156. Although, there is some difficulty with and debate about the Hebrew translated "thirty." See Waltke, *Proverbs 15–31*, 219–20.

Compare the beginning of Proverbs with the beginning of Amenemope, after its prologue, as illustrated in figure 2.4. This comparison shows not only a similarity of content but also of sequence. The instructions are described as "teaching for life" (*Amen* I.1) and "instruction for well-being" (*Amen* I.2) for the purpose of "Knowing how to answer one who speaks, to reply to one who sends a message" (*Amen* I.5–6) and for prosperity, direction, and praise from others (*Amen* I.7–12). A parallel is found in the final part of the prologue in Proverbs: "to make you know what is right and true, that you may give a true answer to those who sent you" (Prov 22:21).[157]

Proverbs 22:17–18	Amenemope[158]
Incline your ear, and hear the words of the wise,	Give your ears, hear the sayings, (III.9)
and apply your heart to my knowledge,	Give your heart to understand them; (III.10)
for it will be pleasant if you keep them within you,[159]	It profits to put them in your heart, (III.11)
	Let them rest in the casket of your belly (III.13)
if all of them are ready on your lips.	They'll be a mooring post for your tongue. (III.16)

Figure 2.3. Proverbs 22:17–18 and Amenemope

Though similar, Proverbs displays some key differences. Most significantly, at the outset of the collection in Proverbs, the writer expresses a purpose that is very different from Amenemope: "That your trust may be in the Lord" (Prov 22:19a)—a difference overlooked or ignored by some.[160] Murphy points out that where the prologue closely echoes Amenemope, the stated purpose of the collection in Prov 22:19 is striking and highly conspicuous.[161] Bartholomew and O'Dowd argue that

---

157. For further discussion of the two collections, see Fox, *Proverbs 10–31*, 757–60; Murphy, *Proverbs*, 290–94; and Waltke, *Proverbs 15–31*, 217–88.

158. "Instructions of Amenemope," trans. Lichtheim, *COS* 1.47:115–22.

159. The Hebrew בְּבִטְנֶךָ translates literally as "in your belly."

160. For example, McLaughlin outlines the similarities with Prov 22:17–18 and with v. 20 onward, but he completely skips Prov 22:19, the very center of the prologue, which notes Israel's unique context and purpose; see McLaughlin, *Israel's Wisdom Tradition*, 57–60. Even where he later mentions that the collection in Proverbs has been adapted to Israel's context and provides examples, he still misses this, *the* fundamental difference.

161. Murphy, *Proverbs*, 170, 293.

the presence of many parallels invites one to critically consider the differences.[162] Waltke argues that Prov 22:19 is the center of the prologue and the theological motivation for the whole collection.[163] He writes, "Beyond making the son charming to others, the sayings enable him to realize a dynamic, trusting relationship with Israel's covenant-keeping God."[164] Rather than reliance on oneself, Proverbs teaches trust in God; and not just any god, but Yahweh. Longman notes, "Nothing could be more particular than this conception of wisdom."[165] Lastly, the final saying that closes the collection in Proverbs begins by echoing this foundational, theological point, forming an inclusion for the collection. The writer declares: "My son, fear the LORD . . ." (Prov 24:21–22). In sum, Israel's "borrowed" wisdom was placed in a new context and given a new foundation and purpose.

When it comes to the question of influence, the matter is certainly more complicated than an uncritical and unilateral cut and paste. While it is easy to accept a measure of shared wisdom, this does not mean that all participating cultures espoused the same ideology. There is a significant difference between adoption and adaption. And there is no reason to assume the former. Moreover, the evidence points unmistakably to the latter. Israel's wisdom has been placed in a new literary context and it is in its new context that it must be interpreted. The foundation of Israel's wisdom is the fear of the Lord. This wisdom is not secular nor universal; rather, it is decidedly theological and particular.

2.5.4 Wisdom and Creation

A second argument against a covenantal foundation for Israel's wisdom needs attention. Given the proclivity to separate wisdom from the rest of the OT, there are some who argue that Israel's wisdom tradition is rooted in creation theology. That is, wisdom's foundation, that which it builds on, is not found in Israel's covenantal relationship with God or any special revelation but rather in observations of the world. Zimmerli is well known for his comment, "Wisdom thinks resolutely within the

---

162. Bartholomew and O'Dowd, *Old Testament Wisdom Literature*, 39.
163. Waltke, *Proverbs 15–31*, 223.
164. Waltke, *Proverbs 15–31*, 223.
165. Longman, *The Fear of the Lord*, 178.

framework of a theology of creation."¹⁶⁶ Accordingly, the sages were guided by the belief that God created the world with order, and sought to study the world so as to discern its order so that they might live by it.¹⁶⁷ But, as Longman argues, this approach is motived more by a lack of a perceived connection between Israel's wisdom tradition and the rest of the OT than by explicit connections between wisdom and creation.¹⁶⁸ To this motivation, one could add the practical nature and universal aspect of the wisdom teachings. But, is creation the foundation upon which Israel's wisdom is built? Is wisdom's *modus operandi* the observation of created orders, even if it holds such orders were created and instilled by God? Is this the most accurate way to speak of its teachings?

To be sure, the theme of creation is discernable at numerous points in the wisdom texts. There are many proverbs that make observations about the created order; for example, "Go to the ant, O sluggard; consider her ways, and be wise" (Prov 6:6). Additionally, God is spoken of as the creator (Prov 14:31; 17:5; 20:12; 22:2; 29:13), and Proverbs contains tree of life imagery (Prov 3:18; 11:30; 13:12; 15:4). Most notably, Prov 3:19–20 speaks of how the Lord created the heavens and the earth with wisdom, understanding, and knowledge. And Prov 8:22–31 describes how wisdom was with God at the beginning of creation.

In Job, the most significant creation imagery is found in the divine speeches (Job 38–41) as well as the wisdom poem of Job 28.¹⁶⁹ In these, God is presented as the sovereign creator and sustainer of all things.

When it comes to Ecclesiastes, there are several verses that refer, either explicitly or implicitly, to God as the creator (3:11; 5:17 [18]; 7:29; 11:5; 12:1, 7). In addition to the theme of creation, many scholars point to intentional connections in Ecclesiastes with the text of Gen 1–11, although, these are not without criticism.¹⁷⁰ One notable proposal put

---

166. Zimmerli, "The Place and Limit of the Wisdom," 148.

167. Note the discussion above on the origins and views of the wisdom crisis and its retribution theology.

168. Longman, *The Fear of the Lord*, 127.

169. For an interesting recent study on the creation imagery in Job, see Breitkopf, *Job: From Lament to Penitence*.

170. In particular, Dell has contributed an essay evaluating and critiquing the many proposed Ecclesiastes-Genesis connections; see Dell, "Exploring Intertextual Links," 3–14. Here, Dell calls for greater criteria in judging intertextual connections and, following Kynes, she delineates three intertextual categories: 1) quotation (explicit, intentional reference); 2) allusion (implicit, intentional reference); and 3) echo (implicit, unintentional reference); see Dell, "Exploring Intertextual Links," 5.

forward by Verheij sees a specific connection between Qoheleth's royal experiment and the creation accounts in Genesis.[171] To Verheij, Qoheleth was trying, but failed, to be like God and recreate paradise.[172] Some, such as Antic and Meek, argue for a connection between *hebel* and Abel in Gen 4.[173] Bundvad sees in Ecclesiastes a fundamental juxtaposition between the cyclicality of created order and the linearity of human life, and Seitz argues that the creational ordering of Gen 1–11 comprises a conceptual backdrop for Ecclesiastes.[174] Qoheleth also speaks of human sinfulness (7:20, 29), toil (1:13; 2:11, 18, 24, *passim*), and that all are from dust, and to dust all return (3:20b; 12:7; see Gen 2:7; 3:19). Surely, the cumulative effect hints at something real.[175]

Individual cases of possible allusions or echoes are open to debate. That is not the purpose here. The larger question, for the present, is that of wisdom's foundation. What picture is portrayed by the various occurrences of the creation theme in the wisdom books? Is creation the foundation of Israel's wisdom?

Schultz, pushing for wisdom's integration within the OT, argues that *both* creation and covenant comprise the foundation, the twin pillars and theological roots of Israel's wisdom.[176] He notes that there are commonly three areas in which these books can be seen to exhibit creation theology; that is, an emphasis on 1) God as Creator, 2) humanity in general, and 3) nature as divinely ordered.[177] He points to several examples of the creation theme in the three wisdom books, and while he concedes its infrequency, he still argues for its significance. He writes,

> Though the creation theme is not referred to frequently in the Old Testament wisdom corpus, its use is significant: in Proverbs

---

171. Verheij, "Paradise Retried," 113–15.

172. Verheij, "Paradise Retried," 114–15. Dell argues that Verheij's position is overstated and the connection is weak because 1) the shared words are common and 2) they are quite spread out over Gen 1–2; see Dell, "Exploring Intertextual Links," 7–8.

173. Antic, "Cain, Abel, Seth, and the Meaning of Human Life," 203–11; Meek, "The Meaning of הבל in Qohelet," 241–56. Dell holds that this connection amounts to nothing more than a small echo; see Dell, "Exploring Intertextual Links," 6–7.

174. Bundvad, *Time*, 46, 72–73; Seitz, *Elder Testament*, 221–42. Dell suggests that the interest in nature may simply be part of a larger theological picture and that the allusion, or even echo, on this account is lacking; see Dell, "Exploring Intertextual Links," 7.

175. For a recent study of the theology of creation in Ecclesiastes, see Fitschen, *"Eine Gabe Gottes ist es": Schöpfungstheologie im Koheletbuch*.

176. Schultz, "Unity or Diversity," 289–306.

177. Schultz, "Unity or Diversity," 303.

1–9, in presenting the case for the primacy of wisdom, in Ecclesiastes, in portraying the world in which one must seek joy under the shadow of fading achievements and irresolvable conundrums, in Job, in proclaiming the utter sovereignty of the Creator who does not need to explain his actions. Especially in its obvious intertextual relationship to Genesis 1–4, wisdom's creation roots are apparent.[178]

However, a portrayal of the primacy of wisdom or a description of the world in which one must live and navigate does not equate to the subsuming of wisdom under creation theology. These tell the reader that wisdom is important and that it is needed for life, but they, by themselves, do not tell the reader what wisdom is nor how to find it.

Despite the various connections, creation as a foundation falls short in upholding the wisdom tradition. There are a number of reasons supporting the view that creation is better received as an important theme and that, as argued above, Israel's covenantal relationship with God constitutes the foundation.

First, creation imagery does not occupy the most crucial positions. While Schultz recognized the infrequency of the creation theme in the wisdom books, he claimed that its use was still significant. If wisdom was rooted in creation, one would expect it to be found in the most significant parts of the wisdom texts. However, a close look reveals a remarkable absence. Further, what is found in these portions describes a wisdom that is rooted in a covenant relationship with God. The prologue of Proverbs (Prov 1:1–7) lays out the aim of the book, piling on words such as wisdom, instruction, understanding, insight, righteousness, justice, equity, etc. Culminating in Prov 1:7, the prologue identifies the fear of the Lord as the beginning/foundational wisdom principle.[179] But the theme of creation makes no appearance.

Ecclesiastes ends with an epilogue (12:8–14), in which the frame narrator gives his assessment of Qoheleth, followed by his concluding thoughts. Here, at the end of the matter, after everything has been heard, the narrator presents the book's grand conclusion with covenantal language; that is, one is to fear God and keep his commandments, for God

---

178. Schultz, "Unity or Diversity," 305.

179. One could also point to the key use of the fear of the Lord in other parts of the book. See discussion above.

will bring everything into judgment. Once again, the theme of creation is absent.[180]

The prologue of Job takes pains to present and reiterate that this man was blameless and upright, one who feared God and turned away from evil (Job 1:1; 8, 9; 2:3). Job would even offer burnt sacrifices in the case that one of his children might have sinned against God (Job 1:5). And after Job lost all he had, he held fast his integrity (Job 2:3, 9) and did not sin (Job 1:22; 2:10). The focus here is not that of creation but of Job's character before God. It is true that in many of the book's speeches, most poignantly in the divine speeches of Job 38–41, the theme of creation is clearly present. Yet, creation is not presented as the foundation of wisdom but is used to show both humanity's lack of understanding and God's supremacy over all things. Indeed, humanity is incapable of truly comprehending the world. For example, the great wisdom poem of Job 28 has much creation imagery as it describes a search for wisdom. People dam up streams, uproot mountains, and unearth countless treasures (v. 1–11). But where shall wisdom be found? (v. 12). It is found not in mines of the earth nor deep in the sea (v. 14). It is not found in the land of the living (v. 13) nor with Abaddon and death (v. 22). It is hidden from the eyes of all, even from birds soaring high above (v. 21). After searching all creation, the poem declares that wisdom is with God and concludes, "Behold, the fear of the Lord, that is wisdom, and to turn away from evil is understanding" (v. 28). Even here, the text declares that wisdom is ultimately not "discovered" in creation but rooted in a proper relationship with God.

In the most significant parts of the wisdom books, the creation theme is largely absent, let alone foundational. Yet, what these sections do present is the fear of the Lord, for this is the beginning of wisdom and the final word on the matter. Creation certainly represents an important theme in the wisdom tradition, but it does not comprise its foundation.[181]

---

180. One could argue that the opening poem of Ecclesiastes (1:4–11) puts forward this creation theme, as does Qoheleth's closing poem about death (12:1–7), and that these are in significant places of the book. While certainly pronounced in these extremities and important to Qoheleth's thought, they describe the world in which Qoheleth conducts his quest for wisdom, but they are not the source of the wisdom he offers in response to his own failures and all that is incomprehensible (Qoheleth's address will be examined in the following chapters). Still, the wisdom of the book *as a whole*, in its final shape, is not rooted in creation but in a covenantal relationship with God, as communicated in the epilogue, and *this* will guide one through life in the created world, with all of its possibilities, difficulties, and mysteries.

181. See Longman, *The Fear of the Lord*, 136.

Second, wisdom is less a search for created orders as it is about receiving instruction. Accompanying the view that wisdom is rooted in creation theology comes the view that wisdom is primarily based on observation and experience and largely constitutes a search for orders distilled in creation, which the sage can discover and live by. Schwáb makes an interesting point as he argues that this is not how Proverbs characterizes the search for wisdom. He writes, "Proverbs actually mainly encourages the reader to listen to instruction rather than to explore reality with an open mind; that besides listening to the fathers' teaching, the key to wisdom is the fear of the Lord and not a search for natural regularities."[182] While observations are common, a cursory glance at Proverbs 1–9, as well as a careful read of the book as a whole, would seem to support Schwáb's claim.

Third, wisdom assumes ethical principles. As discussed earlier in this chapter, Israel's wisdom tradition cannot be properly understood apart from the covenant, for much of the wisdom material alludes to an underlying religious context. Bartholomew and O'Dowd argue, "What is often not noted, though, is that the order that Proverbs finds in the 'carved' creation is not and cannot be simply read out of the creation. This is the point that Fox makes about Israelite wisdom; it is not empirical but *assumes ethical principles which it uses observation to support.*"[183] The very principles that wisdom upholds cannot be discovered in creation; moreover, these principles presuppose instruction.[184] Wisdom does make observations and learns from experience, but as Prov 3:5 teaches, "Trust in the Lord will all your heart, and do not lean on your own understanding."

In sum, creation is not wisdom's foundation. And contra Schultz, creation and covenant are not wisdom's twin pillars. While the theme of creation is unquestionably important to the wisdom tradition, it simply does not represent its foundation. Moreover, a short investigation into the matter reveals, once again, a covenantal base.

---

182. Schwáb, *Toward an Interpretation of the Book of Proverbs*, 63.

183. Bartholomew and O'Dowd, *Old Testament Wisdom Literature*, 287; emphasis added.

184. Bartholomew and O'Dowd, *Old Testament Wisdom Literature*, 287.

2.5.5 Conclusion

This section asked the question of the proper foundation of Israel's wisdom tradition. After outlining the fear of the Lord as wisdom's base, this section considered two counter-foundations represented in scholarship. The first claimed that Israel's tradition was foreign to the rest of Scripture and was more at home in the wisdom traditions of the ANE. However, it was shown that while Israel's wisdom may have possessed an international flavor, borrowing from her many neighbors, Israel adapted rather than merely adopted materials and that these were placed in a new context, one built on Israel's covenantal relationship with God. The second claimed that Israel's wisdom is rooted in creation theology. And while creation is a prominent theme, a quick inquiry revealed that it was simply that: just a theme. The most hermeneutically significant sections of the wisdom books reveal both a striking absence of creational themes and a dominating covenantal presence. In conclusion, the books are clear that the foundation of Israel's wisdom is her covenant relationship with the Lord.

2.6 CONCLUSION

This chapter sought to examine the interpretive context for Qoheleth's address. Three levels were identified: first, Qoheleth's wisdom occurs in the context of a frame narrator; second, Ecclesiastes comes in the context of a wisdom tradition; and third, these wisdom books occur in the larger context of the OT.

Concerning the first contextual level, it was established that Qoheleth's address must be interpreted within its narrative frame. While the section made this point in brief, the larger question of the nature of their relationship has been set to the side, for the time being, to be picked up again in chapter 4, after Qoheleth's address has been given sufficient due. The examination of the second contextual level demonstrated the complementary relationship between Ecclesiastes and Proverbs. Of particular note is the connection between the epilogue of Ecclesiastes and the prologue of Proverbs, which provides a hermeneutical frame and suggests that the two wisdom texts should be read together. And while the two books exhibit many differences, claims of a wisdom crisis fail to recognize both the complexity of Proverbs' understanding of reality as well as the tradition's covenantal foundation. Lastly, the discussion of the third contextual level revealed a much closer relationship between wisdom and the OT than the previous generations of scholarship have, generally speaking, passed down. Wisdom and law are both rooted in a covenantal relationship with the Lord. And wisdom, like much of the OT, teaches the difference between the way of the wise/righteous and the way of the fool/wicked, instructing on the characteristic desires, actions, and outcomes of these two paths. Moreover, it is only through God's covenantal relationship with his people that the rest of the prophets and writings make sense. The many books represent numerous voices, but they still carry an underlying unity of thought and purpose. Much more could be said about these contextual levels and the issues that surround them. This cursory treatment barely begins to describe the deep-rooted relationship wisdom has with the OT. Indeed, there is room for much more study here. However, this short analysis is sufficient for the present purposes.

Admittingly, this chapter has focused on similarities. This is not meant to be at the expense of the differences, of which there are many. Each book has a unique contribution to make. Yet, while there is diversity, there is nevertheless a fundamental unity. The differences have long eclipsed the similarities in scholarship, often leaving the wisdom books in pieces and excised from their biblical context. This project hopes to contribute to their return.

With the results of this inquiry into the context in mind, the following chapters will turn to Qoheleth's address, seeking to discern his wisdom.

3

The Design of Qoheleth

3.1 INTRODUCTION

INQUIRY INTO THE MESSAGE of Qoheleth raises the question of structure. To claim that a section of his address represents his concluding message presupposes a level of structure and movement. But, is the address a cohesive whole or a haphazard collection of sayings and/or pericopes that may convey meaning but not an overarching message? Are Qoheleth's meandering musings aimless, or do they progress purposefully toward an end? And if Qoheleth works with a larger goal in mind, what role do the parts play?

This chapter argues for reading Qoheleth's address as a narrative, the trajectory of which progresses to and culminates in Qoheleth's final section such that it can be read as a conclusion. In the second half of this chapter, the discussion will turn to consider both the meaning of Qoheleth's most prominent motifs and the role they play within this narrative arc, arguing that they contribute to its movements and support its conclusion.

3.2 DISCERNING STRUCTURE

3.2.1 Introduction

Scholarship on the structure of Ecclesiastes has had a difficult past. After noting various approaches to structure and some dynamics that complicate the task, this section will argue for understanding Qoheleth's address as a narrative. This quality provides cohesion to the whole and an overarching structure with purposeful progression to a deliberate end. This basic narrative thread will then be traced through Qoheleth's address.

3.2.2 Past Inquiries into Structure

The dominance of historical criticism in the late nineteenth to early twentieth century promulgated the view that Ecclesiastes consisted of various sayings, collections, and layers of editorial activity, which source- and redaction-criticism worked to decipher.[1] Since many of the difficulties of the book resulted from the redactional layers and glosses, the solution, so it seemed, lay in removing those layers. As a gathering of independent sayings or as a compilation of various collections, the book was thought to contain no overarching structure beyond a loose alignment of various themes. Delitzsch represents the position well. He writes,

> . . . a gradual development, a progressive demonstration, is wanting, and even the grouping together of the parts is not fully carried out; the connection of the thoughts is more frequently determined by that which is external and accidental, and not infrequently an incongruous element is introduced into the connected course of kindred matters. . . . All attempts to show, in the whole, not only oneness of spirit, but also a genetic progress, an all-embracing plan, and an organic connection, have hitherto failed, and must fail.[2]

This view, that there was no overarching structure, was commonplace for some time.[3]

As the twentieth century moved along, the majority of scholars came to accept the basic unity of Qoheleth's address, viewing just the narrative frame as secondary.[4] This shift is what Bartholomew identifies

---

1. See the following select surveys of approaches to the structure of Ecclesiastes: Wright, "Riddle," 314–20; Murphy, *Ecclesiastes*, xxxii–xli, who updates Wright's list; Crenshaw, *Ecclesiastes*, 34–49; Salyer, *Vain Rhetoric*, 143–64; and Beldman, "Framed," 137–44.

2. Delitzsch, *Commentary on the Song of Songs and Ecclesiastes*, 188.

3. For an extensive list of scholars holding similar positions, see Wright, "Riddle," 314n3. Though, some interpreters did organize around various philosophical themes or logical developments; for an overview, see Wright, "Riddle," 315–17.

4. Beldman, "Framed," 139.

as the "literary turn" in wisdom scholarship.[5] This turn of focus to the literary shape of the book as a whole led to a variety of approaches, some of which sought a very detailed view of the book's structure based on repeated vocabulary and/or refrains, though, with quite varying results.[6]

Most notably, Wright employed New Criticism/New Stylistics to analyze the book's structure in an effort to break the deadlock of opposing subjective theories and to once and for all solve the mysterious riddle that is Qoheleth.[7] He sees the book as divided into two halves. The first half (1:12—6:9) is about the vanity of human endeavors and can be divided into eight meaningful units with major observations, each marked by the refrain "(vanity and) chasing wind" (1:14, 17; 2:11, 17, 26; 4:4–6 [2x], 16; 6:9), a refrain not found thereafter.[8] The second half (6:10—11:6) begins with the introduction (6:10–12) of two ideas; namely, man does not know what is good nor does man know what comes after. After this introduction, the second half is comprised of two primary units. The first (7:1—8:17) has four sections, each of which ends with "not find/who can find out." The second (9:1—11:6) has six sections dealing with the problem of what comes after, each of which ends with "do not know" or "no knowledge."[9] He writes, "When these patterns are taken as indicating the framework of the book and when that framework is brought to the material as an overlay as it were, there emerges out of the apparent disorder a straightforward presentation of a very simple theme."[10] And in a pair of subsequent articles, Wright double-downs on his approach, delving into gematria/numerology to support his theory and unlock further mysteries.[11] Some of Wright's insights have certainly been influential, and some

5. See Bartholomew, "Old Testament Wisdom Today," 13–28.

6. For example, Lohfink identifies an artistic interplay of the forms of both a philosophical diatribe taken from Qoheleth's Greek context and an overarching chiastic pattern representative of the sage's Semitic roots; see Lohfink, *Qoheleth*, 7–8. Note also Walton's text-linguistic approach to structure and his hierarchy of clauses; see Walton, *Experimenting with Qohelet*. See also, Loader, *Polar Structures*, 112, who posits a highly complex structure of poles and contra-poles with levels of interlocking brackets; and Rousseau, "Structure de Qohelet 1:4–11 et Plan du Livre," 200–17.

7. Wright, "Riddle," 313–34.

8. Wright, "Riddle," 320–22.

9. Wright, "Riddle," 322–23. For his final outline, see Wright, "Riddle," 325–26.

10. Wright, "Riddle," 313.

11. See Wright, "The Riddle of the Sphinx Revisited," 38–51; and Wright, "Additional Numerical Patterns in Qoheleth," 32–43. Here, the word הבל, representing the number thirty-seven, becomes the key for understanding the structure and development of the book.

scholars have adopted his basic structure.[12] Nevertheless, Wright's results have been widely criticized.[13]

One substantial criticism leveled against many of the proposed detailed structures of Qoheleth's address is that they demand something of the text that is not there. To say this another way, they impose a logical, linear, Western/modern view of structure. However, Beldman notes an increasing trend in scholarship that holds the book's unity but rejects such anachronistic tendencies.[14] Salyer also argues against imposing a Western mindset and outlines many in agreement, such as Lauha, Loretz, Perry, Breton, Caneday, and Viviano.[15] The interpreter must receive the book as is and carefully follow Qoheleth as *he* leads, even if the direction at times seems odd and his turns inexplicable. Fox describes Qoheleth's address as having an "episodic, discontinuous, staccato character"[16] but notes that even without a neat design, a text can still be coherent.[17] He is adamant that "This lack of sequential organization is not a 'riddle' but a characteristic of style."[18] Moreover, this style appropriately reflects the nature of Qoheleth's journey. Bartholomew writes, "The journey into and through despair in anything but linear, and as is typical in such

---

12. Murphy, *Tree of Life*, 52; Johnston, "Confessions of a Workaholic," 14–28; Brown, "Structure in Ecclesiastes," 195–208, who builds on Wright's work but places greater emphasis on the joy passages; and Salyer, *Vain Rhetoric*, 151.

13. For critiques of Wright's theory, see the following: Seow, *Ecclesiastes*, 44–46; Crenshaw, *Ecclesiastes*, 40–42; and Fox, *Time to Tear Down*, 147–49. The following are the most common points of criticism: the formulae used for the structure do not always end a section; the chosen refrains are not as consistent and confined as proposed; other repeated refrains are not considered; the rubric does not always match the topics of the units; it assumes that versification goes back to the autographs; and, there is a lack of control about what does and does not count as numerically significant and of the various adjustments hypothesized to make the numerical versification theory work. Bartholomew argues that as a whole, Wright's structure does not match the back-and-forth nature of Qoheleth's investigations (Bartholomew, *Ecclesiastes*, 82). And Fox writes, "the proposed structure has no more effect on the interpretation than a ghost in the attic. A literary or rhetorical structure should not merely 'be there'; it must *do* something. It should guide readers in recognizing and remembering the author's train of thought, even if there is no unanimity of the precise disposition of the material" (Fox, *Time to Tear Down*, 149; emphasis original). In short, and despite bold claims to the contrary, Wright's theory remains marred by subjectivity.

14. Beldman, "Framed," 143.

15. Salyer, *Vain Rhetoric*, 147–48.

16. Fox, *Time to Tear Down*, 3.

17. Fox, *Time to Tear Down*, 149. Fox points to Wittgenstein's *Philosophical Investigations* as an example.

18. Fox, *Time to Tear Down*, 152.

experiences, moments of great insight are often followed by lapses back into the old struggles so that the journey is far more of a spiral than a straight line ... Thus the structure of Ecclesiastes is *literary and organic*, as befits Qohelet's experience, rather than logical in a scientific sense."[19] This appeal to the book's nature and purpose accounts for the lack of perceived structure and better represents the way readers experience it.[20]

In sum, there is a growing number of scholars that hold the unity of Qoheleth's address and recognize a broad structure without demanding a detailed, linear arrangement. As Longman notes, the general structure is clear, but the search for structure of the minute details predominately leads to frustration (and little to no agreement).[21] Similarly, Fox notes that one can follow Qoheleth's journey and the general progression of thought without dividing up the text's many units.[22] Accordingly, the approach of this chapter considers the macro-structure and general progression of Qoheleth's address, aiming to avoid anachronistic impositions and to allow Qoheleth to investigate, reflect, retell, and advise on his own terms.

3.2.3 Handling Contradictions

Contributing to the difficulty of discerning the structure and message of Qoheleth's address is the presence of contradictions.[23] Tensions rise between the value of life over death (4:2, 3; 6:3; 9:4), wisdom over folly (2:15–16), and righteousness over wickedness (7:16–17; 8:14), to name a few. However, the most significant tension rises between Qoheleth's *hebel* conclusions and his commendations of joy.

Various attempts at resolving the many contradictions have been pursued throughout the history of interpretation. Fox provides a helpful

---

19. Bartholomew, *Ecclesiastes*, 83; emphasis original.
20. Beldman, "Framed," 144.
21. Longman, *Ecclesiastes*, 21.
22. Fox, *Time to Tear Down*, 150–53.
23. There is some variability concerning what scholars mean by "contradiction." The word implies fundamental incompatibility. However, many scholars recognize that the contradictions are only apparent and resolve them in their interpretations—as such, they use the term rather loosely (see Fox, *Time to Tear Down*, 3, 14). Therefore, "tension" may be a more appropriate designation. This acknowledges the difference but allows both sides to carry truth; the tension is how to hold the two together. This fits well with the investigatory nature of Qoheleth's address. Fox writes, "The relation between the two propositions is 'this is true *and*—alas—that is true'" (Fox, *Time to Tear Down*, 17; emphasis original).

discussion and critique of various positions, along with their primary proponents. He identifies the following categories: 1) harmonizing discords (Abraham Ibn Ezra, Hertzberg, Loader); 2) subtracting later additions (Siegfried, Barton, McNeile, Podechard, Crenshaw); 3) discovering quotations (Levy, Gordis, Whybray, Michel); 4) hearing dialogue (Miller, Perry); 5) detecting dialectic (Murphy); and 6) appeals to a fragmented psyche (Galling).[24] These are largely speculative and subjective, lacking substantiation and control.

Now, many scholars attribute it all to Qoheleth and see the many tensions as not only reflecting the character of the address but also representing an integral part of it. Rather than a riddle to be solved or removed, Fox argues that the contradictions play an important role. "My primary thesis is a simple one: The contradictions in the book of Qohelet are real and intended. We must interpret them, not eliminate them."[25] It is not that Qoheleth is contradicting himself but rather reporting contradictions that he has observed in the world around him.[26] Qoheleth does not resolve these tensions "but only describes them, bemoans them, and suggests how to live in such a refractory world. The contradictions do not make the book incoherent. On the contrary, Qohelet's persistent observation of contradictions is a powerful cohesive force, and an awareness of it brings into focus the book's central concern: the problem of meaning in life."[27] Fox rightly concludes, "Qohelet's contradictions are the starting point but not the message of the book."[28] These contradictions are not to be eliminated but recognized for the role they play in tearing down meaning in order that Qoheleth might build up anew.[29]

Bartholomew argues that the book presents a deliberate juxtaposition between the *hebel* conclusions and the carpe diem passages.[30] He writes, "there is always the temptation to flatten the book out in one direction or the other. We should resist both of these temptations. The opposing perspectives are deliberately juxtaposed so that gaps are opened up in the reading, and the book is precisely about how to resolve the tension

---

24. Fox, *Time to Tear Down*, 14–26. See also Murphy, *Ecclesiastes*, xxxiii–xxxiv.

25. Fox, *Time to Tear Down*, 3. See also, Fuhr, *Inter-Dependency*, 10–15, who echoes Fox's approach.

26. Fox, *Time to Tear Down*, 3.

27. Fox, *Time to Tear Down*, 3.

28. Fox, *Time to Tear Down*, 3.

29. Fox, *Time to Tear Down*, 138–40.

30. Bartholomew, *Ecclesiastes*, 81–82.

between these contradictory juxtapositions."[31] Salyer identifies a similar purpose: "What the implied reader encounters is a series of blanks and gaps which prove upon further reflection to be a succession of participatory prods . . . Their effect is to draw the reader into the text, creating a sense of participation with the narrator."[32] Seow's words concerning Job are quite applicable here: "There are all sorts of literary tensions within the book. Hence, instead of performing textual strategies to suit modern preconceptions of coherence, it is necessary to give the ancient narrator-poet the benefit of the doubt and to grapple with those dissonances and asymmetry that may well be part of how the book means."[33] Longman argues, "Close study shows that Qohelet's thought rambles, repeats . . . and occasionally contradicts itself. Such a lack of order, though, far from detracting from the message of the book, actually contributes to it."[34]

In sum, one should allow the tensions to be, to build, and to serve their purpose. The reader must follow Qoheleth to see how these tensions arise, how he reacts to them, and what advice he offers in response. Resisting premature resolution, the reader should join Qoheleth in his investigations and see where the journey leads.

3.2.4 Qoheleth's Address as Narrative

Though one should hesitate to demand of the text a detailed, logical, linear structure, this is not to say that clear movement is absent. Indeed, there is a marked progression throughout Qoheleth's address. In fact, Qoheleth's address possesses strong narrative qualities and is often described as a "quest" or a "journey." This section will consider and build on the scholarship of many who treat Qoheleth's address as a narrative. This understanding supports cohesion and progression in the address, a progression that builds toward and culminates in Qoheleth's final section (11:7—12:7) such that it can be seen as a conclusion to the whole, containing Qoheleth's final and central message.

Fox's contribution is noteworthy as he pushes for reading Ecclesiastes not just as wisdom but also as narration. He writes,

---

31. Bartholomew, *Ecclesiastes*, 81.
32. Salyer, *Vain Rhetoric*, 147.
33. Seow, *Job 1–21*, 38.
34. Longman, *Ecclesiastes*, 22.

It tells something that happened to someone. I would like to take some first steps in the investigation of the literary characteristics of Qoheleth as narrative: Who is speaking (the question of voice), how do the voices speak, and how do they relate to each other? I will argue that the Book of Qoheleth is to be taken as a whole, as a single, well-integrated composition, the product not of editorship but of authorship, which uses interplay of voice as a deliberate literary device for rhetorical and artistic purposes.[35]

Fox argues that "Qohelet's words are presented not as a collection of separate reflections and sentences but as a single search, whose goal is set forth clearly in 1:13 . . . and whose presence shapes our perception of the whole book."[36] He notes that there are about fifty phrases in the book that convey search and observation and that "These phrases provide a matrix that unites the disparate observations that Qoheleth reports. These phrases, which cannot be separated from the sentences they introduce, have meaning only in the context of a single search by one man."[37] Fox argues that the book is by a single hand. "I suggest that all of 1:2—12:14 is by the same hand—not that the epilogue is by Qohelet, but that *Qohelet is 'by' the epilogist*."[38] Accordingly, the book contains a number of levels and perspectives:

Level 1: The frame-narrator who tells about

Level 2a: Qohelet-the-reporter, the narrating "I," who speaks from the vantage point of old age and looks back on

Level 2b: Qohelet-the-seeker, the experiencing "I," the younger Qohelet who made the fruitless investigation introduced in 1:12f.[39]

Thus, the book presents two persons, and the second, Qoheleth, presents two perspectives.[40]

Fox makes two points about Qoheleth's address that are particularly pertinent to the present discussion. First, Qoheleth's address presents a unified, single search. Fox argues that "the book's cohesiveness inheres above all in the constant presence of a single brooding consciousness

---

35. Fox, "Frame Narrative," 83.
36. Fox, "Frame Narrative," 90.
37. Fox, "Frame Narrative," 90.
38. Fox, "Frame Narrative," 91; emphasis original.
39. Fox, "Frame Narrative," 91.
40. Fox, "Frame Narrative," 92.

mediating all the book's observations, counsels, and evaluations."[41] Fox writes, "the book of Qoheleth is about meaning. What unites all of Qoheleth's complaints is the collapse of meaning. What unites all of his counsels and affirmations is the attempt to reconstruct meanings."[42]

The second point from Fox's analysis is the distinction between the two perspectives of Qoheleth; that is, an older Qoheleth reporting and reflecting on an earlier search. Qoheleth makes use of his earlier search and the tensions he found as a vehicle for deconstruction. "At the same time that Qohelet is tearing down, he is building up, identifying things that are good, offering maxims and counsels on how to live, suggesting how we can make the best of the bad deal that is life. Tearing down and building up are the two movements in Qohelet's thought, but they are not two sequential phases. Toward the end of the book, however, the emphasis is increasingly on the constructive."[43] Thus, Qoheleth presents a general, non-sequential movement from past quest to present counsel. Deconstruction is not the end goal. Rather, Qoheleth's ultimate message is found in the reconstruction, in the wisdom of the aged Qoheleth.

Another insightful study comes at the hands of Christianson, who notes that many scholars assume the text to be a narrative and treat it as such; however, he aims to lay out a case and provides a detailed examination.[44] More than simply possessing elements of narrativity, Christianson argues that Ecclesiastes meets narratological criteria to be commended as a narrative text.[45] Specifically, Christianson sees functional narrative events and a proleptic plot.[46] The kernel event of 1:12–13a launches the narrative motion, covering all the events that follow.[47] And as Qoheleth reveals his search (1:13) and its conclusion (1:14), the reader anticipates the account. Further, there is a striking dominance of first-person narration. Boda writes,

---

41. Fox, *Time to Tear Down*, 151. See also Fox, *Contradictions*, 159. Borrowing Fox's language, Salyer argues that "Throughout the book, one meets the brooding reflections of a single consciousness, with the result being an undeniable impression that the writing comes from a single author" (Salyer, *Vain Rhetoric*, 144–45).

42. Fox, *Time to Tear Down*, 133. Similarly, Salyer writes, "Qoheleth's 'I' gives the work a certain structural stability" (Salyer, *Vain Rhetoric*, 147).

43. Fox, *Time to Tear Down*, 140. See also Fox, "Frame Narrative," 83, 90–91.

44. Christianson, *Time to Tell*, 19–50.

45. Christianson, *Time to Tell*, 19.

46. Christianson, *Time to Tell*, 24–33. Christianson also finds the use of motifs as a prominent stylistic feature; see Christianson, *Time to Tell*, 42–45.

47. Christianson, *Time to Tell*, 26–28.

> The opening autobiographical words in 1:12–13 . . . set up the expectation that Qohelet's account is journalistic, autobiographical, and thus, designed to create a sense of journey or exploration that can move in different directions and introduce a variety of perspectives. Thus, the genre signaled at the outset of the autobiography sets for us a strategy for reading this account—a strategy that expects twists and turns and even tensions as the journey progresses toward its conclusion.[48]

This autobiographical form adheres the whole together, even while Qoheleth's explorations vary widely.[49]

Christianson describes the narrative of Qoheleth as a quest. "Qoheleth is embarked on a quest. His is the act of seeking or pursuing a goal, an object of intrinsic but immaterial value. That act touches every corner of Qoheleth's narrative, and its intensity causes readers to recognize in Qoheleth a sincere commitment."[50] Though a predominantly intellectual venture, the text uses a number of verbs related to physical movement—these contribute to the sense of a physical, and wearying, quest.[51] More significantly, this quest forms the basis for the structure and meaning of the address. Qoheleth pursued a quest; one that ultimately failed. Yet, that failure was not the end. Christianson writes,

> Qoheleth gradually moves from quest to expression . . . Most of the texts that directly express the quest occur in the first seven chapters. In the latter part of the book, however, Qoheleth speaks less of the story of his youth and more of his 'present' concern. He addresses the reader with a certainty that betrays the style of questioning that I sketched out above, and that certainty has mostly to do with the fact that he admits his failures and his inability to know—he is certain that he is ignorant . . . That hard-won ignorance forms the basis of his strategy in the latter half of the book: the imparting of advice to the addressee.[52]

---

48. Boda, "Speaking into the Silence," 275.
49. Christianson, *Time to Tell*, 36.
50. Christianson, *Time to Tell*, 216.
51. Christianson, *Time to Tell*, 221–27. For verbs directly expressing his quest, note the following: הלך (2:1), שוב (4:1, 7; 9:11), סבב (2:20; 7:25), תור (1:13; 2:3; 7:25), and פנה (2:11, 12); see Christianson, *Time to tell*, 223. For his list of other words conveying physical movement, see Christianson, *Time to tell*, 222.
52. Christianson, *Time to Tell*, 243.

The primary progression of Qoheleth's address is the movement from quest to expression; the two perspectives of "then" and "now."[53] He recounts his past experiences and failures but then, increasingly, he leaves behind his past skepticism and lifts his head to the reader and, in an act of redemption, imparts advice.[54] This has two significant implications for understanding Qoheleth. First, Qoheleth's pessimism belongs to his younger self. Qoheleth writes, "So I hated life . . . I hated all my toil . . . So I turned and gave my heart up to despair . . ." (2:17–20). However, an older Qoheleth is telling about his *past* quest and failures. "If readers lose their grasp of this narrative structure they become in danger of getting lost in the 'then' of Qoheleth's most pessimistic reflection."[55] This pessimism belongs to the younger Qoheleth but not to the older nor should it necessarily be picked up by the reader. Second, Qoheleth's goal is instruction, and his message particularly comes through in the latter half of his address. "Without a doubt Qoheleth has failed in the act of his quest, but his success lies in the telling of his story."[56] Indeed, this remembering/telling of his story becomes an act of redemption as he is able to bring meaning to his past failures and so transcend the absurd.[57]

This move toward the primary goal of instructing the reader is highlighted by a gradual shift in the narratorial voice.[58] In concert with the shift from the "then" perspective to the "now," comes the diminishment of the first-person and the increase of the second-person. The early chapters of Qoheleth's address are dominated by the first-person. For example, consider 2:4: הִגְדַּלְתִּי מַעֲשָׂי בָּנִיתִי לִי בָּתִּים נָטַעְתִּי לִי כְּרָמִים; lit. "I made great my works. I built for myself houses. I planted for myself vineyards." Six out of the eight words convey the first-person—a concentration not found elsewhere in the MT. And the second-person is not introduced until 4:17 [5:1].[59] The other end of Qoheleth's address reveals a different picture. For example, 11:9—12:1, part of Qoheleth's final section, is governed by

---

53. Christianson, *Time to Tell*, 246.

54. Christianson, *Time to Tell*, 216–54.

55. Christianson, *Time to Tell*, 246.

56. Christianson, *Time to Tell*, 246. Note Seitz's description of Qoheleth as "a persona of an aged wisdom on the other side of failure and achievement both" (Seitz, *Elder Testament*, 232).

57. Christianson, *Time to Tell*, 246, 250–51.

58. Christianson, *Time to Tell*, 244.

59. This statement attributes the imperative "See" in 1:10 to the frame narrator and ignores 2:1, where Qoheleth commands himself.

a string of imperatives: "Rejoice . . . Walk . . . know . . . Remove . . . put away . . . Remember . . ." In fact, the first-person is entirely absent in the final two chapters. While there is not a clear-cut division between the first-person quest in the first half and instruction in the second, a progression is clearly discernable.[60]

Others have highlighted this significant change in the narratorial voice. Castellino notes that 4:17 [5:1] marks an abrupt change as it is the first time Qoheleth, no longer speaking of himself and his quest, directly addresses the implied reader to impart instruction.[61] Consequently, Castellino makes this the primary structural division of the book, resulting in two parts (Part I: 1:1—4:16; and Part II: 4:17 [5:1]—12:12).[62] Indeed, the narratee is only implied at the beginning of Qoheleth's address, but that distance closes as the narratee is brought close in the second half and entreated directly.[63] De Jong builds on Castellino's work, noting the switches between the first-person observational complexes and the instructional complexes addressed to the "you," and while 4:17 is the first switch, he argues that this pattern of alternating complexes continues throughout the address.[64] He also notes that Qoheleth's pessimistic tone tends to come out in the observational complexes and that those of instruction tend toward the positive.[65]

With this general progression from quest to instruction, the second-person stands out as particularly emphatic, pointed directly at the reader, suggesting the communication of key points. Christianson writes, "Sometimes he gets up from his chair to speak directly to the audience, relating soberly what is most important to store away, to remember, to know and to rejoice in."[66] Miller argues that there are four speech types in

---

60. See Christianson, *Time to Tell*, 244, where he provides a graph plotting the percentages of first- and second-person narration for each chapter.

61. Castellino, "Qohelet and His Wisdom," 16.

62. Castellino, "Qohelet and His Wisdom," 16–24.

63. Salyer, *Vain Rhetoric*, 153–54.

64. De Jong, "A Book on Labour," 107–16. Apart from the introduction (1:1), motto (1:2; 12:8), and epilogue (12:8–14), de Jong identifies the following complexes: observation (1:3–4:16); instruction (4:17–5:8 [5:1–9]); observation (5:9 [10]–6:9); instruction (6:10–7:22); observation (7:23–29); instruction (8:1–8); observation (8:9—9:12); and instruction (9:13—12:7); see de Jong, "A Book on Labour," 108. Although, he does note that there is a level of fluidity and that the designation of each complex is reflective of density and not exclusivity.

65. De Jong, "A Book on Labour," 109.

66. Christianson, *Time to Tell*, 258.

the book: reports, inferences, judgments, and injunctions.[67] The first two are primarily concerned with Qoheleth's experiences, and these lead into the third. The fourth is especially pronounced in Qoheleth's use of imperatives but also, to a subtler degree, in the wisdom sayings and reflect the purpose of the book as instruction/persuasion.[68]

Longman's study of comparative ANE wisdom texts supports this basic structure and progression. He analyzes fifteen such Akkadian texts and identifies a common three-part structure, beginning with first-person identification, followed by first-person narration, and concluding with an ending section. Based on the purpose of the final segment, Longman divides them into four subgenres, one of which is wisdom admonitions and instructions for behavior. This subgenre is best represented in three Akkadian fictional autobiographies: the Cuthaean Legend of Naram-Sin; the Adad-guppi autobiography; and the Sin of Sargon. A similar three-part structure can be seen in Qoheleth's address; namely, first-person identification (1:12), first-person narration (1:13–6:9), and an ending of wisdom admonitions (6:10–12:7).[69] If the structural similarities with Akkadian fictional autobiographies are correct, then specific attention is placed on the latter half of Qoheleth's address as instructions for proper behavior. And the advice is rooted in his experience reported in the first half. "His experience is the soil out of which his wisdom grows."[70] The result is a similar progression from "then" to "now," from quest to instruction. Longman notes that while Qoheleth's address may not contain a detailed structure, this general progression may still be observed and was by no means uncommon.[71]

Bartholomew is another who sees Qoheleth's address unified by a single search.[72] The methodological drive of Qoheleth's quest is his autonomous epistemology—a faulty foundation that inevitably caused the quest to fail, as expressed in 7:23–29.[73] His quest repeatedly leads him to

---

67. Miller, *Symbol and Rhetoric*, 47–51.

68. Miller, *Symbol and Rhetoric*, 50.

69. For his discussion, see Longman, *Fictional Akkadian Autobiography*; and Longman, *Ecclesiastes*, 8, 15–20, 58–59. See also Shields, "Qohelet and Royal Autobiography," 117–36; and Koh, *Royal Autobiography in the Book of Qoheleth*, 106–12.

70. Longman, *Ecclesiastes*, 19. See also Christianson, *Time to Tell*, 246, who writes, "Since the 'now' can only emerge from the 'brooding consciousness' (Fox) of the 'then', the 'now' is necessarily refined by the fire of the 'then.'"

71. Longman, *Ecclesiastes*, 22.

72. Bartholomew, *Ecclesiastes*, 82–83.

73. Bartholomew, *Ecclesiastes*, 267–77.

the declaration of *hebel*, but these are then set in deliberate contradictory juxtaposition with his contrary vision expressed in the carpe diem passages. The tension between these poles builds throughout the address and creates a gap for the reader to ponder.[74] It is not until Qoheleth's final section that the tension is broken and Qoheleth provides his primary message and point of reorientation, the proper foundation from which one can approach life.[75] Bartholomew's position will be further examined below. For now, it is sufficient to note first, his view of a unified search and second, a progression that moves from quest to failure to the culminating advice of Qoheleth's final section.

Beldman, taking cue from Aristotle's *Poetics* on the basic building blocks on narrative, sees a beginning, middle, and end in both the frame narrative (1:1–11; 7:27; and 12:8–14, respectively) and in Qoheleth's address, which moves from his quest in the beginning (1:12–18 outlines the quest, which commences in 2:1), to the middle, in which Qoheleth confesses his failure and the bankruptcy of his autonomous epistemology (7:23–29), to the end, where Qoheleth reaches the final step of his journey and the point of reorientation (11:7—12:7).[76]

Many scholars hold to the unity of Qoheleth's discourse and identify a general progression in his address, a progression that finds a quest largely in the first half and instruction largely in the second half. Building on this, there are many indicators that point to Qoheleth's final section (11:7—12:7) as his conclusion to the whole.[77] First, to begin with what is perhaps the most obvious, it comes at the end. If the account is a narrative, the reader expects it to lead somewhere and to conclude in some manner. Most naturally, the reader follows the narrative arc as it leads to the end. Second, noting the gradual progression from first- to second-person, the final section is marked by a succession of imperatives. It comes across as particularly direct, emphatic, and final. Third, the primary motifs, which help to guide the reader, lead to and are brought together in this final unit (see discussion below). Fourth, the final section mentions, for the first time, Qoheleth's addressee, "O young man" (11:9). This explicitness, coming only here at the end of his address, adds

---

74. Bartholomew, *Ecclesiastes*, 81–83.

75. Bartholomew, *Ecclesiastes*, 93–96, 356–58.

76. Beldman, "Framed," 150–60.

77. This is not to say that it answers every problem and solves every mystery. Rather, it conveys Qoheleth's conclusion, as in his final instruction in response to everything covered in his address.

to the sense that everything is drawing to a close and that Qoheleth is imparting his final and most crucial advice.[78] Fifth, the final section is totalizing in its language. That is, rather than introducing new observations or specific examples of wisdom or folly, Qoheleth speaks in a way that encompasses the whole of life. He speaks of the young man and the old, of light and darkness, of joy and *hebel*, of life and death, and of a God who will bring everything into judgment. His advice is emphatic, carries a sense of urgency, and speaks with the totality of life in view.[79] And sixth, many scholars view this final section as Qoheleth's conclusion—scholars who employ differing methodologies and reach varying interpretations.[80]

In sum, many scholars opt for a narrative understanding of Qoheleth's quest. This provides an appealing cohesion as it unites all of Qoheleth's investigations, reflections, judgments, and counsels. While there is little to no agreement on the structure of Qoheleth's address at the micro-level, this macro understanding provides a grasp of the whole while still allowing for the many twists, turns, and roundabouts that mark Qoheleth's address—it is simple enough to make room for the complex. Additionally, this narrative understanding recognizes a general progression that moves from quest to expression and distinguishes between the younger and the older Qoheleth, the "then" and the "now." And the quest with its failure becomes the context out of which Qoheleth's primary goal of instruction rises. This leads to Qoheleth's final section and suggests that it serves as his conclusion.

3.2.5 Following Qoheleth's Quest

This section looks at the key junctures of Qoheleth's address, particularly its beginning, middle, and end. The purpose here is not to present a detailed examination and exegesis of each part but to grasp the macro-structure of the whole and the viability of reading a general progression

---

78. Note also the presence of "my son" (12:12) in the epilogue. This also occurs at a juncture in that the first half of the epilogue focuses on an assessment of Qoheleth while the second half, after the mention of the addressee, contains the narrator's final and central advice, which is also primarily mediated in the form of imperatives.

79. In contrast, for example, note how the exhortations that mark 4:17—5:6 [5:1–7] come in a more specific context, "when you go to the house of God" (4:17 [5:1]), and address a more particular topic; namely, listening/fearing God in contrast to foolish words and vows.

80. Note the survey of scholarship in chapter 1, as well as the examination of Qoheleth's final section in the following chapter.

that leads from quest to failure to instruction, a progression that leads to the end.

Most scholars see 1:12–18 as Qoheleth's initial introduction and overview of his quest.[81] The address begins with a self-introduction: "I [Qoheleth] have been king over Israel in Jerusalem" (1:12). In the next verse (1:13), Qoheleth introduces his quest ("And I applied my heart to seek and to search out"), his methodology ("by wisdom"), and the object and scope of his search ("all that is done under heaven"). Next, Qoheleth reveals the conclusion of his search, "I have seen everything that is done under the sun, and behold, all is [*hebel*] and a striving after wind" (1:14). This conclusion comprises what will become a recurring refrain throughout his quest (2:11, 17, 26; 4:4, 16; 6:9).[82] After closing the first half of the introduction with a proverb (1:15), Qoheleth reiterates his search and his conclusion (1:16–17), followed by a final proverb to close the second half of his introduction (1:18).[83] He says, "I said in my heart,[84] 'I have acquired great wisdom, surpassing all who were over Jerusalem before me, and my heart has had great experience of wisdom and knowledge.' And I applied my heart to know wisdom and to know madness and folly. I perceived that this also is but a striving after wind" (1:16–17).

At first glance, this quest might appear positive. The book of Proverbs, after all, repeatedly encourages one to seek wisdom. One is to "seek it like silver and search for it as for hidden treasure" (Prov 2:4). The father exhorts his son, "Get wisdom; get insight" (Prov 4:5). And Wisdom says, "For whoever finds me finds life" (Prov 8:35). And given the connections between the two wisdom books (see chapter 2), the reader could be inclined to see this wisdom quest in a positive light and expect such a quest to be rooted in the fear of the Lord, the foundation of Israel's wisdom. But, is Qoheleth enacting such a quest? Strikingly, Qoheleth's initial introduction/conclusion indicates that something is awry. Qoheleth declared that he had great wisdom (1:16), conducted his search by wisdom (1:13) in

---

81. Note the following: Fox, *Time to Tear Down*, 169–74; Bartholomew, *Ecclesiastes*, 122–27; Longman, *Ecclesiastes*, 76–85; Beldman, "Framed," 155–56; Seow, *Ecclesiastes*, 142–50; Enns, *Ecclesiastes*, 36–41; and Ogden, *Qoheleth*, 39–42.

82. Note, see Wright, "Riddle," 320–21, who also includes 1:17 and 4:6 although they do not include the statement of *hebel*.

83. While 2:1 marks the beginning of Qoheleth's quest, note the stated purpose in 2:3b, ". . .till I might see what was good for the children of man to do under heaven during the few days of their life." See the narrator's leading question in 1:3.

84. For an investigation of Qoheleth's use of לב, "heart," see Holmstedt, "אֲנִי וְלִבִּי: The Syntactical Encoding of the Collaborative Nature of Qohelet's Experiment," 1–26.

order to know wisdom (1:17), yet concludes that everything is *hebel* and a striving after wind (1:14, 17). The reader has already been prepared for this by the emphatic declaration that everything is *hebel* by the narrator in 1:2. Still, the reader is drawn in and led to wonder how this came to be, to raise objections, to expect an explanation, and ultimately, to look toward resolution.[85]

A number of scholars identify the end of Eccl 7 as representing the midpoint of Qoheleth's address.[86] In this important section, Qoheleth reflects honestly upon his quest and its results. He begins, "All this I have tested by wisdom" (7:23a; see 7:25). While most immediately referring to what came prior in the chapter, it also looks back over the entire quest up to this point and echoes his opening introduction (1:13, 17).[87] In fact, some argue that the writer worked hard to intentionally connect this with the introduction of Qoheleth's quest.[88]

---

85. Note Christianson's discussion of the use of prolepsis as part of the narrative strategy and the deliberate tension between the stated quest and results; see Christianson, *Time to Tell*, 24–33. See also Bartholomew, *Ecclesiastes*, 81–82, 124–25, and his discussion of "gaps."

86. For example, note the following: Christianson, *Time to Tell*, 93–95; Bartholomew, *Ecclesiastes*, 264–77; and Beldman, "Framed," 156–59. In contrast, many scholars see 6:10 as the midpoint of the book: Wright, "Riddle," 322–26; Longman, *Ecclesiastes*, 22, 176, 208; Seow, *Ecclesiastes*, 46–47; and Murphy, *Ecclesiastes*, xxxv–xli. There is a measure of support for this latter position. First, the refrain that has recurred throughout Qoheleth's quest, "(vanity and) chasing wind," finds its final occurrence at the end of 6:9 (though *hebel* can be found in the second half). Second, in terms of length, this is the midpoint of the book. The *Masorah finalis* of the Leningrad Codex reads, רכב, indicating 222 verses. This would make 1:1—6:9 the first half and 6:10—12:14 the second half. Third, this juncture is accompanied by a change of form, as evidenced by the dominance of proverbial sayings in the first half of Eccl 7. This coincides with a shift in the larger narrative as Qoheleth's quest fades and he transitions to his primary goal of instruction, part of which involves reflecting upon his quest and its failure (7:23–29). While a shift at 6:10 has some support, some remain unconvinced. Fox, for example, argues that while a move in the latter parts of the book toward the constructive is obvious, reading through the address does not produce the sense that there is a sudden shift at this point nor does viewing it as the midpoint have any real effect on one's reading—Fox opts for a more gradual progression (Fox, *Time to Tear Down*, 152; see also Bartholomew, *Ecclesiastes*, 82–84). Ultimately, the question of a decisive shift in 6:10 does not make or break the larger view of narrative progression nor does it take anything away from reading 7:23–29 as an important moment of confession and reflection.

87. Scholars disagree about the referent of כָּל־זֹה and whether it refers to what precedes or follows and to the extent of its reach. For an overview of positions, see Spears, "Theological Hermeneutics," 133–34.

88. Beldman, "Framed," 156–57. Spears notes that the verb נסה ("to test, try") is only used elsewhere in the book in 2:1, the beginning of Qoheleth's quest, and the stated methodology, בחכמה, echoes Qoheleth's introduction of his quest in 1:13 (also

As the reader who has followed Qoheleth's quest knows, the results have been less than satisfactory. Now, in language reminiscent of Job 28, Qoheleth confesses his failure. "I said, 'I will be wise,' but it was far from me. That which has been is far off, and deep, very deep; who can find it out?" (7:23b–24). The understanding that Qoheleth sought was beyond his grasp. He was not able to make sense of life's mysteries nor control its irregularities. The quest has failed. Noting the irony, Spears writes, "the 'wise man' who has journeyed with 'wisdom' in his search for 'wisdom' cannot grasp wisdom."[89] Beldman argues that here, "Qohelet honestly admits the bankruptcy of his autonomous method, which relies on human machination apart from the fear of the Lord."[90] And after the initial reflection and assessment of 7:23–24, Qoheleth continues and elaborates in more detail. He says, "I turned my heart to know and to search out and to see wisdom and the scheme of things, and to know the wickedness of folly and the foolishness that is madness" (7:25; see 1:13, 17); once again he echoes back to his quest.[91]

In this assessment of his quest, Qoheleth does not merely reflect on what he did not find but also on what he did find. In fact, this section has a pronounced interplay between finding and not finding as the verb מצא ("to find") is used eight times. After initially confessing his failure (7:23) and asking "who can find it out" (7:24), his next use of the verb comes in 7:26, where he presents what he did find: "And I find something more bitter than death: the woman whose heart is snares and nets, and whose hands are fetters. He who pleases God escapes her, but the sinner is taken by her." This verse has caused scholars no small amount of angst, and various interpretations have been proposed.[92] However, the most

---

used in 2:3, 21); see Spears, "Theological Hermeneutics," 135. Spears argues that while the initial כָּל־זֹה begins 7:23 with ambiguity, each successive word points to a referent of 1:13 and the announcement of Qoheleth's quest (Spears, "Theological Hermeneutics," 135–36). Note the following supporters: Christianson, *Time to Tell*, 94; Beldman, "Framed," 157; Bartholomew, *Ecclesiastes*, 264; and Seow, *Ecclesiastes*, 270.

89. Spears, "Theological Hermeneutics," 177. See also Murphy, *Ecclesiastes*, 72; Fox, *Time to Tear Down*, 264; and Holmstedt et al., *Qoheleth*, 217–19.

90. Beldman, "Framed," 159.

91. Salyer, *Vain Rhetoric*, 343, describes this as a "narrative flashback." Note also, Spears, "Theological Hermeneutics," 147–57; and Walton, *Experimenting*, 85–86.

92. Note the following proposals. First, women in general. Christianson writes, "It seems that in order to make some sense of this flaw in Israel's great wisdom teacher the 'historian' turned to a seemingly simple and time-honoured solution: ascribe the problem to women" (Christianson, *Time to Tell*, 144). Fox writes, "Despite the valiant efforts of some exegetes, this passage remains irreparably misogynistic" (Fox, *Time to Tear*

convincing interpretation, in the opinion of this writer, understands an allusion to lady folly as presented in the book of Proverbs.[93] Seow writes,

---

Down, 266). Although, Fox continues and tries to downplay and even reverse the tone by claiming that "Qoheleth is crabby" and does not intend for his words to be taken seriously and that such persiflage is commonplace and occurs because one actually cares deeply about the opposite sex (Fox, *Time to Tear Down*, 267). Second, some identify not all women but rather a particular type of women; namely, the adulterous women referred to in Proverbs. For proponents, see Enns, *Ecclesiastes*, 87–88; Shields, *End of Wisdom*, 186–87; and Murphy, *Ecclesiastes*, 76. Third, the connections with Proverbs from the prior option are accepted, but the woman is taken metaphorically to be lady folly (see below). Fourth, some have argued that the referent is a single woman, such as Qoheleth's wife. Davis holds that Qoheleth speaks an "honest statement of disappointment" about "an embittered romantic relationship" (Davis, *Proverbs, Ecclesiastes, and the Song of Songs*, 205). And fifth, one can note a few more outlying proposals. Ogden takes this verse as a metaphor for untimely/premature death (Ogden, *Qoheleth*, 130–31). Dahood renders "bitter" as "strong" (Dahood, "Qoheleth and Recent Discoveries," 308–10). Similarly, Crenshaw sees a traditional saying (which Qoheleth rejects) that "woman is stronger than death" (Crenshaw, *Ecclesiastes*, 146; so also, Lohfink, *Qoheleth*, 101–3).

93. Note the following points of support. First, the context of the reference to the woman in 7:26 in about finding/not finding wisdom/folly. Qoheleth's whole quest was about wisdom and in 7:23–24, he confesses that wisdom was beyond his grasp. In 7:25, Qoheleth reiterates his search and the topic of wisdom and folly. For Qoheleth to suddenly be talking about women would be out of place. Ingram notes that no woman has been mentioned yet in the book and this reference suddenly comes as if readers are supposed to know who she is (Ingram, "Riddled with Ambiguity," 229; although Ingram argues that the verse, just like the entire section, is intentionally ambiguous). Second, there are strong connections with Proverbs (see Prov 2:16–19; 5:1–6, 20; 6:24–35; 7:5–27; 9:13–18; 22:14; 23:27–28). However, it is particularly Prov 1–9 that sets a fundamental contrast between two women; that is, lady wisdom and lady folly. These two women, representative of the "two ways," are foundational wisdom metaphors in an OT wisdom tradition, in which Qoheleth belongs and apart from which he cannot be understood (Spears, "Theological Hermeneutics," 161). The many connections between Ecclesiastes and Proverbs discussed in chapter 2 further solidify this relation. Third, Seow points out that "woman" is definite in the Hebrew (7:26), suggesting a certain woman or type, and that the immediate context points to a referent of "folly" in 7:25, which is the only definite noun in the verse (Seow, *Ecclesiastes*, 271). Fourth, the presence of moral language suggests that the topic is wisdom and folly. In reference to the woman, the second half of 7:26 reads, "He who pleases God escapes her but the sinner is taken by her." Additionally, just prior, 7:20 informs that there is no one righteous who never sins. And this section builds up to 7:29 with its climactic pronouncement of what Qoheleth found; namely, that God made humanity upright but they have sought out many schemes. Lastly, the unsatisfactory results of other proposals make this the best option. Spears sums up the matter well when he writes, "In summary, the identity of this woman is only ambiguous when it is read apart from its wisdom context, out of its immediate context, or with a developmentalism that issues forth in a 'crisis of wisdom' view" (Spears, "Theological Hermeneutics," 163).

Some work to get away from the moral language of this section (and of the book). Crenshaw writes that "the one who pleases God" and "the sinner" "refer to lucky and

"The *femme fatale* is not, therefore, an individual woman. She is not necessarily a specific type of woman or women in general. Rather, she is a composite image of Folly herself (Prov 9:13–18). Folly is out on a hunt, as it were, trying to lure and trap people and lead them down the deadly path."[94] In short, Qoheleth sought wisdom, but instead of finding wisdom, he found himself entrapped by folly.

The remainder of this section (7:27–29) builds to Qoheleth's final statement, which begins, "See, this alone I found . . ." (7:29a). This thought began in 7:27 with "Behold, this is what I found," before Qoheleth paused to reiterate that he sought an account of things (7:27), which his soul sought repeatedly but was not able to find (7:28a); indeed, he was able to find one man in a thousand but not one woman (7:28b).[95] The

---

unlucky (as in 2:26) rather than to virtuous as opposed to wicked" (Crenshaw, *Ecclesiastes*, 146). Murphy argues that these terms here should be understood "not as moral qualifications, but as designations of human beings in terms of the inscrutable divine will. Some will fall victim to this type of woman but others will not, as God pleases." (Murphy, *Ecclesiastes*, 76; so also, Longman, *Ecclesiastes*, 204–05). However, as argued in chapter 2, the wisdom tradition cannot be separated from its religious context and moral terminology is common in Proverbs and Ecclesiastes. Many of the views that seek a morally neutral interpretation are faulty in their presuppositions (for a discussion, see Spears, "Theological Hermeneutics," 163–70). A plain sense reading easily recognizes the presence of religious and moral terms not only in the previous section (esp. 7:20) and in the conclusion of this section (7:29) but also here in 7:26 and in the contrast between wisdom and folly that runs throughout. Extra ingenuity is required to circumspect this plain sense. For discussions, see Seow, *Ecclesiastes*, 263; and Bartholomew, *Ecclesiastes*, 267.

94. Seow, *Ecclesiastes*, 272. See also, Bartholomew, *Ecclesiastes*, 265–67; Beldman, "Framed," 157; and esp. Spears, "Theological Hermeneutics," 158–71.

95. 7:28 presents interpreters many of the same difficulties as 7:26, and again, various proposals are offered. Baltzer interprets אלף ("a thousand") as referring to a military unit and concludes that only men and no women were in the military and women were thus, "stronger" than death (Baltzer, "Women and War in Qohelet 7:23–8:1a," 130–31). Murphy proposes that Qoheleth is quoting a saying, which Qoheleth then rejects as demeaning to women and then corrects in 7:29; thus, it actually comprises a defense of women (Murphy, *Ecclesiastes*, 75–77). Seow holds that the verse is a gloss by a later scribe who failed to understand the passage (Seow, *Ecclesiastes*, 264–65, 274); although Seow does note that it may also be a reference to lady wisdom (Seow, *Ecclesiastes*, 51, 274–75). Some conclude that Qoheleth is clearly a misogynist (Longman, *Ecclesiastes*, 206–07). Shields writes, "Qoheleth's words were specifically chosen to offend and in offending to deter the original audience from becoming aligned with the wisdom movement" (Shields, *End of Wisdom*, 187). More convincingly, this verse is seen as a continuation of the lady wisdom/lady folly imagery already introduced. Bartholomew interprets that Qoheleth is capable of finding one *person* (interpreting אדם to be general, as it is everywhere else is Ecclesiastes, including 7:29) in a thousand but not one woman, with the woman most likely being lady wisdom of Proverbs and the counterpart of lady folly, in whose snare Qoheleth has found himself entrapped

delay builds anticipation. And the momentary intrusion by the frame narrator in 7:27 suggests the significance of Qoheleth's point.[96] Fox also notes that the emphatic character of Qoheleth's declaration in 7:29 is further highlighted by the way the main clause begins with לְבַד, a use not found elsewhere in the MT.[97] This leads to Qoheleth's final, emphatic statement: "See, this alone I found, that God made man upright, but they have sought out many schemes" (7:29).

Bartholomew notes a wordplay that uses phonetic similarities to highlight Qoheleth's failure.[98] Occurring three times in this section is the word(s) that is often translated as "scheme(s)" (7:25, 27, 29). The first two have the word חֶשְׁבּוֹן (7:25, 27), which means an "account" or "explanation" and has the idea of an accounting term, as if one is adding up

---

(Bartholomew, Ecclesiastes, 267–68). Spears also argues that the natural assumption for the reader would be to read that Qoheleth could not find lady wisdom, and so balance the prior portrayal of lady folly in 7:26 (Spears, "Theological Hermeneutics," 176–83). Whether or not Qoheleth is employing a saying, "The context of 7:23–29 determines that the contrast is not between male and female but between finding and not finding. Furthermore, in this context the object of finding/not finding is wisdom and/or folly" (Beldman, "Framed," 158; see also Spears, "Theological Hermeneutics," 181). "Clearly, these images are intended to evoke the inaccessibility of wisdom" (Bartholomew, Ecclesiastes, 265–66).

96. The brief appearance by the narrator, evidenced by the third-person reference to Qoheleth in 7:27 ("says Qoheleth"), is curious as it is the only occurrence within Qoheleth's address (1:12–12:7). Scholars typically offer a handful of explanations. First, some argue that the narrator is simply reminding the reader of the narrator; see Fox, "Frame Narrative," 83–91; and Enns, Ecclesiastes, 88. Others simply admit ignorance. Whybray, Ecclesiastes, 126, resolves to conclude that its purpose is not clear. Ogden, Qoheleth, 132, says that its significance is uncertain. Some argue that the narrator is intentionally distancing himself from Qoheleth and his views (Shields, End of Wisdom, 189; and Longman, Ecclesiastes, 7–8, 205). However, many scholars more persuasively argue that the narrator's presence suggests the importance of this section/point. Christianson, Time to Tell, 93–95, argues that it is like a partition in the middle of a window frame. "The frame narrator's insertion here supplements the overall strategy of 'setting aside,' marking its importance for Qoheleth's narrative" (Christianson, Time to Tell, 95). Seow writes, "Neither in 1:2 nor 12:8 can the words attributed to Qohelet be taken lightly, for they are clearly central for the book. We must not, therefore, regard the viewpoint expressed in this passage as incidental . . . On the contrary, it may be that the editor is deliberately invoking the authority of the author, calling attention to this passage as the main point of his message" (Seow, Ecclesiastes, 272). Others describe it as "profoundly and incomparably important" (Spears, "Theological Hermeneutics," 152); "a highly significant point of reflection" (Bartholomew, Ecclesiastes, 265); and "of utmost importance" (Beldman, "Framed," 151–52; see also Salyer, Vain Rhetoric, 344–46).

97. Fox, Time to Tear Down, 271–72; Bartholomew, Ecclesiastes, 268.

98. Bartholomew, Ecclesiastes, 268–69. See also Seow, Ecclesiastes, 265, 275–76; and Spears, "Theological Hermeneutics," 185.

the ledgers line by line or taking inventory.⁹⁹ And while some take the third word חִשְּׁבֹנוֹת (7:29) to be the plural of חֶשְׁבּוֹן,¹⁰⁰ it is a different word (though with the same root) meaning "plan" or "invention."¹⁰¹ Supporting the case for a wordplay, Bartholomew notes that each of these three occurs as the object of the verb בקש ("to seek"), which occurs in this section only these three times.¹⁰² First, Qoheleth sought (בקש) wisdom and an account (חֶשְׁבּוֹן) of things (7:25). Second, he added things together to find an account (חֶשְׁבּוֹן), which he diligently sought (בקש) but did not find (7:27–28a). And third, what he did find is that God made humanity upright but they have sought (בקש) out many schemes (חִשְּׁבֹנוֹת; 7:29). Qoheleth is the one who sought an account of things but ended up chasing many schemes. While he sought wisdom, he is the sinner ensnared by lady folly!

In sum, 7:23–29 marks a significant midpoint in Qoheleth's address. Here, he reflects upon and confesses the failure of his quest. While this failure has already been noted at various points, most notably in the recurring conclusory refrains "(*hebel* and) striving after wind" (1:14, 17; 2:11, 17, 26; 4:4, 16; 6:9), Qoheleth now offers a more explicit, intentional, and sustained reflection. The wisdom he sought was beyond his grasp. And instead, he found himself ensnared by folly. He claimed to be wise, but it was far from him. He sought an account of things but ended up chasing schemes. Turning from created uprightness, he is the sinner ensnared. Though this confession brings a measure of clarity, resolution still evades. Where does Qoheleth go from here? What advice does he offer his addressee in light of this unsettling discovery?

The second half of Qoheleth's address reveals a shift from experience to expression.¹⁰³ With his quest largely behind, Qoheleth's focus increasingly turns to the imparting of advice. There is less first-person narration and more second-person exhortation, in addition to the greater inclusion of proverbial sayings. As noted above, there is not a clear dividing line but rather a persistent progression such that the final two chapters are void of the first-person.

Rather than the pursuit of knowledge that drove Qoheleth's quest, the latter half of the address betrays a greater acceptance of one's

99. *HALOT*, חֶשְׁבּוֹן, I:360; Seow, *Ecclesiastes*, 260–61.
100. For example, Longman, *Ecclesiastes*, 207.
101. *HALOT*, חֶשְׁבּוֹן, I:361.
102. Bartholomew, *Ecclesiastes*, 268.
103. Christianson, *Time to Tell*, 243–52.

limitations, a theme revealed in Qoheleth's introduction (1:15). In 6:12, Qoheleth highlights that one cannot know. In 7:13, the final saying in the block, Qoheleth says, "Consider the work of God: who can make straight what he has made crooked." The next verse speaks of God's sovereignty over all things and one's inability to find out what will be after him (7:14). In 8:16–17, Qoheleth says, "When I applied my heart to know wisdom, and to see the business that is done on earth, how neither day nor night do one's eyes see sleep, then I saw all the work of God, that man cannot find out the work that is done under the sun. However much man may toil in seeking, he will not find it out. Even though a wise man claims to know, he cannot find it out." Beldman says it well when he describes the second half as "tempered with an epistemological humility."[104] And Christianson speaks of a "hard-won ignorance."[105] Qoheleth's failed quest becomes the context from which he instructs. He has accepted the limitations of humanity, recognizing what is unknowable and uncontrollable, and counsels how one should live.

This progression leads to Qoheleth's climactic end, where he emphatically provides his concluding instruction. In this final section (11:7—12:7), Qoheleth reveals his addressee, "O young man" (11:9), exhorts him on his approach to life, brings together the primary motifs of his address, and concludes with a reflection on death. A detailed look at this section has been reserved for the following chapter.

The understanding of Qoheleth's address as a narrative and a quest works well. It provides a framework for interpreting the whole, its parts, and its general progression. While this brief section has overlooked much of Qoheleth's address, enough has been noted to convey its basic movement.

3.2.6 Conclusion

This section has considered the structure of Qoheleth's address. While efforts at discerning a highly detailed structure have proven unsatisfactory, readings of Qoheleth's address as a narrative are promising. The narrative understanding outlined here ascribes a cohesion to the whole as it unites all of Qoheleth's investigations and counsels and discerns a general

---

104. Beldman, "Framed," 159.
105. Christianson, *Time to Tell*, 243.

progression from quest to expression, a progression that ultimately leads to Qoheleth's final section.

3.3 QOHELETH'S PRIMARY MOTIFS

3.3.1 Introduction

Ecclesiastes is a book of motifs. Christianson writes, a "*Leitmotif* . . . denotes a phrase or idea, or (as with music) a figure or refrain that is repeated throughout a single work having the effect of pronouncing a theme."[106] Not only do these contribute to the book's wonderful artistry, they may play a crucial role in the shape of the work and in its message. If, as this chapter has argued, there is purposeful movement in the narrative toward a conclusion, and if the primary motifs are integrally connected with Qoheleth's message, then one should expect the two to work together in a complementary manner. Rather than simply being there, the key motifs should at the least be compatible with and even contribute toward the proposed structural progression.

Now, Ecclesiastes has many themes or motifs. Which should be taken as primary or secondary? Or should all be treated equally? Fuhr, for example, identifies seven key motifs: *hebel*; under the sun; wisdom; divine determinacy and the imposition of limitations on humanity; the inevitability of death; the enjoyment of life; and the fear of God.[107] However, Fuhr's description of Qoheleth's work as "a wise man's approach to living in a הבל world"[108] reveals that in practice, he subsumes many of the motifs under *hebel*, which he uses in a general way to speak of all that Qoheleth found in the world. Additionally, while he dubs these seven as prominent, he interprets only the final two as representing Qoheleth's advice. First, life's unpredictability, life's fleetingness, and death's inevitability lead the wise to enjoy life as a responsibility given to him.[109] Second, life's fleetingness, death's inevitability, God's enigmatic ways, and future

---

106. Christianson, *Time to Tell*, 42–45 (42). The term "leitmotif" or "leitmotiv," meaning "leading motif," is often utilized in a broader sense to denote a recurring theme, dropping any distinction between "motif" and "leitmotif." This project uses these terms in this broad sense.

107. Fuhr, *Inter-Dependency*, 22–26.

108. Fuhr, *Inter-Dependency*, 27.

109. Fuhr, *Inter-Dependency*, 27, 191.

THE DESIGN OF QOHELETH 97

judgment lead the wise to fear God and keep his commandments.[110] In essence, the result is three primary motifs: *hebel* as a description of the world and joy and the fear of God as the advice. As chapter 1 showed, the vast majority of scholars associate Qoheleth's message with one or more of these three motifs. Accordingly, this project will follow suit and treat these three as primary. Other themes, motifs, and refrains are interpreted as secondary and are generally placed under one of these larger categories. For example, Qoheleth has a number of motifs in connection with his quest.[111] Yet, *hebel* is used as a wide-reaching conclusion—the way this motif is utilized as the book's primary *inclusio* (1:2; 12:8) makes this clear. In a similar way, the joy motif represents a category that encompasses various notes of eating, drinking, rejoicing, etc.

The purpose of this section is to look at the meaning and use of Qoheleth's three primary motifs: *hebel*, joy, and the fear of God. The aim is to show how they work within and contribute to the larger narrative movement. Each of these motifs will be discussed in turn.

3.3.2 Hebel

The most characteristic motif of the book is *hebel*. As soon as the second verse the reader is confronted with its emphatic declaration—five of the eight words in the verse are *hebel*. The word הֶבֶל literally means breath or vapor, but beyond the concrete, it can carry the figurative sense of vanity.[112] With thirty-eight of its seventy-three occurrences in the MT found in

---

110. Fuhr, *Inter-Dependency*, 27, 191.

111. For example, "striving after wind" (רְעוּת רוּחַ: 1:14; 2:11, 17, 26; 4:4, 6; 6:9]; רַעְיוֹן רוּחַ: 1:17; 4:16). This refrain is restricted to the first half of the book and is almost exclusively connected with a declaration of *hebel* (1:17 and 4:6 are the two exceptions). "Profit" or "advantage" (יִתְרוֹן/יוֹתֵר) recurs throughout (1:3; 2:11, 13, 15; 3:9; 5:8 [9], 15 [16]; 6:8, 11; 7:11, 12, 16; 10:10, 11; 12:9, 12). This speaks to the question behind the quest. "Toil" (עָמָל) is a regular theme (1:3; 2:10, 11, 18, 19, 20, 21, 22, 24; 3:9, 13; 4:4, 6, 8, 9; 5:14, 15, 17, 18 [5:15, 16, 18, 19]; 6:7; 8:15, 17; 9:9; 10:15). While it may be a source of frustration, it is also one's portion and a gift from God and to be enjoyed. "Under the sun" (תַּחַת הַשֶּׁמֶשׁ) occurs twenty-nine times (1:3, 9; 2:11, 17, 18, 19, 20, 22; 3:16; 4:1, 3, 7, 15; 5:13 [14], 18 [19]; 6:1, 12; 7:11; 8:9, 15 [x2], 17; 9:3, 6, 9 [x2], 11, 13; 10:5; note also the comparable expressions, "under heaven" [תַּחַת הַשָּׁמַיִם: 2:3; 3:1] and "on earth" [עַל־הָאָרֶץ: 5:1 [2]; 8:14, 16; 11:2; בָּאָרֶץ: 7:20]). This speaks to the scope of Qoheleth's quest; he searched and explored everything, leaving no stone unturned. While some interpret this phrase in a *restrictive* sense (Longman, *Ecclesiastes*, 66), an *inclusive* sense is more appropriate (Fox, *Time to Tear Down*, 165).

112. *HALOT*, הֶבֶל, I:236–37.

Ecclesiastes, it is one of the most common words in the book.[113] To state the obvious, the word is used in a metaphorical/figurative sense. And herein lies the difficulty and point of scholarly disagreement; namely, what aspect(s) of the metaphor is being employed?

The early Greek translations of Aquila, Symmachus, and Theodotion translate הֶבֶל literally as ἀτμός/ἀτμίς ("vapor"), while the LXX offers ματαιότης, ("emptiness, futility, purposelessness, transitoriness").[114] However, it was Jerome's translation in the Vulgate as *vanitas*, reflecting his *contemptus mundi* reading, that proved most influential, dominating for roughly the next one thousand years. Though Jerome's reading was challenged by the likes of Bonaventure and Luther, from the Latin *vanitas* comes the English "vanity," prominent among modern translations (ESV, NASB, NKJV, NRSV).[115]

Modern scholarship has strongly challenged the validity of the "vanity" translation/interpretation and has put forward a wide array of proposals even though some, such as Whybray, still opt for the traditional "vanity."[116] Some translate *hebel* as "vanity" but argue that it does not necessarily mean "vanity." For Murphy, "vanity" is a codeword that encompasses various nuances of meaning—in short, it means whatever *hebel* means.[117] Seow also uses this traditional translation for want of a more adequate alternative but reinterprets it to mean all that *hebel* means.[118] Others retain the wholly negative meaning of "vanity" but opt

---

113. Eccl 1:2 (x5), 14; 2:1, 11, 15, 17, 19, 21, 23, 26; 3:19; 4:4, 7, 8, 16; 5:6 [7], 9 [10]; 6:2, 4, 9, 11, 12; 7:6, 15; 8:10, 14 (x2); 9:9 (x2); 11:8, 10; 12:8 (x3). While dominant, it is surpassed by, for example, time (עת, 40x), God (אלהים, 40x), heart (לבב, 41x), good (טוב, 45x), man (אדם, 49x), to do (עשׂה, 43x), and to see (ראה, 47x).

114. BDAG, ματαιότης, 621.

115. Bonaventure turned Jerome's reading upside-down by arguing that the one who despises the world despises God (St. Bonaventure, *Commentary on Ecclesiastes*, 77). This paved a way for Luther, who then argued that *hebel* referred to humanity's vanity and not to creation (Luther, "Notes on Ecclesiastes," 10–11).

116. Whybray, *Ecclesiastes*, 34–36.

117. Murphy, *Ecclesiastes*, lix.

118. Seow, *Ecclesiastes*, 102.

for other vocabulary, such as "meaningless,"[119] "worthless,"[120] "futile,"[121] "useless,"[122] "pointless,"[123] "senseless"[124] or "absurd."[125]

Against such exclusively negative readings, some argue that the imagery of *hebel* is multifaceted. Notably, Miller sees *hebel* as a symbol with three primary referents: insubstantiality, transience, and foulness.[126] Fuhr argues for a multivalent metaphor that carries negative, neutral, and positive connotations as it describes the whole of fallen creation.[127] Bundvad also interprets multivalence but with a primary understanding of transience.[128] Salyer argues for a similar approach but foregrounds "absurd."[129] Shields proposes that Qoheleth uses *hebel* because its wide semantic range allows him to aptly apply it to disparate contexts and that Qoheleth plays on the term's ambiguity.[130] Meek proposes that *hebel* is an intertextual reference to Abel in Gen 4 and that along with the idea of transience, it speaks of the reversals of the expected order of life, the incongruities between actions and results or as he puts it, the "Abel-ness" of all things.[131] Some even translate *hebel* using multiple English words in an attempt to capture manifold nuances. For example, Krüger translates 1:2 with both "futile" and "fleeting."[132]

Fredericks argues against such multivalence and that the word demands a singular, consistent meaning, which he takes as "breath," which

119. NIV; NLT; Longman, *Ecclesiastes*, 32, 61–64.

120. Sneed, "הבל as 'Worthless' in Qohelet: A Critique of Michael V. Fox's 'Absurd' Thesis," 891–94.

121. CSB; JPS; NET; TLB; Crenshaw, *Ecclesiastes*, 57–58.

122. GNT

123. CEB; ISV

124. Shields, *End of Wisdom*, 112–21.

125. Fox, *Time to Tear Down*, 30–32; Christianson, *Time to Tell*, 83–87; Enns, *Ecclesiastes*, 31.

126. Miller, *Symbol and Rhetoric*, 15. Depending on the context, *hebel* may have a single meaning (valency), two or more meanings (multivalency), or even all of its meanings (omnivalency).

127. Fuhr, *Inter-Dependency*, 181–82.

128. Bundvad, *Time*, 80.

129. Salyer, *Vain Rhetoric*, 254.

130. Shields, *End of Wisdom*, 120–21.

131. Meek, "The Meaning of הבל in Qohelet," 245–56.

132. Krüger, *Qoheleth*, 3, 42. As a more extreme example, note the AMP, "'Vanity of vanities,' says the Preacher. 'Vanity of vanities! All [that is done without God's guidance] is vanity [futile, meaningless—a wisp of smoke, a vapor that vanishes, merely chasing the wind]'" (1:2).

means "fleeting"; thus, he takes a more neutral rather than negative interpretation.[133] Continuing along the neutral lines, Bartholomew argues for an understanding of *hebel* as "enigmatic" as he aims to keep open the possibility of meaning.[134] In a similar vein, Ogden argues for "mysterious."[135] Some prefer to stick with a more literal translation, such as "breath"[136] or even "smoke."[137] In a positive way, these retain the metaphorical image; however, the question of interpretation remains.

There is no shortage of material written on this matter, and there is no need to rehearse it at length here.[138] While the differences of translations may seem inconsequential, the implications are anything but. To say, for example, that something is meaningless is a wholly different claim than to say that something is mysterious or enigmatic. The former is decisive in its claim of the subject's character: it is completely (and only) negative. The latter simply states that something is unknowable but does not claim this to be positive or negative and thus, leaves both doors open. The former claims knowledge while the latter acknowledges ignorance. Still different from these is the assertion that something is fleeting or transient. This also is a neutral claim as it merely speaks to the referent's temporality. Needless to say, one's interpretation of this key word greatly affects one's interpretation of Qoheleth's entire message.

This project favors the retention of the metaphorical image and describes *hebel* as "ungraspable." Although Seow opts for the traditional translation of "vanity," he explains *hebel* well. "He [Qoheleth] does not mean that everything is meaningless or insignificant, but that everything is beyond human apprehension and comprehension."[139] Elsewhere he writes, "What is *hebel* cannot be grasped—neither physically nor

---

133. Fredericks, *Coping with Transience*, 11–32; Fredericks and Estes, *Ecclesiastes and the Song of Songs*, 24–31, 46–54.

134. Bartholomew, *Ecclesiastes*, 93–94, 104–07.

135. Ogden, *Qoheleth*, 21–26. Ogden writes, "for Qoheleth the term has a very specific meaning: it identifies the enigmatic, the ironic dimension of human experience; it suggests that life is not fully comprehensible. It in no sense carries the meaning 'vanity' or 'meaningless'" (Ogden, *Qoheleth*, 17).

136. Lohfink, *Qoheleth*, 36; Provan, *Ecclesiastes*, 38.

137. MSG.

138. Note the following discussions: Seybold, הֶבֶל, *TDOT* III:313–20; Miller, *Symbol and Rhetoric*, 1–14; Christianson, *Ecclesiastes Through the Centuries*, 98–141; Meek, "Twentieth- and Twenty-First Century Readings of *Hebel*," 279–97; Fox, *Time to Tear Down*, 27–42; and Fuhr, *Inter-Dependency*, 29–63.

139. Seow, *Ecclesiastes*, 59.

intellectually. It cannot be controlled."[140] This favoring of a multi-faceted metaphor is influenced by a handful of factors. First, it can be interpreted broadly—incomprehensible, uncontrollable, ephemeral, and empty— and thus, can be used in a wide range of contexts; for example, of pleasure (2:1), wealth and toil (2:11), wisdom (2:17), people die just as the beasts (3:19), not being able to enjoy one's possessions (6:2), the righteous receiving what the wicked deserve and vice versa (8:14), youth (11:10), and, in an all-encompassing way, everything (1:2; 12:8). Qoheleth cannot grasp an account of things; it is incomprehensible. He cannot wrest control of life's events so as to secure a specific outcome. Everything in life, even life itself, is fleeting; Qoheleth cannot hold on to it. Qoheleth searched but came up empty-handed—a striving after wind.

Second, the retention of the metaphorical image preserves an aspect of the book's character. Imagery has the remarkable ability to capture and convey meaning, to stir emotion, to uniquely impress upon the reader, while still retaining a level of mystery that draws one into further contemplation. The multi-faceted image communicates not just *what* Qoheleth had to say but also *how* he said it.

Third, a broad understanding avoids being painted into a corner, a difficulty that plagues some more narrowly defined understandings. Take "fleeting," for example. While fitting in many cases, it seems sorely out of place in others, such as in reference to injustice (8:14).[141]

Fourth, since this broad understanding of *hebel* is not exclusively negative, it does not rule out meaning. Describing *hebel* as "ungraspable" has some commonality with Fox's "absurd,"[142] which he describes as "an affront to reason."[143] While Fox notes a measure of overlap with terms such as "incomprehensible" or "enigmatic," these, he argues, are too soft for they allow, even suggest, that meaning could lie beyond Qoheleth's grasp; in contrast, for Fox, the term is wholly negative—it is oppressive.[144]

---

140. Seow, *Ecclesiastes*, 102.

141. Yet, Fredericks insists that the text demands a single meaning throughout and "Even injustice, as prevalent and tortuous as it can be, is a temporary experience" (Fredericks, "Preaching Qoheleth," 438–39).

142. Fox, *Time to Tear Down*, 30–35; See also Christianson, *Time to Tell*, 83–87.

143. Fox, *Time to Tear Down*, 31.

144. Fox, *Time to Tear Down*, 33–35. Perhaps this is why Fox—though he claims that tearing down and building up are the two fundamental movements in Qoheleth's address—is able to tear down but struggles to build up; see Fox, *Time to Tear Down*, 138–40. Shields writes, "The one irrefutable aspect of Qoheleth's use of the term הבל is its clearly negative connotation. This fact undermines any attempt to find a message in

Yes, "ungraspable" leans toward the neutral, but this is an advantage precisely because it remains open to the possibility of meaning.[145] To declare that there is no meaning ultimately undercuts any and all instruction that Qoheleth might give. If this were so, then there is no real advice; one option is not better than any other. A read of Qoheleth's address challenges this view. While Qoheleth certainly makes some striking observations, he offers much advice in response. The large blocks of sayings offer counsel. Better-than sayings claim that one thing is better than another. Qoheleth's sections of imperatives call for a specific response. In short, Qoheleth has much wisdom to offer.

Given the state of scholarship, a final point is worth noting. As this chapter argues, *hebel* does not represent Qoheleth's final message. Accordingly, the thesis of this book does not stand or fall on a particular translation/interpretation of *hebel*. And while debates continue and consensus evades, there is a measure of wisdom in holding the term loosely.

So what role does *hebel* play in Qoheleth's address? Two points will be provided here. First, *hebel* represents the results of Qoheleth's search. Qoheleth embarks on a quest to search out all that is done under heaven (1:13), to know wisdom (1:17), and to know the sum/account of things (7:25). After introducing himself (1:12) and his quest (1:13), he provides an initial summary of his findings: "I have seen everything that is done under the sun, and behold, all is [*hebel*] and a striving after wind" (1:14). This marks his first use of this term, and it comes as a summary of his findings. Additionally, this initial summary is followed by a saying in 1:15, "What is crooked cannot be made straight, and what is lacking cannot be counted." Functioning as a commentary on 1:14, this saying describes things as uncontrollable/unchangeable and possibly, incomprehensible.[146] And as Qoheleth continues through his quest, he repeatedly pronounces *hebel* as a conclusion: everything is ungraspable; nothing lasts; one cannot control events to secure a desired outcome/advantage; life and the time of things are enigmatic; and one cannot come to an account of things. And

---

Qoheleth's words that is consistent with the remainder of the Hebrew Bible" (Shields, *End of Wisdom*, 121). For Longman, Qoheleth's entire address is meaningless and can simply be discarded and ignored in favor of the epilogue (Longman, *Ecclesiastes*, 32–39). See also Crenshaw, *Ecclesiastes*, 23–28.

145. Bartholomew, *Ecclesiastes*, 93–94.

146. Seow, *Ecclesiastes*, 147, notes that the saying "continues and reinforces the thought of the preceding verses." Fox, *Time to Tear Down*, 172, describes 1:15 as an elaboration on verse 1:14. Murphy, *Ecclesiastes*, 13, sees 1:15 as justification for Qoheleth's conclusion in 1:14.

then, in a moment of remarkable honesty, Qoheleth reveals that he did not find wisdom (7:23–29). *Hebel* is the conclusion of Qoheleth's (failed) quest.

Second, *hebel* represents the problem that serves as the context for Qoheleth's subsequent instruction. Qoheleth's quest is not the sum of his address. The quest represents the "then" of the younger Qoheleth that dominates the first half. In the second half, Qoheleth shifts to the "now" as he reflects on his quest and increasingly pursues his primary goal of instruction. As such, the quest with its conclusion of *hebel* becomes the context for Qoheleth's instruction. This understanding accounts for the predominance of *hebel* in the first half and how it significantly recedes in the second half. Additionally, the second half conveys a greater acceptance of the limitations of human wisdom, coming to terms with what one cannot know and cannot find (see 6:12; 7:13–14; 8:16–17; 11:5). And it is in this position that Qoheleth gives his advice. Thus, *hebel* is *not* the message of the older Qoheleth but the result of his prior quest and subsequently, the context from which he now offers his hard-earned wisdom.

In response to this claim that *hebel* represents the findings of what Qoheleth found and not his final message, one may object and point to 1:2 and 12:8 as evidence that *hebel* comprises a summary of Qoheleth's address/conclusion. Yes, these two verses are uniquely emphatic: 1) the unmatched repetition of the word *hebel*; 2) the only three superlatives of *hebel* are found in these two verses; 3) they both state the matter in ultimate terms, that is, הַכֹּל הָבֶל; and 4) they form a key *inclusio* around Qoheleth's address. And while some take this evidence as a clear indication that *hebel* represents Qoheleth's central message,[147] that is by no means the only available reading. Some take 1:2 and 12:8 as conveying the main motto/theme of the book and not its final message. Bartholomew interprets them as "the theme of Qohelet's investigation."[148] He views "1:2 and 12:8 as the title of the book, as indicating the journey of exploration on which Qohelet takes the reader, but without assuming that this is his

---

147. Longman argues that the narrator "indicates that he understands this typically Qohelethine expression to be a proper summary of his message. That message is: there is no ultimate meaning in this world. Once all is said and done, Qohelet's conclusion is that *everything is meaningless*" (Longman, *Ecclesiastes*, 276; emphasis original). Fox speaks of 1:2 and 12:8 as "an encapsulation of the book" (Fox, *Time to Tear Down*, 332). Christianson sees them as the narrator's (inadequate) summary of Qoheleth (Christianson, *Time to Tell*, 98). See also, Crenshaw, *Ecclesiastes*, 57; Enns, *Ecclesiastes*, 31; and Shields, *End of Wisdom*, 234.

148. Bartholomew, *Ecclesiastes*, 360–61.

conclusion."[149] Beldman argues that they convey the motto of the book but not its conclusion.[150] Ogden sees them as conveying the problem that Qoheleth encountered and not his message in response to this problem.[151] Given the above discussion on the nature and progression of Qoheleth's address, it is entirely reasonable to interpret these two verses as representing the key problem/theme. The first, 1:2, introduces the conclusion of Qoheleth's quest: the pervasiveness of *hebel*. After Qoheleth has finished, 12:8 serves to restate the key theme and to transition back to the narrator. And just as Qoheleth encountered a world of *hebel* and from that context offered his wisdom, the narrator restates the key context of *hebel* (12:8) and then proceeds to offer his final advice in response.

In sum, *hebel* is an image creatively employed by the writer. Its metaphorical use draws the reader in and invites the reader to ponder the ways in which it might represent the many aspects of Qoheleth's search and, to be sure, the reader's own reality. While this project prefers to retain *hebel*'s metaphorical image and describes it as ungraspable—broad enough to convey nuances of incomprehensible, uncontrollable, ephemeral, and empty—scholarly disagreement will likely continue for some time. However, whatever it means, *hebel* represents the conclusion of Qoheleth's quest but *not* the primary message of his address. His failed quest and the pervasiveness of *hebel* become the context for his aged wisdom.

3.3.3 Joy

If *hebel* is Qoheleth's most conspicuous motif, joy is a close second. These two key motifs have dominated the center of scholarship on Qoheleth's message. This section will briefly touch on what this important motif entails before focusing on the role it plays in Qoheleth's address.

While not comprising a specifically repeated refrain, Qoheleth has much to say on the topic of joy, mentioning שׂמח and חפץ frequently.[152] He also speaks of eating and drinking (2:24; 3:13; 5:17 [18]; 9:7); enjoying life with one's wife (9:9); taking pleasure in one's work/toil (2:24; 3:13, 22; 5:17 [18], 18 [19]); that this is one's portion (2:10; 5:17 [18], 18 [19]; 9:9);

---

149. Bartholomew, *Ecclesiastes*, 362.

150. Beldman, "Framed," 152.

151. Ogden, *Qoheleth*, 224.

152. שׂמח: 2:1, 2, 10, 26; 3:12, 22; 4:16; 5:18 [19], 19 [20]; 7:4; 8:15; 9:7; 10:19; 11:8, 9. חפץ: 3:1, 17; 5:3 [4], 7 [8]; 8:3, 6; 12:1, 10.

and that this is a gift from God (2:24–26; 3:13; 5:18 [19]). Yet, Qoheleth also has some strong words that seem to express a contrary viewpoint. He describes pleasure and enjoyment as *hebel* (2:1) and of laughter and pleasure he asks, "what use is it?" (2:2). He notes that one will have to give an account (11:9) and also speaks of the value of mourning (7:2–4). What then is this joy that Qoheleth commends?

Chapter 1 outlined various scholars and their interpretations of the joy passages, ranging from a meaningless resignation to a positive commendation to a divine command. In the end, much is tied up with how one interprets many other matters of the book. In the view of this writer, Qoheleth's differing perspectives on enjoyment do not represent different types of joy[153] but suggest that while certainly good and a gift from God, enjoyment is not the whole picture nor an end in and of itself. The following chapter will revisit Qoheleth's message of joy as it examines his final section. The focus here will turn to the question of progression.

Many scholars argue for a progression of the joy passages throughout Qoheleth's address. And when it comes to a discussion on the matter, Whybray's work is a common starting place. In his article, "Qoheleth, Preacher of Joy," Whybray identifies seven joy passages:

1. "There is nothing better for a person than . . ." (2:24)
2. "I perceived that there is nothing better for them than . . ." (3:12)
3. "So I saw that there is nothing better than . . ." (3:22)
4. "Behold, what I have seen to be good and fitting is . . ." (5:17 [18])
5. "And I commend joy, for man has no good thing under the sun but . . ." (8:15)
6. "Go, eat your bread with joy, and drink your wine with a merry heart . . . Let your garments be always white. Let not oil be lacking on your head. Enjoy life with the wife whom you love . . . Whatever your hand finds to do, do it with your might . . ." (9:7–10)
7. "Rejoice, O young man in your youth, and let your heart cheer you in the days of your youth. Walk in the ways of your heart . . . Remove

---

153. Fox mentions three efforts at harmonization regarding contradictory statements about pleasure: 1) frivolous/foolish vs. deep; 2) passively received vs. actively pursued; and 3) practical vs. absolute (Fox, *Time to Tear Down*, 123–25). Fox argues that Qoheleth makes no such distinction and that these imposed categories are not supported by the text.

vexation from your heart, and put away pain from your body . . . Remember also your Creator . . ." (11:9—12:1)[154]

Whybray argues that these joy passages punctuate the text as a leitmotif.[155] Indeed, they are quite evenly distributed, more so than the *hebel* pronouncements. Moreover, Whybray argues that there is a purposeful progression in the joy passages throughout Qoheleth's address. While the first passage states the matter plainly, the second and third prefix an asseverative phrase (יָדַעְתִּי כִּי [3:12]; וְרָאִיתִי כִּי [3:22]).[156] Whybray sees in the fourth a more solemn introduction and the fifth is expressed in more decided terms.[157] Becoming more emphatic, the sixth switches to the imperative mood, and the seventh and final joy passage, also in the imperative, is more personal with its address to the young man and introduces and dominates the final section of Qoheleth's address.[158] Whybray also argues that each joy passage relates to a specific section and theme/problem of the book.[159] And these provide the reasons for enjoyment: 1) the gift is from God; 2) the necessity to accept one's lot; 3) the brevity of life; and 4) one's ignorance of the future.[160] In this way, Whybray sees joy passages that are "incapable of reconciliation with a fundamentally pessimistic standpoint" and so, *hebel* is recognized as the problem and background against which Qoheleth proclaims joy.[161]

This concept of a crescendoing note of joy coincides with the narrative understanding of the book presented earlier in this chapter. As the quest of the first half fades, *hebel* recedes from the forefront. And as the focus in the second half turns increasingly to instruction, the notes of joy

---

154. See Whybray, "Preacher of Joy," 87–88.
155. Whybray, "Preacher of Joy," 88.
156. Whybray, "Preacher of Joy," 87.
157. Whybray, "Preacher of Joy," 87.
158. Whybray, "Preacher of Joy," 87–88.
159. These passages divide up the book as they speak on the vanity of 1) toil and human effort (1:12—2:26); 2) man's ignorance of the future (3:1–15); 3) the presence of injustice in the world (3:16–22); 4) the pursuit of wealth (5:9–19 [10–20]); 5) unpunished wickedness (8:10–15); 6) the fact that all men share a common fate (9:1–10); and 7) the brevity of human life (11:7—12:7); see Whybray, "Preacher of Joy," 91–92. Whybray informs that he is not attempting to offer a comprehensive theory of the book's structure, but notes that this may be possible (Whybray, "Preacher of Joy," 95–96n8).
160. Whybray, "Preacher of Joy," 88.
161. Whybray, "Preacher of Joy," 92–94 (92).

build. While many scholars do not interpret the same "Preacher of Joy" that Whybray finds, many, nevertheless, attest to a similar progression.[162]

Christianson notes the key role joy plays in the latter parts of Qoheleth's address. "Indeed, when Qoheleth breaks out with joy it is almost exclusively when he narrates in a 'now' to the 'reader.'"[163] For Christianson, the "now" portion of Qoheleth's address contains a shift in the actantial model from that of his prior quest. "The new Object of the new Subject, instead of understanding, which brings only grief, is practical living and enjoyment of life."[164] This view shares similarities with Ogden's three-part framework of question, answer, and response. The programmatic question of advantage (1:3) launches the quest, which results in the answer of *hebel*.[165] However, it is the third part of the framework that constitutes Qoheleth's culminating advice and the true thesis of the book; namely, the series of passages commending enjoyment.[166] For Fuhr, "The 'enjoy life' motif is stated as [a conclusion] through the repetition seen in the thematic refrain and the escalation of that refrain from consideration (2:24–25; 3:12–13, 22; 5:18–20) to commendation (8:15), and finally to imperative command (9:7–10; 11:9)."[167] Not only does Lee identify eight key joy passages—adding 7:14 to Whybray's seven—Lee also notes other expressions denoting a similar perspective; for example, "look into good" (2:1), "see good" (2:24), "do good" (3:12), "be in good" (7:14), and "see life" (9:9).[168] The result is that Lee perceives the note of enjoyment in almost every unit of the book.[169] Like others who came before, she sees an intentional progression in this theme until it reaches its "dramatic culmination" in Qoheleth's final section (11:7—12:7), which presents "his final and decisive counsel, appropriately summing up the whole of his teachings."[170] Lee writes, "Qohelet's love of life pulsates throughout his

---

162. For example, all of the scholars from chapter 1 who elevate *hebel* to first position as comprising Qoheleth's central message fundamentally disagree with interpreting Qoheleth as any type of a preacher of joy.

163. Christianson, *Time to Tell*, 246–47.

164. Christianson, *Time to Tell*, 247.

165. Ogden, *Qoheleth*, 16.

166. Ogden, *Qoheleth*, 17.

167. Fuhr, *Inter-Dependency*, 177.

168. Lee, *Vitality of Enjoyment*, 3, 33.

169. Lee, *Vitality of Enjoyment*, 33.

170. Lee, *Vitality of Enjoyment*, 72. See also Murphy, *Ecclesiastes*, 114, who speaks of Qoheleth's final section as summing up his message and as bringing together the key themes, which, for Murphy, are joy and death.

discourse, at the start in a muted beat but growing steadily until it swells into a veritable celebration of life."[171]

For Bartholomew, *hebel* and joy are set in deliberate contradictory juxtaposition, resulting in tension.[172] He is adamant that joy is *not* a response to *hebel* but an alternate shalomic vision based on Qoheleth's view of Edenic paradise from Gen 2 and from the good land promised to Israel (see Deut 6:10–11; 30:9).[173] Bartholomew notes that not only do the joy passages "increase in intensity as the book progresses," but that the "tension between them and the *hebel* conclusions also increases and comes close to deconstruction in 9:7–10."[174] The *hebel*-joy tension increases until 11:7, where it finally breaks and an important shift takes place, one that is made clearer in 11:8—12:7, which resolves the tension by putting forward the fear of God as the proper foundation.[175] Thus, this final joy passage is *not* part of a tension-producing juxtaposition with *hebel*; it is free to make a positive commendation. In sum, he sees a progression to the final section of the address, which provides resolution and Qoheleth's central message.

The positions of these scholars will be engaged with further in the following chapter. For now, this shows that many scholars see the joy motif building throughout Qoheleth's address, becoming longer, more emphatic, and direct—a crescendo that culminates in Qoheleth's final section and constitutes, at least in part, Qoheleth's central advice.

3.3.4 Fear God

When it comes to the question of Qoheleth's message, many scholars disparage the fear God motif, seeing it as largely negative. This section will consider the common handlings of this motif and the reasons behind

---

171. Lee, *Vitality of Enjoyment*, 81.

172. Bartholomew, *Ecclesiastes*, 81–82.

173. Bartholomew, *Ecclesiastes*, 152. See also Meek, "The Meaning of הבל in Qohelet," 250–52.

174. Bartholomew, *Ecclesiastes*, 81.

175. Bartholomew, *Ecclesiastes*, 94–95, 354–58. He roots this view of joy in the way the final section mentions joy before *hebel* instead of the other way around; see Bartholomew, *Ecclesiastes*, 353–54. Bartholomew agrees with Whybray about the increasing emphasis of joy and of the great significance of the final joy passage but disagrees about the nature of the role that the joy passages play; see Bartholomew, *Ecclesiastes*, 355; and Whybray, "Qoheleth, Preacher of joy," 87–88.

THE DESIGN OF QOHELETH

them. And after touching on the importance of this motif, this section will survey its use in Qoheleth's address and finally, draw some observations.

Many scholars downplay and dismiss the importance of the fear God motif to Qoheleth. For those who have recourse to glosses to make their interpretation work, the verses that speak of the fear of God and judgment are often the first eliminated.[176] Murphy remarks that "It is hard to escape the impression that the interpreter's subjectivism is at work" and encourages treating the text as one piece.[177] Yet, Murphy reaches much the same result. In some of the very passages he criticizes past scholars for attributing to glosses, Murphy posits that Qoheleth simply quoted the past wisdom tradition only to reject it.[178] Lee picks up on the tendency to downplay the fear God motif, noting various *ad hoc* approaches such as seeing glossators or quotations of traditional views for the purpose of deconstruction.[179] Moreover, Lee notes that many who do, in fact, take the fear God motif to be important filter Qoheleth's view of God through a perception of Qoheleth as pessimist/skeptic and think that the motif "regresses to its primitive notion of enervating terror before an unpredictable God" and thus, fail to recognize Qoheleth's positive counsel.[180] For example, Longman argues that when Qoheleth's words about God are understood in context, they reveal a God who is "distant, occasionally indifferent, and sometimes cruel."[181] While God may be sovereign, he does not really care; while there may be future judgment, do not expect justice.[182] For Fox, Qoheleth's God is a hard ruler, unpredictable, and unloving; mostly indifferent but not hostile.[183] And rather than looking to God, one should "look inward to find one's own strengths."[184] Crenshaw asserts that there is no moral order and that God "stands distant, abandoning humanity to chance and death."[185] Enns holds that the fear of God is "not a healthy, covenantal fear, as we see

---

176. See Murphy, *Ecclesiastes*, xxxiii–xxxiv.

177. Murphy, *Ecclesiastes*, xxxiv.

178. Murphy, *Ecclesiastes*, lxvi. For various approaches to dealing with contradictions, see Fox, *Time to Tear Down*, 14–26.

179. Lee, *Vitality of Enjoyment*, 84.

180. Lee, *Vitality of Enjoyment*, 84.

181. Longman, *Ecclesiastes*, 35.

182. Longman, *Ecclesiastes*, 35.

183. Fox, *Time to Tear Down*, 136–37.

184. Fox, *Time to Tear Down*, 137.

185. Crenshaw, *Ecclesiastes*, 23.

elsewhere in the OT, but something dysfunctional, born out of frustration. God is not to be trusted, so keep out of his way."[186]

This same negative lens leads to (even requires) the reinterpretation of much of Qoheleth's religious and moral language. For example, commenting on "the one who pleases God" and "the sinner" (7:26), Murphy argues that these are to be understood "not as moral qualifications, but as designations of human beings in terms of the inscrutable divine will."[187] Similarly, Fox writes that the sinner is "not a transgressor against the law or moral norms, but rather one who has somehow incurred God's disfavor."[188] And, this person "may be more or less virtuous than others. Qohelet calls a man pleasing or offensive to God in accordance with his fate rather than his deeds."[189] Bartholomew notes a number of reasons for the removal of religious and moral nuances: 1) the developmental view of wisdom; 2) the variety of nuances the word "wisdom" can carry, such as "crafty" (2 Sam 13:3); 3) the view of Torah, prophecy, and wisdom as overly distinct and thus, separate categories; and 4) the complexity of Ecclesiastes as a book.[190] As the previous chapter argued, Israel's wisdom tradition presupposed the covenant. Proverbs and Ecclesiastes echo laws and religious concepts, have no small amount of religious and moral vocabulary, and put forward a fundamental two-ways wisdom framework. The entire wisdom endeavor was rooted in the covenantal understanding of the fear of the Lord. The context of Qoheleth's address—within the narrative frame, in relation to Proverbs, and in connection with the rest of the OT—suggests that the many moral/religious terms, including the fear God motif, should be allowed (even expected to have) their moral/religious sense.[191] Recourses to creative reinterpretations should be reconsidered.

God plays a large part in Qoheleth's investigations, reflections, and admonitions. While Qoheleth does make observations and utilizes rational arguments, Qoheleth talks about God, assumes things about God, and has an established idea about God's rule over the world and relation to humanity. In fact, God (40x) is mentioned more frequently than *hebel* (38x).[192] As the Creator, he gives life (3:11; 5:17 [18]; 7:29; 8:15; 9:9; 11:5;

186. Enns, *Ecclesiastes*, 84.
187. Murphy, *Ecclesiastes*, 76.
188. Fox, *Time to Tear Down*, 189.
189. Fox, *Time to Tear Down*, 269.
190. Bartholomew, *Ecclesiastes*, 89–93.
191. See the fuller discussion in chapter 2.
192. That is, in the book. In Qoheleth's address (1:12–12:7), God occurs 38x and

12:1, 7). God also gives work, one's portion, and enjoyment (2:24–25; 3:13; 5:18 [19]). Indeed, God is very active and involved; 18x God gives/does. Qoheleth speaks of God's sovereignty/control (1:15; 3:14; 7:13–14), and his ways are beyond human comprehension (3:11; 8:17; 11:5). Qoheleth's view of the world is integrally connected with his view of God. When it comes to Qoheleth's message, the fear God motif cannot be suppressed.

If the fear God motif is given room to speak, the question follows, what does it convey? While the final lines of the narrator (12:13–14) are undeniably the most memorable in this respect—these will be discussed later—the fear God motif occurs throughout Qoheleth's address. The first occurrence comes in 3:14: "I perceived that whatever God does endures forever; nothing can be added to it, nor anything taken from it. God has done it, so that people fear before him." Following a poem about a time for every matter (3:1–8), Qoheleth asks the question, "What gain has the worker from his toil?" (3:9; see 1:3; 2:3). In response, Qoheleth declares two things that he knows (יָדַעְתִּי כִּי; 3:12, 14). First, since one cannot find out all that God has done (3:10–11), one should be joyful and do good, taking pleasure in one's toil—a gift from God (3:12–13). Second, one cannot control the times and thus, should fear God (3:14). Note the two themes of unknowable and uncontrollable (i.e., ungraspable) and the two responses of joy and fearing God.[193]

Amidst the narrative of Qoheleth's quest comes a conspicuous turn: 4:17—5:6 [5:1–7]. Not only is there a noticeable shift in the topic as Qoheleth addresses cultic activities but also a pronounced shift in the narratorial voice as Qoheleth speaks, for the first time (ignoring 2:1), in the second-person as he emphatically and directly commands his addressee. Urging caution when going to the house of God, Qoheleth warns against making rash (and thus, unfulfilled) vows, describing it as the sacrifice of fools (4:17 [5:1]), displeasing to God (5:3 [4]), evil (4:17 [5:1]), and sin (5:5 [6]). Rather, recognizing God's transcendence, one should guard one's steps (4:17 [5:1]), draw near to listen (4:17 [5:1]), be not hasty to speak (5:1 [2]), and not delay in fulfilling one's vows (5:3 [4]). Then, by way of summary, Qoheleth implores, "God is the one you must fear"

---

hebel 30x.

193. For positive readings of this passage, see the following: Bartholomew, *Ecclesiastes*, 159–74; Whybray, *Ecclesiastes*, 75; Provan, *Ecclesiastes*, 91; and Lee, *Vitality of Enjoyment*, 86–91. For negative readings, see Longman, *Ecclesiastes*, 123–24; and Enns, *Ecclesiastes*, 56. Ogden translates 3:14b as, "God has done (this) so that they might see (what proceeds) from him" (Ogden, *Qoheleth*, 62).

(5:6b [7b]). While there are differing views concerning Qoheleth's handling of this Deuteronomic law[194] and of his view of God here,[195] the fear

---

194. Levinson sees in Qoheleth a new spirit of theological autonomy as he focuses on the degree of transformation in Qoheleth's use of the Deuteronomic law, noting 1) linguistic updating, 2) a rewritten motive clause, and 3) a reordered sequence (Levinson, "Better That You Should Not Vow," 28–41). The result is that the law is presented not as a divine command but as Qoheleth's personal advice and breach is not presented as sin mandating divine punishment but as folly that merely displeases God (Levinson, "Better That You Should Not Vow," 38). "In that way, the Torah's absolute prohibition . . . is relativized by Qoheleth to a mere transgression against wisdom and good sense" (Levinson, "Better That You Should Not Vow," 38). Note also Fox, *Time to Tear Down*, 229, who holds that "the misdeed is condemned for its folly rather than its sinfulness." However, 4:17 [5:1] describes the action as evil (רע) and 5:5 [6] describes it as sin (חטא). Additionally, the words of Qoheleth that speak of God being angry and destroying the work of the sinner (5:5 [6]) clearly denote judgment. Schultz offers a much more convincing assessment. Looking at the law of the vow in Eccl 5:3–5 [4–6] and Deut 23:22–24 [21–23], Schultz argues that the almost verbatim opening serves as a literary marker to help readers recognize the Deuteronomic parallel, while the rest has been adapted from a legal to a more poetic style to serve Qoheleth's own context and purposes (Schultz, "The Reuse of Deuteronomy's 'Law of the Vow,'" 123–27). This close connection with Deuteronomy suggests that Qoheleth's summative clause of the section, that one is to fear God, carries a sense similar to that found in Deuteronomy. For a concise overview of various scholarly positions, see Schultz, "The Reuse of Deuteronomy's 'Law of the Vow,'" 122–23.

195. When Qoheleth says that "God is in heaven and you are on earth" (5:1 [2]), some argue that Qoheleth views God to be distant, far off, removed, uninvolved, and thus, interpret the command to fear God (5:6 [7]) in this negative light. Longman argues that the "universe is ruled by a God that just does not seem to care much about earthly concerns" and "the fear advocated here is that of fright before a powerful and dangerous being, not respect or awe" (Longman, *Ecclesiastes*, 36). Enns concludes that "This is a different kind of fear, one that concerns a God . . . whose inscrutable acts produce pain, anxiety, frustration—fear" (Enns, *Ecclesiastes*, 69). Christianson writes, "This could hardly be summarized as 'Fear God and keep his commands.' Indeed, this passage emits a strong 'aroma of paranoia' out of keeping with the very positive effects that fearing God is meant to engender elsewhere, not the least of which is the beginning of knowledge (Prov 1:7; cf. 1 Sam 12:24; Prov 3:7–8)" (Christianson, *Time to Tell*, 116). Shields sees here an "exhortation to abstain from speaking to God" (in prayers and vows) because of his distance and lack of care (Shields, *End of Wisdom*, 159). He argues that Qoheleth's words are ultimately "incompatible with the canon" (Shields, *End of Wisdom*, 163). However, many scholars offer a more positive interpretation. Bartholomew argues that when Qoheleth speaks of drawing near to the house of God to listen (4:17 [5:1]), he is speaking of drawing near to the temple to listen to the instruction of the Torah (Bartholomew, *Ecclesiastes*, 204). The temple was the place where God's presence dwelt and his voice heard (thus, God was not far off and uninvolved). And the posture of listening is the posture of the learner who submits to one greater, so that one may learn wisdom. This listening is not merely "hearing" but also "receiving" and "following"—it affects one's behaviors. It "means to hear and obey the words of God" (Whybray, *Ecclesiastes*, 92; see also Provan, *Ecclesiastes*, 116). In contrast, the one who does not listen is a fool who does evil (4:17 [5:1]). This concept of "listening" is a key aspect of gaining wisdom (Bartholomew, *Ecclesiastes*, 204). Proverbs 28:9 says, "If one turns away his ear from

God motif encapsulates the heart of Qoheleth's message in this section. He exhorts a listening posture before God and that one's conduct should be void of folly/evil/sin. God is the source of wisdom and the one who judges—fear him.

The next occurrence is found in 7:18. In light of one's inability to control or understand the works of God (7:12-14), and in a contrast between the righteous and the wicked (7:15-17), Qoheleth concludes that "the one who fears God shall come out from both of them" (7:18b). A common interpretation is that Qoheleth is endorsing some form of moderation. "His advice boils down to this: be moderate in both and excessive in neither."[196] Though, there are good reasons some reject the view that Qoheleth is advising one to take a little folly and righteousness.[197] In the view of this writer, Qoheleth, while noting that one cannot control/change the works of God (7:13), that both the day of prosperity and adversity are from him (7:14a), that one cannot find out what is to be (7:14b), and noting that the righteous may perish in their righteousness and the wicked may live long (7:15), Qoheleth states that being overly righteous/too wise will not enable one to control the times and secure a desired outcome (7:16); indeed, there is no one righteous, who never sins (7:20). However, this does not mean that one should go the opposite way and be overly wicked and a fool and so destroy himself (7:17). Rather, the proper response to these incomprehensible and inapprehensible matters is that one should fear God (7:18).

The next three occurrences appear together. In a moment of reflection upon the pervasiveness of evil and the delay of justice (8:10-11), Qoheleth affirms that "Though a sinner does evil a hundred times and prolongs his life, yet I know that it will be well with those who fear God, because they fear before him. But it will not be well with the wicked, neither will he prolong his days like a shadow, because he does not fear before God" (8:12-13). Here, the deeds of the wicked and the righteous are explicitly connected with their fear of God, or lack thereof, and with

---

hearing the law, even his prayer is an abomination" (see also Prov 2:2; 4:20; 5:1; 15:31; 18:15; 21:13; 22:17; 23:12; 25:12. Note also Ps 73:16-17 as well as Solomon's request for a "listening heart" to govern and discern between good and evil [1 Kgs 3:9]).

196. Bartholomew, *Ecclesiastes*, 253-62 (254). He takes "fears God" in 7:18 to be ironic; see Bartholomew, *Ecclesiastes*, 256. Cf. Longman, *Ecclesiastes*, 196-97.

197. Ogden argues that "Qoheleth does not advocate a *via media*. He does, however, call upon his reader to take both warnings seriously: they should shun pretensions to righteousness and also keep free from evil" (Ogden, *Qoheleth*, 125; similarly, Provan, *Ecclesiastes*, 151-52).

resulting divine judgment, even if Qoheleth cannot see it (8:14, 16–17). The primary difficulty in this small section is in translating 8:10, one of the most difficult verses in the book.[198] Nevertheless, its difficulty does nothing to obscure the clarity of 8:12–13.[199]

Lastly, Qoheleth's final section needs consideration. In 12:1, as the ultima in a string of closing imperatives, Qoheleth exhorts, "Remember also your Creator." Although this does not contain the specific wording "fear God," it does present a message that some argue to be functionally equivalent.[200] A more detailed examination of this verse will be left to the following chapter.

With these fear God passages in hand, a few observations are in order. First, they are spread out in the address as opposed to being relegated to one section, such as part of Qoheleth's quest. Second, in contrast to Qoheleth's meandering deliberations of positive and negative assessments, Grant notes that in every case where the fear of the Lord is put forward, there is never an accompanying negative flip side.[201]

Third, the mention of fearing God is often accompanied by notes about moral conduct as well as God's judgment. 1) The first occurrence of the motif in 3:14 is preceded by "doing good" (3:14; see 7:20)[202] and followed by a contrast between the righteous and the wicked (3:16–17), to which Qoheleth asserts that God will judge (3:17). 2) The next section (4:17—5:6 [5:1–7]), which culminates in the command to fear God (5:6

---

198. Note the following discussions: Seow, *Ecclesiastes*, 284–86, 294; Longman, *Ecclesiastes*, 216, 218–19; Fox, *Time to Tear Down*, 283–85; and Bartholomew, *Ecclesiastes*, 289–90.

199. Most scholars recognize 8:12–13 as clearly orthodox; however, responses vary. Crenshaw believes it to be a gloss (Crenshaw, *Ecclesiastes*, 155). Murphy argues that Qoheleth is dialoguing with the wisdom tradition to acknowledge that he is aware of its claims but denies its truth (Murphy, *Ecclesiastes*, lxvi, 85; see also Lohfink, *Qoheleth*, 108; and Shields, *End of Wisdom*, 198). Similarly, Longman holds that Qoheleth is "stating an argument that is not his own" (Longman, *Ecclesiastes*, 219). Bartholomew sees Qoheleth juxtaposing what he knows with what he sees, his confessional view with his enigmatic view, and that Qoheleth does not resolve this contradiction but struggles with its tension (Bartholomew, *Ecclesiastes*, 290–91). For Ogden, "Qoheleth basically supports the traditional view about divine justice" (Ogden, *Qoheleth*, 137).

200. See Fuhr, *Inter-Dependency*, 166; Bartholomew, *Ecclesiastes*, 345–46, 354, 356–58; and Beldman, "Framed," 159–60.

201. Grant, "Wisdom and Covenant," 860.

202. While, for example, Provan, *Ecclesiastes*, 37, takes this to mean morally good, many interpreters resist and/or excuse the moral language in Qoheleth's address. See discussions above and in the previous chapter for arguments in favor of interpreting moral language.

[7]), stresses one's conduct, encouraging one to listen to (and follow) instruction (4:17 [5:1]) rather than do evil (4:17 [5:1]) and sin (5:5 [6]). For, as Qoheleth asks, with a clear reference to judgment, "Why should God be angry at your voice and destroy the work of your hands?" (5:5 [6]). 3) Next, 7:15 notes that Qoheleth has seen the righteous perish in their righteousness and the wicked prolong his life in his evildoing. With the apparent disconnect between deeds and outcomes in view, Qoheleth's advice is to fear God (7:18). 4) In 8:10-13, Qoheleth affirms that it will not be well (that is, judgment) with the wicked and the sinner who does evil because they do not fear God (8:12-13). Conversely, it will go well with those who fear God (8:12b). 5) In Qoheleth's final section, the commendations of joy and of walking in the ways of one's heart and eyes (11:9) are grounded by a recognition of God's future judgment (11:9). Additionally, Qoheleth commands proper conduct, that is, turning from vexation and evil (11:10) and that one remembers the Creator (12:1), the equivalence of fearing God. This pattern suggests that Qoheleth's understanding of fearing God includes aspects of both right conduct and divine judgment.[203] Additionally, this suggests that Qoheleth's understanding of the fear of God is reflective of a covenantal background and similar to that found in Proverbs, Psalms, Deuteronomy, and indeed, much of the OT.[204]

Fourth, the fear God motif does not appear to possess any significant progression, such as what can be seen in the joy motif—its first occurrence (5:6 [7]) is an emphatic imperative that concludes the section. Grant writes, "These orthodox statements in the midst of the complexity of Qoheleth's thought serve as beacons for the reader to chart a way through the text."[205] And Kidner notes, "And, as we have seen, the blackness of what (in the author's words) '*I saw*' does not succeed in quenching the tiny spark of '*Yet I know. . .*'"[206] The fear God motif is presented as a consistent part of Qoheleth's instruction.

Fifth, the fear God motif occurs in significant places, such as the culmination of the first major shift in the narratorial voice (4:17—5:6

---

203. One could also point to the closing words of the book (12:13-14), where these same themes occur together; namely, fear God and keep his commands, for he will bring everything into judgment. The similarities suggest that the narrator's perspective in 12:13-14 is quite similar to that of Qoheleth's (that is, an understanding similar to that found in Proverbs and the Torah) and that this is a significant motif. See chapter 4.

204. Of course, this is supported by many other connections between these books; see chapter 2.

205. Grant, "Wisdom and Covenant," 860.

206. Kidner, *The Wisdom of Proverbs, Job and Ecclesiastes*, 141; emphasis original.

[5:1–7]). And it features prominently in Qoheleth's final section (11:7–12:7)—to say nothing of 12:13–14.[207]

Qoheleth's understanding of God is integral to his address and message. The passages that speak of fearing God are interwoven to such an extent that they cannot be dismissed as glosses. This motif is spread throughout the address, appears consistently with elements of judgment and moral actions, and culminates in Qoheleth's final section. And while this motif does not have the same level of progression as that of joy, it is like a steady note, one that Qoheleth keeps returning to sound. It is like a thread woven through the address, guiding and giving hope. And it is this call that rings both at the end of Qoheleth's address and at the close of the book.

3.3.5 Conclusion

This section has considered the three primary motifs of Qoheleth's address: *hebel*, joy, and the fear of God. *Hebel* represents the conclusion of the search of Qoheleth's younger self. Accordingly, this conclusion becomes the context from which he imparts advice and instruction to the reader on how to live in this world of *hebel*. As such, *hebel* is not the message of the aged Qoheleth. Moreover, while this motif was dominant in the first half of the address, coinciding with Qoheleth's quest, its waning gives room for the rise of Qoheleth's instruction. The joy motif, expressed in its many forms, builds throughout the address, comprises a notable part of Qoheleth's advice, and leads to his final section. The fear God motif, accompanied by tones of moral conduct and divine judgment, resounds throughout the address as a consistent part of Qoheleth's instruction. Not only is this understanding of these motifs compatible with the general progression of Qoheleth's narrative outlined above, it contributes to it as they lead to and culminate in Qoheleth's final section.

3.4 CONCLUSION

This chapter began with a discussion of structure and rather than pursuing a detailed linear arrangement, a loose macro-perspective was favored. Specifically, an argument was made for viewing Qoheleth's address

---

207. Whether or not the other occurrences come in significant places is open to debate.

as a narrative, which offers both cohesion of the whole and a progression from quest to expression. This broad narrative framework recognizes two perspectives of Qoheleth. The first is the wisdom quest of Qoheleth's younger self. The second is that of the aged Qoheleth as he reflects upon his past quest with its failure and focuses on his present concern of instruction. Within this framework comes Qoheleth's primary motifs: *hebel*, joy, and the fear of God. *Hebel* represents the conclusion of Qoheleth's quest and becomes the context for his later counsel. And while this motif diminishes with Qoheleth's quest, the others rise with his instruction. As a whole, Qoheleth's address leads to and culminates in his final section (11:7—12:7), in which he brings together the primary motifs and offers his parting exhortations.

This chapter does not claim to be the only viable reading of the design of Qoheleth's address. Indeed, the circularity of Qoheleth's investigations, as he drifts from one topic to another and back again, opens itself up to a number of possible structural conceptions. However, the proposal here presents a tasteful simplicity that provides a basic structure with a general progression that satisfactorily culminates at its end—all the while giving ample room for the complexities of Qoheleth's wide-ranging ruminations.

Yet, questions remain. How do the motifs, particularly that of joy and fear, relate to each other? What is, in fact, Qoheleth's central message? While Qoheleth's final section has only been noted in brief, the following chapter examines 11:7—12:7 to see how Qoheleth brings together the primary motifs and to discern his final instructions.

4

The Message of Qoheleth

4.1 INTRODUCTION

THE PREVIOUS CHAPTER EXPLORED the design of Qoheleth's address and argued for a purposeful progression that leads to and culminates in his final section. This chapter turns to a close examination of that concluding unit with the aim of discerning the contours of Qoheleth's message and its connection with his primary motifs. This chapter will argue that in his final section, Qoheleth brings together the primary motifs as he communicates his central message. In doing so, he reveals his understanding of their interrelation, an understanding that corresponds with their use throughout his address; namely, *hebel* represents the context, joy comprises the advice, and the fear of God, also part of his advice, constitutes the foundation.

This chapter will first consider the unity and structure of Qoheleth's final section before pursuing a detailed examination. Subsequently, the state of scholarship will be revisited and the present thesis differentiated from similar perspectives. Finally, this chapter will address the narrator's evaluation of Qoheleth and his message, particularly as it weighs upon the reading of Qoheleth offered here.

4.2 THE UNITY AND STRUCTURE OF QOHELETH'S FINAL SECTION

If one is to speak of Qoheleth's final section, the first question is one of identification. Accordingly, this section will demarcate the boundaries of his final unit, noting areas of disagreement in scholarship. Additionally, a few points concerning its shape will be highlighted.

Most scholars identify 11:7—12:7/8 as Qoheleth's final section.[1] Murphy speaks of a "broad consensus" and Ogden notes an "almost universal" recognition.[2] Seow argues that "it is clear that the passage as a whole is a carefully-constructed cohesive unit" and titles it "Conclusion."[3] There are, however, a few small points of disagreement.

Discerning the closing boundary is relatively simple since Qoheleth concludes his address and the narrator resurfaces to present some closing remarks. The primary question concerns the attribution of 12:8. Some view 12:8 as closing the poem.[4] Others see 12:8 as belonging to the narrator.[5] Still, others prefer to highlight the verse's transitional nature. For example, Fox describes 12:8 as "a linchpin" between the two and notes that it could be attached to either.[6] This project attributes 12:8, along with its counterpart 1:2, to the narrator and holds that Qoheleth's address runs from 1:12 to 12:7.[7] That being said, the verse possesses a transitional quality as it serves to close Qoheleth's address, restate the theme of *hebel*, and reintroduce the voice of the narrator. Ultimately, this is not a major issue as not much is at stake for the present concerns.

Discerning the beginning of Qoheleth's final section requires slightly more attention. Though a few prefer to deal in larger blocks and

---

1. The following are a few among many who take 11:7–12:7 as the final unit: Crenshaw, *Ecclesiastes*, 181–89; Shields, *End of Wisdom*, 227; Bartholomew, *Ecclesiastes*, 339–42; Beldman, "Framed," 159–60; Miller, *Symbol and Rhetoric*, 23; Longman, *Ecclesiastes*, 262; Treier, *Proverbs & Ecclesiastes*, 219; and Lee, *Vitality of Enjoyment*, 72.

2. Murphy, *Ecclesiastes*, 114; Ogden, *Qoheleth*, 207.

3. Seow, *Ecclesiastes*, 346, 368.

4. Seow, *Ecclesiastes*, 346–47; Ogden, *Qoheleth*, 207–08; Lohfink, *Qoheleth*, 136; Provan, *Ecclesiastes*, 211–19; and Loader, *Polar Structures*, 107–08.

5. Christianson, *Time to Tell*, 92–93; Longman, *Ecclesiastes*, 274; Bartholomew, *Ecclesiastes*, 359; and Beldman, "Framed," 150.

6. Fox, *Time to Tear Down*, 316. Still, Fox tends to treat 12:8 as the climax of the poem; see Fox, "Aging and Death," 55–56, 71–72n1.

7. See chapter 2 for discussion.

see Qoheleth's final section as reaching back to 11:1[8] or even 9:7,[9] and while some view 11:7–8 as belonging to the previous section[10] or even as its own small unit,[11] the majority position identifies a final unit beginning at 11:7.[12] While this position typically notes differences of content between 11:7–8 and what precedes, it is ultimately rooted in thematic and vocabulary links between 11:7–8 and what follows.[13] As such, 11:7–8 is commonly taken as an introduction presenting the twin themes of rejoicing and remembering that then govern and divide the remainder into two sections.[14] The result is as follows: introduction (11:7–8); rejoice (11:9–10); and remember (12:1–7). One could also note the recurrence of *hebel* (11:8, 10; 12:8) and how the whole section begins with life (11:7) and concludes with death (12:7).

A marked shift between 11:8 and 11:9 is easily recognizable, supporting the view that 11:7–8 comprises an introduction and 11:9—12:7 represents the body. The jussives of 11:8 give way to a series of imperatives that drive and center the whole unit: rejoice; walk; know; remove; put away; and remember. After the first imperative to rejoice in 11:9, all the rest are linked with a *waw*. The final imperative launches the closing poem of 12:1–7. It begins, "Remember also your Creator in the days of your youth" (12:1a). After this opening, the rest of the poem consists of a series of three subsections, each beginning with the phrase עַד אֲשֶׁר לֹא ("before"; 12:1b, 2a, 6a). As such, the entire poem is comprised of a single sentence with its main clause in 12:1a, which serves as the foundation for

---

8. For example, Krüger, *Qoheleth*, 191; and Enns, *Ecclesiastes*, 104. Yet, these still note a thematic distinction between 11:1–6 and 11:7–12:7.

9. Lohfink sees a much larger section of 9:7—12:8—held together by the framing joy sections of 9:7–9 and 11:7–12:8—entitled "Ethic" (Lohfink, *Qoheleth*, 114–15). However, even this structure still groups 11:7—12:8.

10. Crenshaw notes that 11:8 ends with a *hebel* statement and that these often conclude sections (Crenshaw, *Ironic Wink*, 91; see also Provan, *Ecclesiastes*, 204). Lohfink interprets the opening conjunction of 11:7 as linking it with what precedes (read as consequence) and identifies a vocabulary link in the word טוב, which closes 11:6 and features prominently in 11:7 (Lohfink, *Qoheleth*, 133–36). Additionally, Hobbins points to the introductory vocative in 11:9 as a common component of a new unit (Hobbins, "The Poetry of Qohelet," 189).

11. See Whybray, *Ecclesiastes*, 161, who roots his view in stylistic differences.

12. Note the following: Longman, *Ecclesiastes*, 258; Bartholomew, *Ecclesiastes*, 342; Holmstedt et al., *Qoheleth*, 290; and Loader, *Polar Structures*, 66.

13. See Murphy, *Ecclesiastes*, 114; and Seow, *Ecclesiastes*, 346–47.

14. Ogden, *Qoheleth*, 207–08; Fox, *Time to Tear Down*, 315–17; Lee, *Vitality of Enjoyment*, 72; and Bartholomew, *Ecclesiastes*, 342–43.

the whole. Thus, it is this string of imperatives that represent the heart of this final section.

In sum, the evidence supports the view of 11:7—12:7 as Qoheleth's final section—and so this chapter will proceed with the majority. However, the divisions between units in Qoheleth's address will continue to be a matter of much discussion—the circularity of Qoheleth's investigations and thought gives the impression of each unit leading into the next. Strong structural divisions risk disrupting that flow. And so, whether 11:7–8 concludes the previous, serves to introduce what follows, or stands on its own as a transitional section, the general effect on the reader remains the same; thus, not much is at stake. In each case, however, the imperatives of 11:9—12:1a carry the heart and force of Qoheleth's concluding instructions.

4.3 THE MESSAGE OF QOHELETH'S FINAL SECTION

4.3.1 Introduction

Attention will now turn to the examination of Qoheleth's final section with the aim of identifying his central message. As argued in the previous chapter, Qoheleth's address, as a whole, has been leading and building to this point. If 11:7—12:7 does, in fact, communicate Qoheleth's central message, one would expect it to be broad enough to cover the many facets of his address. One would also expect the primary motifs/themes of his address to play a significant part in his closing message. And then, if Qoheleth does bring together the primary motifs, his handling of them should first, be compatible with his prior use of them and second, bring greater clarity to his understanding of their interrelation. This section argues that this is just what happens.

4.3.2 Ecclesiastes 11:7–8

While the focus of this section will be on the main body of Qoheleth's final unit, its introduction deserves brief consideration. It reads as follows: "Light is sweet, and it is pleasant for the eyes to see the sun. So if a person lives many years, let him rejoice in them all; but let him remember that the days of darkness will be many. All that comes is [*hebel*]" (11:7–8).

Qoheleth begins with a pleasant affirmation. Most take "light" and "see the sun" as clear imagery depicting life.[15] It is true that Qoheleth has had some strong words about life in his address. He said that he hated life (2:17) and all his toil (2:18) and that he gave his heart up to despair (2:20). He said that the dead are more fortunate than the living (4:2) and better than both is the one who has not yet been (4:3). However, Qoheleth's words were not all negative. He also spoke of how the living have hope (9:4), and he regularly commended enjoyment. Here, at the end, Qoheleth unreservedly affirms life.

On the heels of life's affirmation, Qoheleth endorses enjoyment in all the years of one's life (11:8). This, however, is coupled with a recognition of life's other side; "but let him remember that the days of darkness will be many" (11:8). The future orientation of this call to remember suggests an understanding of "ponder" or "consider" with the idea that the matter should have some effect on the present.[16] As a counterpart to the affirmation of light in the previous verse (11:7), Qoheleth now speaks of many days of darkness. What are these days of darkness? Some identify old age[17] while others point to Sheol/death.[18] And some hold a referent of both old age and death.[19] Seow, pointing to 5:16 [17] and 12:1, argues that the referent is not death nor Sheol but all "the gloomy and miserable days in one's lifetime."[20] While this may encompass parts of old age, it is certainly not limited to it. In a similar way, Bartholomew holds that "The phrase includes death but so much more as well: evil days, oppression,

---

15. Seow, *Ecclesiastes*, 347; Longman, *Ecclesiastes*, 259; Krüger, *Qoheleth*, 195; Whybray, *Ecclesiastes*, 161; Shields, *End of Wisdom*, 228; Lohfink, *Qoheleth*, 135; Lee, *Vitality of Enjoyment*, 73; and Fox, *Time to Tear Down*, 316. These are not uncommon as images for life; see Job 3:16; 33:28, 30; Ps 56:14 [13]; Eccl 6:5; 7:11. In contrast, Crenshaw holds that light characterizes youth while darkness represents the waning years (Crenshaw, *Ecclesiastes*, 182).

16. Ogden, *Qoheleth*, 209.

17. Enns, *Ecclesiastes*, 106.

18. See Whybray, *Ecclesiastes*, 161, who argues that darkness/death is the counterpart to the light/life of 11:7 and finds precedent for darkness as a metaphor for death in 6:4. See also Ogden, *Qoheleth*, 208; Fox, *Time to Tear Down*, 40, 317; and Loader, *Polar Structures*, 109.

19. Longman, *Ecclesiastes*, 259–60; Shields, *End of Wisdom*, 228; Murphy, *Ecclesiastes*, 116; and Lohfink, *Qoheleth*, 135. Crenshaw argues that darkness refers to Sheol but may possibly include old age (Crenshaw, *Ecclesiastes*, 348). Lee argues that the metaphor refers to death and days of unpleasantness (Lee, *Vitality of Enjoyment*, 73).

20. Seow, *Ecclesiastes*, 348. Note Krüger, *Qoheleth*, 196, who interprets an old man looking back over his life and remembering its many dark days.

aloneness, abusive rule, and so on."²¹ The broader views of Seow and Bartholomew are more convincing as they speak to the many facets of life's difficulties covered by Qoheleth throughout his address.

Qoheleth concludes this introduction with a familiar statement of *hebel*. Just as views of the referents of 11:7–8a differ, so too with the "all" that is *hebel*. While some argue that the "all" that comes refers to death,²² it is more likely a broad reference that covers the entirety of life. As Seow argues, not only has Qoheleth communicated ignorance of what happens after death (3:21; 10:14), he has emphasized the *hebel* of life.²³ Qoheleth's *hebel* statements typically came with more specificity, declaring that "this is *hebel*" or "I have seen a *hebel*"; however, the statement in 11:8 carries a summative quality and reads similar to Qoheleth's initial summary of his quest in 1:14 as well as the narrator's thematic statements in 1:2 and 12:8 that "all is [*hebel*]."²⁴ *Hebel* dominated in the first half of Qoheleth's address but diminished in the second—the most recent occurrence being 9:9. As *hebel* represented the conclusion of Qoheleth's quest and became the context for his instruction, so here, in the introduction to his final section, he reiterates this primary motif and context before moving to his concluding advice.

What then is the message of this introduction? For Fox, one should seize pleasure as a distraction from the absurdity of life and death. "We are reminded of death in order to persuade us to lay hold of the pleasures that will divert our thoughts from death."²⁵ Against Fox's diversionary interpretation, Ogden argues that one's recognition of death should help form one's understanding of the present.²⁶ Whybray holds that "Qoheleth's intention here is not to introduce a note of gloom to negate or qualify the cheerful notes struck in v. 7, but to use the backdrop of inevitable death to highlight the positive opportunities for joy in this life."²⁷ Against

---

21. Bartholomew, *Ecclesiastes*, 344.

22. Whybray, *Ecclesiastes*, 161. For Crenshaw, this means, "everything that the future holds in Sheol is utterly absurd" (Crenshaw, *Ecclesiastes*, 183).

23. Seow, *Ecclesiastes*, 348. Specifically, he sees "all that comes" as referring to one's coming into existence, pairing with 12:5, in which humanity is going to his eternal home (note 1:2, "A generation goes and a generation comes").

24. Note also the *hebel* statement in 2:11, where Qoheleth reflects on "all" that he has done. The two other cases in which Qoheleth says that "all is *hebel*" are 2:17 and 3:19, which also share a large view of life in general.

25. Fox, *Time to Tear Down*, 317.

26. Ogden, *Qoheleth*, 209.

27. Whybray, *Ecclesiastes*, 161. Similarly, Lohfink writes, "The thought of death in no

such positive interpretations, Longman argues that while 11:7 was optimistic, in 11:8, Qoheleth "immediately notes the impossibility of his own counsel."[28] For Crenshaw, this rejoicing is but a meaningless resignation, and he likens it to the sentiment of the doomed who say in Isa 22:13, "Let us eat and drink, for tomorrow we die."[29] In many ways, as noted above, the majority of scholars appear to take 11:7–8 as introductory to Qoheleth's final section. If this is so, one would expect Qoheleth to then continue and build on these ideas, making clear his final message. And so, that is where the focus of this chapter will lie.

In sum, this introduction (11:7–8) to Qoheleth's final section consists of two primary points: first, an affirmation of life, conveyed through the imagery of light in 11:7 and the note about enjoyment in 11:8a; and second, a recognition of life's difficulties, communicated in 11:8b by both the days of darkness and the statement of *hebel*. Thus, life is good and to be enjoyed, but there is also *hebel*. Apart from introducing key notes of rejoicing and remembering, the introduction resurfaces the *hebel* motif. And in this final section, Qoheleth acknowledges this context of *hebel* before continuing to impart his final instruction.

4.3.3 Ecclesiastes 11:9a

Moving past the introduction and into the body of the final section, Qoheleth focuses his attention on the emphatic and direct imparting of advice. The opening line reveals his addressee as a young man.[30] This is the first mention of the implied reader in Qoheleth's address, which adds to the sense that he is drawing to a close and imparting that which is most important. While the characteristic student of a sage may well have been a young man, the idea also represents a typical wisdom trope. For example, Proverbs repeatedly presents a father instructing his son (Prov 1:8; 4:1; 5:1; *passim*), urging him to keep his commandments (Prov 2:1; 3:1; 6:20; 7:1).[31] And this imagery was not unique to Israel but common

---

way relativizes joy, but rather gives it its strength and justification" (Lohfink, *Qoheleth*, 135).

28. Longman, *Ecclesiastes*, 259–60.

29. Crenshaw, *Ecclesiastes*, 183.

30. The words בחור and ילדות convey not childhood but a young adult, with military eligibility, one in the prime of life; see Seow, *Ecclesiastes*, 349; and Fox, *Time to Tear Down*, 318.

31. While dominant, the imagery did not have a monopoly. Note Proverb's depiction

in the ANE.³² Why is Qoheleth addressing the young? Christianson holds that it merely represents an ideal, implied reader.³³ For Fuhr, instruction is given to the young because they are best able to capitalize on all that life has to offer.³⁴ Bartholomew highlights that the use of the young here draws particular attention to wisdom as the foundation for life and encourages one to lay this foundation while young.³⁵ However, the specified recipient as one who is young should not be mistaken as restrictive. To be sure, there is an emphasis on the young—11:9a makes three references to the young, followed by "youth" in 11:10 and "days of one's youth" in 12:1. Yet, Qoheleth's words in 11:8, that one should rejoice in *all* the days of one's life, indicate that his advice is not reserved for the young but for the aged as well. Heeding instruction while young is certainly advantageous, but as one ages, the teaching was not to be cast aside. Wisdom was to guide one through all the days of one's life. In this way, wisdom calls to all.

The body of Qoheleth's final section begins with his first imperative, accompanied by a jussive calling for rejoicing. "Rejoice, O young man, in your youth, and let your heart cheer you in the days of your youth" (11:9a). The two halves are clearly parallel.³⁶ This familiar note of rejoicing has sounded throughout Qoheleth's address (2:24–26; 3:12–13, 22; 5:17–19 [18–20]; 7:14; 9:7–9); its appearance here should come as no surprise. Still, interpretations vary. Crenshaw argues that Qoheleth expresses enjoyment here with "lean vocabulary," that the mood is "hardly celebratory," and that the context suggests irony.³⁷ Ogden argues for an understanding of "mind" rather than "heart" and thus, enjoyment here is an intellectual pursuit.³⁸ In reality, one finds here the same breadth of interpretations that have plagued the rest of Qoheleth's discussions on joy—a spectrum ranging from a meaningless resignation to a positive commendation to a divine command. However, as Qoheleth proceeds through his final section, he provides further information clarifying the nature of this enjoyment. More attention will be devoted there.

---

of a mother teaching her son (Prov 6:20; 31:1–2) as well as the portrayal of lady wisdom calling to all (Prov 9:1–6) and the woman with wisdom in Prov 31:10–31 (esp. v. 26).

32. Longman, *Ecclesiastes*, 280.
33. Christianson, *Time to Tell*, 245.
34. Fuhr, *Inter-Dependency*, 180.
35. Bartholomew, *Ecclesiastes*, 344.
36. Ogden, *Qoheleth*, 210.
37. Crenshaw, *Ironic Wink*, 91–92.
38. Ogden, *Qoheleth*, 210.

In short, after an introduction that included an acknowledgment and reiteration of the context of *hebel*, Qoheleth leads his final instruction with a call to rejoice. This motif has resounded throughout his address, crescendoing to this climax. This first imperative recalls the rest of Qoheleth's instruction on the matter. And while enjoyment is promoted and undoubtedly comprises a key part of Qoheleth's central message, it is qualified shortly—joy is not the final word.

4.3.4 Ecclesiastes 11:9b

In 11:9b, the reader encounters the second imperative: "Walk in the ways of your heart and the sight of your eyes." This second exhortation is generally understood as an elaboration on the first, speaking of one's conduct as it concerns the pursuit of enjoyment.[39] Gordis identifies the heart and the eyes as the "organs of desire."[40] Whybray reads, "do whatever seems good to you."[41] And Fox interprets, "Go where your heart goes."[42] This idea of pursuing something desirable leads well from 11:1–6, which instructs that while one may not know what will happen nor what will succeed, one need not be crippled with inaction but should work hard and try something. Still, what does it mean to walk in the ways of one's heart and eyes? Is this path good or bad? Does this promote hedonism and licentiousness or is this enjoyment more restrained?

In an attempt to understand Qoheleth's message in this verse, it has often been juxtaposed with the seemingly contrary admonition in Num 15:39, which instructs, "And it shall be a tassel for you to look at and remember all the commandments of the Lord, to do them, not to follow after your own heart and your own eyes, which you are inclined to whore after." Accordingly, some Greek witnesses add "blameless" and/or "not" to 11:9b, reversing Qoheleth's instruction: "walk in the ways of your heart blameless, and not in the sight of your eyes."[43] And in what is a likely response to Qoheleth, Sir 5:2 says, "Do not follow your soul and your strength, to walk in your heart's desires."[44] While these early wit-

---

39. Seow, *Ecclesiastes*, 349.
40. Gordis, *Koheleth*, 325; see also Longman, *Ecclesiastes*, 261.
41. Whybray, *Ecclesiastes*, 162.
42. Fox, *Time to Tear Down*, 317.
43. See Fox, *Time to Tear Down*, 318; Schoors, *Ecclesiastes*, 789; and Longman, *Ecclesiastes*, 261.
44. Fox, *Time to Tear Down*, 318n45.

nesses attest to the saying's difficulty, Murphy describes them as "futile attempts to rectify a faulty interpretation."[45] Provan argues that "It is not foolish behavior that Qohelet advocates here, but life lived out joyfully in the world God has made and governs."[46] Is this so? Or does Qoheleth, as Christianson holds, play havoc with the Torah's command, twisting it for his own purposes?[47]

The perceived incompatibility between Qoheleth and Numbers is given as evidence of Qoheleth's waywardness, wisdom crisis, and departure from the faith. However, there is much evidence indicating that Qoheleth has been misunderstood. 1) The previous joy passage (9:7–10) speaks of divine approval, "God has already approved what you do" (9:7). And its encouragement that "Whatever your hand finds to do, do it with your might" (9:10) is similar to the idea of pursuing found in 11:9b and 11:1–6. 2) More broadly, Qoheleth has presented enjoyment as a gift from God (2:24–26; 3:12–13; 5:18 [19]). Murphy argues that the joy of 11:7–9 is thus, to be understood in the context of Qoheleth's prior joy passages.[48] 3) Qoheleth has earlier expressed his disapproval of indulgence that is excessive, inappropriate, and untimely (10:16–17). 4) Qoheleth's regular criticism of folly and encouragement of wisdom make the interpretation of hedonism unlikely (see 7:1–13; 9:17–10:20).[49] 5) The expression of the sight of one's eyes in 11:9 is similar to 6:9, where Qoheleth says, "Better is the sight of the eyes than the wandering of the appetite." Here, the sight of the eyes is positive and in contrast to being led by wandering desires. 6) Seow argues that "The Egyptian parallels . . . show that the point here is enjoyment. The idiom has nothing to do with how one makes ethical decisions (i.e., whether one follows one's heart or obeys divine orders)."[50] 7) And ultimately, as will be argued below, 11:9c qualifies the matter.

---

45. Murphy, *Ecclesiastes*, 116.
46. Provan, *Ecclesiastes*, 212.
47. Christianson, *Time to Tell*, 116.
48. Murphy, *Ecclesiastes*, 117.
49. Whybray, *Ecclesiastes*, 162.
50. Seow, *Ecclesiastes*, 350; see also 370–71. Note the contrary and curious view of Lee, who sees Qoheleth as intentionally countering the Torah command, which sets the desires of the heart against God's will. She argues that "gladness in the human heart redeems that inner space (cf. 5:19), making it and its desires an appropriate vehicle of moral agency. Indeed, joy in the heart becomes the divine answer to the problem of wayward desire and the destructive side of the human appetite (cf. 6:7)" (Lee, *Vitality of Enjoyment*, 76).

In sum, Qoheleth's call to walk in the ways of one's heart and in the sight of one's eyes represents not an endorsement of sinful behavior but a call to enjoyment that extends from the prior imperative. This call should be understood in the context of the breadth of Qoheleth's teaching on enjoyment and in light of its subsequent qualification in the rest of the verse.

4.3.5 Ecclesiastes 11:9c

The last part of 11:9 brings the third imperative and a different timbre: "But know that for all these things God will bring you into judgment." Given the endorsement of enjoyment in the first half of 11:9, coupled with the supposed departure from the Torah's command, some find this turn to impending divine judgment conspicuously divergent, leading to the view that it represents a gloss by the hand of a subsequent, orthodox redactor, who sought to temper and counteract Qoheleth's hedonistic proclivities.[51] The problem with such theories is that they are purely speculative. There is no textual evidence that this is the work of a later glossator. Further, the topic of judgment is by no means novel; the matter has risen at several points in Qoheleth's address (3:17–18; 5:5 [6]; 8:12–13; see also 12:13–14). Fox is sympathetic to the difficulty that this verse brings but appeals to the evidence. He writes, "The sentence is indeed somewhat intrusive in the series of imperatives, and of all the proposed glosses in the book this is the most likely. But the arguments are not compelling."[52] Thus, one may conclude with Seow, "The line should not be deleted."[53]

Persuaded by the evidence, most scholars retain the verse; however, some still find the matter uneasy and employ alternative tactics to circumvent Qoheleth's wisdom. For example, Longman holds that Qoheleth has no room for final, divine judgment and that this verse's account is merely a "theological reflex" of a confused old man.[54] As such, Longman

---

51. Crenshaw writes, "The second half of Eccl 11:9 may well be a moralistic gloss, inserted to counteract Qohelet's shocking advice" (Crenshaw, *Ecclesiastes*, 184; see also Lauha, *Kohelet*, 205). Lohfink holds that this is a gloss by the same hand who wrote 12:13–14, intending "to protect the text from a libertine interpretation" (Lohfink, *Qoheleth*, 139).

52. Fox, *Time to Tear Down*, 318.

53. Seow, *Ecclesiastes*, 350.

54. Longman, *Ecclesiastes*, 261.

argues that these vacillations revealing traditional doctrine can simply be dismissed in favor of the "reality" that Qoheleth sees.[55]

If Qoheleth's imperative recognizing judgment should not be excised and if it is allowed to speak, one must consider what it means and how it relates to the calls for joy that drive the first half of the verse.[56] Apart from a few outliers,[57] there are three dominant interpretations. First, some hold that one will be judged for enjoying. Longman states that after the call to enjoy life (11:9ab), Qoheleth says that God will judge you for that very youthful enjoyment.[58] Similarly, Crenshaw notes, "There is irony in the juxtaposition of encouragement to follow your desires, knowing that you are simply heaping up offenses for which you will be held accountable."[59] However, this understanding contradicts Qoheleth's repeated description of enjoyment and the ability to enjoy as a gift from God (2:24; 3:13; 5:18–19 [19–20]; 9:7).

Second, some hold that one will be judged for how well one enjoys and for failure to enjoy. As expected, this position understands the call to enjoy not as merely a positive commendation but as a divine command. Gordis interprets judgment for the failure to enjoy life, for such enjoyment is the portion that God has given (9:9).[60] Similarly, Whybray writes, "The best thing for men to do is to accept this and to enjoy to the full what *good* things God has given; and indeed this is what God *requires* of them."[61] For support, Whybray points to other passages speaking of enjoyment as one's lot/portion (חלק), which Whybray takes to mean "his

---

55. Longman, *Ecclesiastes*, 261.

56. While the imperative to "know" is linked with the preceding by a *waw*, the relationship could be understood grammatically as adversative or conjunctive/coordinative (see Williams, *Williams' Hebrew Syntax*, 152–53). Thus, the sentence could be translated with "and" or "but" (Seow, *Ecclesiastes*, 350). It is "a matter of broad contextual understanding rather than grammatical form" (Fuhr, *Inter-Dependency*, 179).

57. Shields argues that while God controls one's fate, one simply cannot know what God requires nor what pleases him (Shields, *End of Wisdom*, 229). Enns argues that the divine judgment of 11:9 is not about one's actions at all but identifies God's judgment as the onslaught of old age and, eventually, death; thus, one should enjoy one's youth (Enns, *Ecclesiastes*, 106–07).

58. Longman, *Ecclesiastes*, 260.

59. Crenshaw, *Ironic Wink*, 91.

60. Gordis, *Koheleth*, 93. Seow takes a similar view as he writes, "Human beings are supposed to enjoy life to the full because that is their divinely assigned portion, and God calls one into account for failure to enjoy. . . . For Qohelet, enjoyment is not only permitted, it is commanded; it is not only an opportunity, it is a divine imperative" (Seow, *Ecclesiastes*, 371; see also 58, 395).

61. Whybray, *Ecclesiastes*, 28; emphasis original.

proper function" (see 5:17–18 [18–19]; 9:9).[62] For Lee, enjoyment is seen as a religious duty and a divine command; as such, "those who fail to enjoy have refused to accept the will of God, and will be called to account."[63] Further, failure to keep this command results not only in personal judgment but also in cosmic chaos, evidenced by the various societal troubles witnessed in Qoheleth's address.[64] But interpreting divine judgment for the failure to enjoy life to the full is not without its problems. Not all of Qoheleth's words regarding enjoyment line up with this position. Qoheleth refers to enjoyment as *hebel* (2:1) and upholds the value of mourning (7:2–4). And Qoheleth does not endorse all enjoyment for he speaks against inappropriate indulgence (10:17). Further, this is not the first time Qoheleth has spoken of divine judgment. In his previous mentions of the matter, it has always been in discussion of the righteous and the wicked, that is, one's moral conduct, and never in reference to enjoyment or the failure to enjoy.[65] This consistency makes it quite unlikely that in 11:9, Qoheleth believes divine judgment is coming to those who fail to enjoy life to the full. Fuhr is right that "there is no evidence aside from this verse that man will be judged over his obedience to the enjoy life imperative."[66]

The third major position is more convincing as it interprets the call to recognize divine judgment as meant to ground and guide all of one's enjoyment, pursuits, and indeed, life. Fuhr argues that this note of judgment, implying that one fear God, serves as "an adversative compliment to balance the enjoyment of life, not as a warning that one's obedience or disobedience to the שׂמח imperative will be judged. In this sense, the fear of God dictates that the wise man establish boundaries in his experience of joy, knowing that the line of distinction between the legitimate enjoyment of God's gifts and the ill-fated enjoyment of sin is an easy one to cross."[67] Holmstedt et al. argue that the advice of the first two imperatives in 11:9 is "tempered, however, by Qoheleth's unswerving belief that

62. Whybray, *Ecclesiastes*, 162.

63. Lee, *Vitality of Enjoyment*, 49; see also 72, 77.

64. Lee, *Vitality of Enjoyment*, 49–50. For Lee, proper enjoyment carries a strong sense of social responsibility; see Lee, *Vitality of Enjoyment*, 129–35.

65. The explicit mention of divine judgment in 3:17 is in reference to the righteous and the wicked of 3:16–17. The judgment of 5:5 [6] is against the fool who does evil (4:17 [5:1]) and sins (5:5 [6]), breaking the Torah's command. And the judgment of 8:12–13 is also explicitly against the sinner who does evil and does not fear God.

66. Fuhr, *Inter-Dependency*, 179.

67. Fuhr, *Inter-Dependency*, 179–80.

everything falls within the purview of God's oversight, including the morality of one's actions in life."[68] And for Provan, "The following of the heart and the eyes is to be carried out in the sure knowledge that there is moral accountability in the universe."[69] Pursue joy but within these boundaries. This understanding of judgment is more in keeping with the rest of Qoheleth's discussion on the matter.[70]

What then does this third imperative uncover about Qoheleth's understanding of joy? This reveals that while enjoyment is good, a gift from God, and can be pursued, it is not an end in and of itself. Instead, joy is qualified. *Hebel* is the result of Qoheleth's quest and the context that one encounters in the world. Joy, to be sure, is a central part of Qoheleth's advice that rises from this *hebel*-context. Yet, this joy motif is grounded by an understanding of divine judgment for one's actions, implying that one is to fear God. Thus, while the two motifs of joy and the fear of God represent the center of Qoheleth's message, the latter is unmistakably foundational.

While the relation between judgment and joy has been discussed, this third imperative still requires further attention. What is the nature of this judgment that Qoheleth speaks of? To begin with the more obvious, there is a judgment of sorts and it is administered by God. Further, this judgment concerns human activity. The judgment is עַל־כָּל־אֵלֶּה ("upon all these"); that is, its scope is broad and surely encompasses the rejoicing and walking of 11:9ab. Throughout the address, the proper human response to God's activities is to fear God. And as discussed in the prior chapter, this includes right conduct; one should act righteously and not do evil. Yet, though one may live righteously, justice and divine judgment may be hard to see in the world (7:15; 8:14); God's ways remain a mystery (8:17). Although Qoheleth cannot discover nor define the bounds of divine judgment, and though it appears at times to be violated, Qoheleth repeatedly returns to affirm its reality. This resolve in the face of mystery has led some scholars to believe that Qoheleth is pointing to a final judgment that lies on the other side of death. Ogden holds that Qoheleth hopes in post-death judgment/resolution; Qoheleth cannot prove this but insists its possibility and in this way, he is at least an early

---

68. Holmstedt et al., *Qoheleth*, 291–92.

69. Provan, *Ecclesiastes*, 212. Provan, however, appears to hold his view rather loosely as he elsewhere states that this judgment could just as easily be about the failure to enjoy (Provan, *Ecclesiastes*, 220).

70. For further discussion, see chapter 3.

forerunner of such thought.⁷¹ Fuhr argues that Qoheleth has not given up on justice; "Therefore, it is best to understand these texts as suggestive of some form, however veiled in the details, of judgment executed beyond the grave."⁷² Bartholomew interprets life after death in Qoheleth's words, though, primarily from his final poem. He writes, "to see death in this section as the end makes nonsense of Qohelet's insistence that finally judgment comes before God. For this judgment to be a reality, there must be life beyond death, and although Qohelet lived prior to the revelation of the NT, he envisions, albeit without elaboration, that life which is a gift of God returning to God, its eternal home (12:5)."⁷³ To be sure, there is a palpable tension between the lack of discernable justice in the world and Qoheleth's affirmation of divine judgment. Despite what Qoheleth sees, he holds to what he knows to be true. Qoheleth may not articulate the how or when of divine judgment, but its reality is sure. While post mortem judgment is not explicitly stated, the tension leaves room for its possibility; furthermore, it is even suggestive of it.

In sum, the third imperative of Qoheleth's final section calls attention to divine judgment. This note is not out of place but is in keeping with key themes found in his address. It serves to qualify not only the commendation of enjoyment but all of one's actions. By implication, one should fear God and conduct oneself righteously/wisely and not wickedly/foolishly. This reveals that the commendation of joy (11:9a) is not the final word and the advice to pursue one's desires (11:9b) is not a licence to sin. Rather, one's relation to God is the foundation that directs all.

---

71. Ogden, *Qoheleth*, 18, 30. For arguments against this view, see Enns, *Ecclesiastes*, 106–07. For Seow, the judgment of 11:9 concerns enjoyment and not sin; Qoheleth "does not speak of God's judgment in the future, as in a judgment day, only a deity who reserves the right to judge at any time and in any way" (Seow, *Ecclesiastes*, 394–95). But Seow concedes that the possibility of an eschatological judgment is not explicitly rejected (Seow, *Ecclesiastes*, 395). However, Seow does hold that the judgment of 12:14—particularly evidenced by its statement that everything hidden will be revealed—concerns an eschatological judgment, even though its phraseology is similar to 11:9 (Seow, *Ecclesiastes*, 395; see also Lee, *Vitality of Enjoyment*, 116; and Longman, *Ecclesiastes*, 283). Note also the discussion of judgment and the afterlife in Hartermann, "Auch dies erkannte ich, dass es von Gottes Hand kommt (Koh 2,24a) die Theologie des Buches Kohelet," 138–97.

72. Fuhr, *Inter-Dependency*, 174; see also 26n102. For his fuller discussion and response to those who restrict judgment to life, see Fuhr, *Inter-Dependency*, 172–76.

73. Bartholomew, *Ecclesiastes*, 353.

4.3.6 Ecclesiastes 11:10

The next verse brings two more imperatives in parallel form: "Remove vexation from your heart, and put away pain from your body, for youth and the dawn of life are [*hebel*]" (11:10).

To begin, the first imperative is a *hiphil* of the verb סור, which occurs only here in the book and means to remove.[74] The second, "put away," is also a *hiphil* and of the root עבר, which also occurs only here in the book and can means to take away, remove, or put away.[75] It carries the same sense of removal as the first verb and can also convey a sense of avoidance.

From where is the object to be removed? Line A indicates לב ("heart"), and line B has בשר (lit. "flesh"; though, many translate as "body"). The heart is often seen as the seat of one's intellect and emotions.[76] Accordingly, some interpret these two locales are referring to the psychological (heart) and the physical (flesh).[77] Others, however, interpret the matter more broadly and argue that "The phrase means little more than 'from yourself.'"[78] Either way, Qoheleth's imperatives here concern that which is clearly undesirable.

The more significant question concerns the objects of removal and avoidance against which Qoheleth implores. The first object is the noun בַּעַס, which means vexation, anger, or grief.[79] This word appears at several points in Qoheleth's address (1:18; 2:23; 5:16 [17]; 7:3, 9), some of which carry more negative connotations, while others are more neutral. For example, Qoheleth says that "Sorrow [כעס] is better than laughter, for by sadness of face the heart is made glad" (7:3; see 7:2, 4). Here the term carries neutral, and even positive, nuances. In contrast, Qoheleth says in 7:9, "Be not quick in your spirit to become angry [כעס], for anger

---

74. *HALOT*, סור, II:747–49.
75. *HALOT*, עבר, II:778–80.
76. Longman, *Ecclesiastes*, 261.
77. Fox, *Time to Tear Down*, 318; see also Crenshaw, *Ecclesiastes*, 184.
78. Whybray, *Ecclesiastes*, 163.
79. *HALOT*, בַּעַס, II:491. Translations vary. Note the following: "anger" (Shields, *End of Wisdom*, 228; Longman, *Ecclesiastes*, 261); "vexation" (ESV; Seow, *Ecclesiastes*, 346; Bartholomew, *Ecclesiastes*, 345); "irritation" (Fox, *Time to Tear Down*, 316); "frustration" (Longman, *Ecclesiastes*, 261, who also interprets "anger"; Provan, *Ecclesiastes*, 212–13); "agitation" (Enns, *Ecclesiastes*, 107); "emotional stress" (NET); "anxiety" (CEB; NIV; NRSV); "trouble" (Murphy, *Ecclesiastes*, 111); "sorrow" (AMP; ASV; CSB; NASB; NKJV); "worry" (NLT); and "care" (NJPS).

[כעס] lodges in the heart of fools." Here, the term is negative. There is something in כעס that marks the way of fools. Thus, the removal of כעס should be associated with the wise and their actions. The question follows, in 11:10, is Qoheleth using כעס more neutrally or negatively? The evidence suggests the latter. First, the fact that Qoheleth commands its removal strongly suggests that it is negative. Second, one could look to 7:9 as Qoheleth's most similar saying to 11:10a; both speak of כעס in the heart, though 7:9 uses a different word, חֵיק (lit. "bosom"), to convey the same idea. Thus, while 7:9 speaks of כעס lodging in the heart of fools, 11:10 commands one to remove כעס from one's heart. Third, it follows immediately on the heels of judgment—this is its most immediate context. This suggests an understanding of כעס as something associated with foolishness/wickedness, something for which one will be judged. Lastly, the parallel in line B supports this reading.

As a parallel to כעס, line B presents as the undesirable object רָעָה. The noun רָעָה possesses a broad semantic range, carrying nuances such as evil, wickedness, misfortune, and disaster.[80] The word is common in Ecclesiastes and is used in a myriad of ways as Qoheleth employs both its moral and nonmoral aspects.[81] Surely, the important question is what aspect of the word is Qoheleth utilizing here. The majority of scholars opt for a nonmoral reading, with varying translations.[82] Additionally, most connect the verse closely with the call to enjoyment that began 11:9. Longman holds that רעה likely means "pain" here and that Qoheleth is advocating the removal of two characteristics, anger and pain, that particularly afflict the aged.[83] Crenshaw sees this verse as a counterpart to the previous one in that for one to achieve the goal of enjoyment of life, one must remove "certain annoyances"; namely, "mental anxiety and physical distress, that

---

80. *HALOT*, רָעָה, III:1262–64.

81. The noun רָעָה, 13x: 2:21; 5:12 [13; 2x], 15 [16]; 6:1; 7:14, 15; 8:6, 11; 10:5; 11:2, 10; 12:1. Note also the adj. רַע, 18x: 1:13; 2:17; 4:3, 8, 17 [5:1]; 5:13 [14]; 6:2; 8:3, 5, 9, 11, 12; 9:3 [2x], 12 [2x], 10:13; 12:14.

82. Note the following: "pain" (AMP; CEB; CSB; NASB; NRSV; Longman, *Ecclesiastes*, 261; Crenshaw, *Ecclesiastes*, 181); "misery" (Whybray, *Ecclesiastes*, 162); "unpleasantness" (Fox, *Time to Tear Down*, 318; Seow, *Ecclesiastes*, 350; Lee, *Vitality of Enjoyment*, 77; Enns, *Ecclesiastes*, 107); "troubles" (NIV; Provan, *Ecclesiastes*, 213); "sorrow" (NJPS); "suffering" (Murphy, *Ecclesiastes*, 111); and "keep your body healthy" (NLT). In contrast, some translations select "evil" (ASV; ESV; NKJV; Bartholomew, *Ecclesiastes*, 345).

83. Longman, *Ecclesiastes*, 261. While this may be true of "pain," the case is less convincing for "anger." And if these particularly afflict the aged rather than the young, it makes little sense to command the young to remove them.

is, that which negatively affects the mind and the body."⁸⁴ Shields writes, "The exhortations here—to expunge anger and physical pain from one's body—serve to facilitate the enjoyment of life."⁸⁵ More than simply facilitating, Ogden reads the advice to avoid pain as synonymous with the call to enjoy.⁸⁶ Against synonymy, Fox argues that the verses are complementary. He writes, "Though that verse advises pleasure and this one counsels the removal of displeasures, psychological and physical, they are not saying the same thing in different words . . . Qohelet here goes beyond his usual advice and teaches that in addition to embracing pleasures, one must also pull the thorns out of body and soul."⁸⁷

While such readings of non-moral counterparts to enjoyment are possible, scholars have been far too quick to dismiss potential moral readings, whether this propensity be attributed to a reflex to seeing glosses, presuppositions of a wisdom crisis, or views of a secular/universalistic wisdom tradition that was only later tied to Israel's covenantal faith.⁸⁸ For many, Qoheleth *could not* have offered a message in line with Israel's Torah. However, the evidence suggests that there is good reason for translating רעה as "evil" and understanding the line in a religious and moral sense. As noted above, moral evil falls within the purview of the word and thus, cannot be automatically ruled out. Second, a moral understanding of "evil" is common in Qoheleth's address. For example, 7:15 laments the wicked one who prolongs his life in his evil. And 8:11–12 says, "Because the sentence against an evil deed is not executed speedily, the heart of the children of man is fully set to do evil. Though a sinner does evil a hundred times and prolongs his life, yet I know that it will be well with those who fear God, because they fear before him." Additionally, as argued in chapter 2, religious/moral vocabulary is common in both Proverbs and Ecclesiastes. The tradition is rooted in the covenantal understanding of the fear of the Lord and expounds upon its primary two ways: the way of obedience, righteousness, and wisdom and the way of disobedience, wickedness, and folly. Clearly, the moral aspect of רעה is not foreign but is a real possibility.

However, merely speaking to the possibility of a moral interpretation is insufficient. The command in 11:10 must be examined to reveal

84. Crenshaw, *Ecclesiastes*, 184.
85. Shields, *End of Wisdom*, 230; see also Whybray, *Ecclesiastes*, 162.
86. Ogden, *Qoheleth*, 211.
87. Fox, *Time to Tear Down*, 318.
88. See discussions in chapter 2.

what is preferable in this particular context. There are many points of evidence that strongly suggest a moral reading is to be preferred. 1) The only other collocation in the MT of עבר (*hiphil*) and רעה comes in Esther 8:3 and displays a moral understanding. Here, Esther pleads before the king to עבר (*hiphil*) the רעה that Haman had plotted against the Jews.[89] 2) Most scholars read the two lines together.[90] Indeed, their structure is identical:

| וְהָסֵר כַּעַס מִלִּבֶּךָ | And remove | vexation | from your heart |
| וְהַעֲבֵר רָעָה מִבְּשָׂרֶךָ | And put away | evil | from your body |

Many (above) who read רעה as non-moral take cue from a non-moral reading of כעס, interpreting synonymies. However, one could just as easily read the reverse, taking cue from the latter that both should be understood in moral terms. And as discussed above, both lines have good reasons of their own to be read in moral terms.

3) The lines highlight a connection between the initial verb סור and the final object of רעה. The verb סור is commonly used to convey a moral turning and while its use in the *hiphil* is typically in connection to the removal of idols, it is also used of evil.[91] Isaiah 1:16 reads, "Wash yourselves; makes yourselves clean; remove [סור, *hiphil*] the evil of your deeds from before my eyes; cease to do evil." Ezekiel 45:9 calls for the princes of Israel to "Put away [סור, *hiphil*] violence and oppression, and execute justice and righteousness" (see also Job 33:17, note the LXX translation of מַעֲשֶׂה as ἀδικίας, "unrighteousness"; and Prov 4:27). Additionally, in Israel's wisdom writings, the verb סור (*qal*) is commonly used in connection with evil and in connection with the fear of the Lord.[92] Job was repeatedly announced as "one who feared God and turned away from evil" (Job 1:1; see also 1:8, 2:3). And the climax of Job's great wisdom poem declares, "Behold, the fear of the Lord, that is wisdom, and to turn away from evil is understanding" (Job 28:28). Proverbs says, "Be not wise

---

89. That the books of Ecclesiastes and Esther are both quite late serves to strengthen this connection.

90. For a recent critique of Lowthian parallelism and a proposed appositional-centered approach, see Holmstedt, "Hebrew Poetry and the Appositive Style," 617–48.

91. For a discussion on the language of repentance, see Boda, *Return to Me*, 24–34.

92. While one must be cognizant of a verb's different meanings in its various stems, the calls for one to "remove [סור, *hiphil*] evil" and "turn [סור, *qal*] from evil" carry the same basic idea; both speak to a moral realignment. The root סור is the second most common in the MT (after שוב) associated with the language of repentance; see Boda, *Return to Me*, 25–26.

in your own eyes; fear the Lord, and turn away from evil" (Prov 3:7; see also 13:19; 14:16; 16:6, 17). Turning from evil, as part of what it means to fear God, is at the very heart of wisdom's message not only in Job and Proverbs but also in Ecclesiastes. As outlined in the previous chapter, all of Qoheleth's references to fearing God have come with encouragement toward moral conduct. It should come as no surprise that here, in Qoheleth's final section, where he imparts his final and central message, he implores the reader to remove evil.

4) The call to remove רעה comes in the context of divine judgment. Many scholars hold that the context of 11:10 is the joy of 11:9ab. However, rejoicing and enjoyment only begin the verse, which subsequently alters course to bring to the fore the reality of divine judgment. It is within *this* context that Qoheleth continues and charges one to turn/remove vexation/evil. In light of future judgment, Qoheleth encourages proper conduct. In fact, all of Qoheleth's references to divine judgment have been accompanied by encouragement for moral conduct.[93] Strengthening this connection, the final word in 11:9 is משפט ("judgment"). The very next word, the first of 11:10, is סור. Building on point three above, how could one familiar with the tradition, after reading משפט, followed immediately by the imperatives סור and עבר, then read רעה and not readily connect the dots? It would seem that non-moral readings unnecessarily sidestep the obvious.

5) The imperatives of 11:10 are followed by the call to remember one's Creator in 12:1, which is equivalent to the call to fear God (see discussion below), further supporting a moral reading. This puts the two imperatives of removal from 11:10 between two imperatives calling for recognition of and submission to God and his role as Creator and judge.

6) The final words of the book offer support as the narrator implores one to fear God and keep his commandments, for God will judge everything (12:13–14). While outside the bounds of Qoheleth's address, the narrator serves as the first interpreter of Qoheleth and strongly affirms and echoes Qoheleth and his message. Shead argues that in the final form of the book, the epilogue is hermeneutically significant for the whole and encourages a moral reading.[94] The epilogue will be discussed at the end of this chapter.

---

93. See discussion in chapter 3.
94. Shead, "Reading Ecclesiastes 'Epilogically,'" 86.

7) Lastly, understandings of רעה in 11:10 as "pain," "sickness," or "disaster" are illogical. For one, even a fool would not want to be the recipient of such things. Why would Qoheleth feel the need to instruct one to remove them? Secondly, for the most part, these things are not under one's control and therefore, it is illogical to command one to remove them. Picking up on this, Crenshaw describes the advice as "pathetic" and chides, "as if that were possible."[95] Is one to really believe that Qoheleth's grand conclusion is to instruct the sick and the suffering to remove the sickness, pain, and/or disaster that has befallen them?[96] In sum, reading a call for one to turn from moral evil is not only possible and defensible but given the context, it is preferable.[97]

The final line of 11:10 reads, "for youth and the dawn of life are [*hebel*]." The Hebrew הַשַּׁחֲרוּת (fm. pl. noun) is a hapax legomenon of an unclear root, resulting in various translations.[98] It may stem from שָׁחֹר ("blackness"; that is, black hair) and serve as a figure for youthfulness, in contrast to שֵׂיבָה, "gray hair," meaning "old age."[99] Alternatively, it may stem from שַׁחַר ("dawn") and figuratively convey the dawn of life. In either case, one finds a figure for youthfulness, a reading supported by the parallel הַיַּלְדוּת ("youth").[100] Still, Fox argues that "black hair" is better

---

95. Crenshaw, *Ironic Wink*, 91.

96. It is possible to read in רעה the nuance "distress" as meaning "sorrow" or "grief"; commanding the removal of this may not necessarily be illogical. However, as noted above, most scholars interpret "pain" and understand the line to refer to one's physical flesh, differentiated from the psychological and the heart/mind from line A.

97. If one still chooses to read 11:10 non-morally as the negative counterparts to the commendations of joy in the first part of 11:9, the overall reading of this thesis remains intact. The exhortation to proper moral conduct is not lost but easily falls under the purview of judgment in 11:9c as well as remembering one's creator/fearing God in 12:1a.

Additionally, the reading put forward here challenges the widely held view that Qoheleth's final section is structured with an introduction (11:7–8) followed by two sections conveying rejoicing (11:9–10) and remembering (12:1–7). If, as argued here, 11:10 does not primarily concern enjoyment, this structure does not work. Instead of reading rejoicing and remembering as the two halves, it would be better to read them as the first and the last. As such, they represent the beginning and end of Qoheleth's final imperatives and the two primary motifs of Qoheleth's instruction; that is, joy (11:9a) and the fear of God (12:1a).

98. Note the following: "dawn of life" (ASV; CEB; ESV; NRSV; Provan, *Ecclesiastes*, 213); "black hair" (NJPS; Murphy, *Ecclesiastes*, 112); "vigor" (NIV); "youth" (NKJV); "prime of life" (AMP; CSB; NASB); and "vitality" (Enns, *Ecclesiastes*, 107; Longman, *Ecclesiastes*, 261).

99. Seow, *Ecclesiastes*, 351.

100. *HALOT*, שַׁחֲרוּת, IV:1469.

than "dawn of life," which would more likely indicate infancy as opposed to the youth whom Qoheleth advises.[101]

The *hebel* statements typically garner a wide range of interpretations; however, the final line of 11:10 has received remarkable agreement. Most scholars agree that in this verse, *hebel* means "fleeting" or "ephemeral"—and this comes even from scholars who exclusively translate *hebel* in other ways.[102] Once again, *hebel* comes as the context from which Qoheleth instructs. Here, there is a sense of urgency—youthfulness is ungraspable, that is, fleeting. Death looms (12:1–7), and there will be divine judgment (11:9). Therefore, heed this advice today!

In sum, Qoheleth's two imperatives in 11:10 carry on from 11:9. Those who opt for a non-moral interpretation of 11:10, such as "pain" or "suffering," tend to connect the verse with 11:9ab, expressing the same sentiment (whether synonymous [Ogden] or complementary [Fox]) but in the negative.[103] To be sure, the removal of כעס and רעה is not without effect on one's enjoyment; however, that does not appear to be Qoheleth's intent here. A closer look has revealed that a moral reading is not only possible but the context makes it preferable. Qoheleth does advise enjoyment but one grounded in a recognition of divine judgment. And in light of future judgment, Qoheleth offers further instruction for one's conduct; namely, the removal and avoidance of evil.

4.3.7 Ecclesiastes 12:1a

Qoheleth's closing poem begins with his final imperative, וּזְכֹר אֶת־בּוֹרְאֶיךָ, commonly translated as "Remember also your Creator" (12:1a). The first order of business is to discuss the words of this opening clause and second, to discuss their meaning.

---

101. Fox, *Time to Tear Down*, 319.

102. While understood as "meaningless" everywhere else, Longman notes that this could be the one verse where *hebel*'s temporal aspect is intended (Longman, *Ecclesiastes*, 261–62). While normally "absurd," Enns sees *hebel* here as "fleeting/transient" (Enns, *Ecclesiastes*, 107; see also Fox, *Time to Tear Down*, 319). Likewise, Whybray departs from his typical reading of "vanity" (Whybray, *Ecclesiastes*, 36, 163) and Shields from "senseless" (Shields, *End of Wisdom*, 230). And as expected, those who read *hebel* as a multivalent image typically highlight *hebel*'s temporality in this instance (see Miller, *Symbol and Rhetoric*, 145–51).

103. Ogden, *Qoheleth*, 211; Fox, *Time to Tear Down*, 318; see also Murphy, *Ecclesiastes*, 117; Crenshaw, *Ecclesiastes*, 184; and Whybray, *Ecclesiastes*, 162.

The main point of contention concerns בּוֹרְאֶיךָ. The word is a *qal* participle from the root ברא ("to create") with a second-person masculine singular pronominal suffix. The contention rises in two forms: 1) the participle's number (plural) is strange (lit. "your Creators"); and, 2) referencing God as "Creator" appears, to some, out of place. The perceived awkwardness of the reference to one's creator has led to the opinion that this phrase may be a gloss.[104] However, scholars have by and large abandoned that direction as it lacks textual support. Additionally, Fox argues that it would not make sense semantically to remove it for the entire poem (12:1–7) is built upon it and the poem would then be left without a main clause; it also cannot be joined directly to 11:10b.[105]

In place of excision, a handful of emendations have been proposed. 1) "Your pit." The BHS proposes the emendation בּוֹרְךָ, "your pit/cistern," often understood to mean one's grave.[106] In a poem that speaks of death, there is some logic behind this suggestion. 2) "Your well/cistern." Crenshaw, drawing from Prov 5:15–18, takes the word as בְּאֵרְךָ, "your well," and understands it metaphorically as "your wife."[107] He concludes that Qoheleth probably "urges young people to reflect on the joys of female companionship before old age and death render one incapable of sensual pleasure."[108] 3) Still, one may read בְּרוּאֶיךָ and understand it to mean "your health/well-being" or "your vigor."[109] Accordingly, the NJPS reads, "So appreciate your vigor" (12:1a). Additionally, some claim multiple meanings. Lohfink suggests that the words for both "Creator" and "pit" can be recognized at the same time.[110] Seow, followed by Lee, appeals to Qoheleth's proclivity for wordplays and suggests intentional multivalence.[111]

Appeals to emendations have greatly dwindled as the majority of scholars have come to reject such recourse.[112] It is true that the proposed emendations may work logically with Qoheleth's address; however, there

---

104. Lauha, *Kohelet*, 204–05.

105. Fox, "Aging and Death," 72n2; Fox, *Time to Tear Down*, 322; see also Krüger, *Qohleth*, 198; and Longman, *Ecclesiastes*, 267.

106. Wright, "Riddle," 333.

107. Crenshaw, *Ecclesiastes*, 185.

108. Crenshaw, *Ecclesiastes*, 185.

109. See postbiblical בּוֹרִי; Crenshaw, *Ecclesiastes*, 185.

110. Lohfink, *Qoheleth*, 139.

111. Seow, *Ecclesiastes*, 375; Lee, *Vitality of Enjoyment*, 78.

112. For example, see Longman, *Ecclesiastes*, 264; Fox, *Time to Tear Down*, 322; Fox, "Aging and Death," 72n2; Seow, *Ecclesiastes*, 351; Ogden, *Qoheleth*, 214; Shields, *End of Wisdom*, 232; and Krüger, *Qoheleth*, 198.

is no need to change the text. First and foremost, there is no textual evidence to support emendation.[113] Second, the reference to God as Creator is not out of place, contrary to the claims of some.[114] Consider the following. 1) Creation is a common wisdom theme—many even consider it foundational.[115] 2) There are many references to God's role as Creator in Qoheleth's address. God has made everything beautiful in its time (3:11), has given the days of one's life (5:17 [18]; 8:15; 9:9), and has made humanity upright (7:29); indeed, he makes everything (11:5). To this could be added a plethora of passages about God's sovereignty (for example, 3:14; 7:13–14). God's role as the creator is a consistent part of Qoheleth's worldview. 3) The final poem references God as Creator. The poem concludes, "and the dust returns to the earth as it was, and the spirit returns to God *who gave it*" (12:7; emphasis added). Thus, there is a portrayal of God as the Creator at both the beginning and the end of the poem. Additionally, 12:7 (see also 3:20b) echoes Gen 2:7; 3:19, adding further to the creational imagery. 4) Qoheleth's final poem begins with the Creator and ends with death. "Creation and death, the two extremities of existence, are bound together."[116] To speak of humanity's end, Qoheleth starts by referencing its beginning. Though Longman thinks the reference to God as Creator "seems odd, and even forced," he concludes that it is the best understanding.[117] Seow concludes, "If the consonantal text is correct, as all the witnesses attest, it is difficult to think that something other than 'creator' is the primary meaning."[118] Whybray argues that Creator is "extremely appropriate."[119] And Gordis argues that anything else is unsuitable.[120] In short, 12:1a, with its reference to God as Creator, is neither abrupt nor out of place but quite fitting.

Third, the plural is not a mistake nor a problem. Many identify a plural of majesty.[121] Others point to its use for emphasis, intensification,

---

113. While the *BHS* proposes "your pit," it cites no textual variants—it is simply an editor's opinion. And the *BHQ* directs one to read with the versions (LXX, Vulg., Syr.) the singular "your Creator" (*BHQ*, fasc. 18, 109*–10*).

114. See Crenshaw, *Ecclesiastes*, 184.

115. See discussion in chapter 2.

116. Ogden, *Qoheleth*, 214.

117. Longman, *Ecclesiastes*, 267–68.

118. Seow, *Ecclesiastes*, 351.

119. Whybray, *Ecclesiastes*, 163.

120. Gordis, *Koheleth*, 330.

121. Murphy, *Ecclesiastes*, 112; Lohfink, *Qoheleth*, 139; see also GKC §124k; *IBHS* §7.4.3. Though, some are against it, such as Seow, who holds that the word should not

or excellence like אלהים.¹²² Fox argues that there is no mistake in the text and that the *yod* represents "a fuller representation of the segol."¹²³ While the precise reason for the plural is debated, its presence is not a problem.

In sum, the reference to God as Creator is not out of place and the plural is easily accounted for. The recourse to emendations is unsupported—it seeks a solution to a problem of its own making. What the text *says* is clear. However, what it *means* is still a matter of much debate.

Before discussing the meaning of this clause, the imperative deserves attention. The verb זכר is common and means "to remember."¹²⁴ The verb can carry a meaning beyond mere intellectual recollection; that is, it speaks of a remembrance that is carried out in one's actions. It is a dynamic concept.¹²⁵ It is "active contemplation by which the object shapes the subject."¹²⁶ Whybray notes that perhaps a better understanding would be "obey."¹²⁷ For, he says, to remember your Creator means to do God's will.¹²⁸ The word has wide theological usage, commonly pertaining to aspects of the covenantal relationship between Israel and God.¹²⁹ For example, Deut 8:18 implores, "You shall remember the Lord your God . . ." In that context, remembering/forgetting is particularly connected with keeping/rejecting God's commandments.¹³⁰ As a negative example, Judg 8:33–34 describes how the Israelites did not remember God and what he had done for them (see also Isa 17:10; 48:1; Jer 51:50). Qoheleth's call for one to remember the creator in the days of one's youth is not merely intellectual recollection but is rather a remembrance that is to affect one's actions and the very way in which one orients one's life. This is, after all,

---

be viewed as a plural but rather the result of a confusion in Late Hebrew between III-א and III-ה verbs (Seow, *Ecclesiastes*, 351; see also Gordis, *Koheleth*, 340–41).

122. Longman, *Ecclesiastes*, 264n10; Schoors, *Ecclesiastes*, 795. Note also the similar honorific plural of a participle in Job 35:10, עֹשָׂי ("my Maker"; see Ps 149:2; Isa 54:5; *IBHS* §7.4.3).

123. Fox, *Time to Tear Down*, 321.

124. *HALOT*, זכר, I:269–70.

125. Ogden, *Qoheleth*, 214.

126. Treier, *Proverbs & Ecclesiastes*, 223.

127. Whybray, *Ecclesiastes*, 163.

128. Whybray, "Preacher of Joy," 91–92. Schoors argues that "in the present context, it denotes remembering God by doing his will" (Schoors, *Ecclesiastes*, 795).

129. Schottroff, זכר, *TLOT*, 385–89; see also Eising, זָכַר, *TDOT*, IV:64–82. In this way, it is not that dissimilar to the verb שמע, which can mean far more than simply hearing but obeying (see Rütersworden, שָׁמַע, *TDOT*, XV:254–79).

130. See Bartholomew, *Ecclesiastes*, 356.

part of Qoheleth's *instruction* that he commands his addressee. Surely, a response is envisioned.

Now that "remember" and "your Creator" have been addressed, what does Qoheleth's imperative to remember your Creator mean? For some, this imperative amounts to a commendation of enjoyment. Whybray writes, "It is imperative to enjoy life, because that is the way to 'remember your Creator,' that is, to do his will."[131] Likewise, Lee argues, "To remember one's 'Creator' is to do the will of God and enjoy life now."[132] For others, Qoheleth's imperative highlights human mortality. Shields writes, "the reference to the Creator appears to serve primarily as a reminder of one's mortality, that life is in God's hands and thus beyond the control of even the wisest sage."[133] And Fox argues that "to think of one's creator is to think of death, for the life-spirit returns to its giver (12:7)."[134] For Krüger, it urges a consciousness of one's "creatureliness" and thus, one's transitoriness.[135] But for most, this reminder of mortality is simply meant to spur one to enjoyment. As Murphy concludes, "Therefore, mindfulness of the creator conditions the enjoyment of youth."[136]

In contrast to these two understandings, some do not make much of this final imperative. Longman interprets the reference "as a pious, but fairly empty, impersonal, and objective reference to God."[137] Rather than positive advice in the final poem, Bundvad interprets complaint. Its mention of God as the giver (12:7; see also 12:1) is "a final sarcastic sting" in what is at best "a thinly veiled accusation" as it blames God for the order that results in human death.[138]

Rather than a mere reminder of mortality and/or encouragement to enjoy life, this writer argues that Qoheleth's imperative to remember one's Creator is functionally equivalent to the call to fear God. There are a few

---

131. Whybray, "Preacher of Joy," 91. This position is reflective of his view of joy as a divine command; thus, "To enjoy life is to obey God" (Whybray, *Ecclesiastes*, 163).

132. Lee, *Vitality of Enjoyment*, 80.

133. Shields, *End of Wisdom*, 233.

134. Fox, *Time to Tear Down*, 322; see also Fox, "Aging and Death," 72n2; Enns, *Ecclesiastes*, 108; and Christianson, *Time to Tell*, 252–54.

135. Krüger, *Qoheleth*, 197. However, he also sees it touching on various other theological points from Qoheleth's address, such as the call to seize opportunities for pleasure, the immutability of God's works (3:14–15; 7:13), and the incomprehensibility of his ways by humanity (3:11; 8:17; 11:5); see Krüger, *Qoheleth*, 198.

136. Murphy, *Ecclesiastes*, 118.

137. Longman, *Ecclesiastes*, 268.

138. Bundvad, *Time*, 70.

scholars who agree. Fuhr interprets 12:1 as a near-synonym to fear God.[139] And Bartholomew argues that the fear of God is given here as the proper foundation, in contrast to the misguided enterprise of Qoheleth's past; he writes, "Remembering one's Creator, in all its richness, subverts Qohelet's autonomous epistemology and provides a new starting point for wrestling with the very real issues his journey explored."[140] But can this position be supported? There is good reason to read the phrase as a call to fear God. 1) As outlined in the above discussion on זכר, remembering is dynamic and should affect one's actions, and the concept of remembering God was closely tied with covenantal faithfulness. 2) Qoheleth's call to remember God should bring to the reader's mind the rest of his teachings about God from his address. Qoheleth spoke of God's sovereignty, divine judgment, that one should fear God, etc. There is a consistent notion in his address that one must recognize God's position over everything and humanity's position before him. 3) There is also a correspondence between the imperatives of removal in 11:10 as a form of "turning from" and the remembering of 12:1 as a "turning to." Youth is fleeting (11:10) and death approaching (12:1b–7); therefore, remove/turn from evil (11:10) and to God (12:1a). 4) Following the previous imperatives, 12:1a comes in the context not of enjoyment but of a call to recognize divine judgment and to remove evil. The fear of God provides a natural foundation that encompasses these aspects, and all of Qoheleth's references to the fear of God are accompanied by them. 5) And as will be discussed below, these are the same three notes (fear, obedience, judgment) struck in the narrator's final message in 12:13–14. The fear of the Lord is the heart of Israel's wisdom tradition as represented in the books of Job, Proverbs, and Ecclesiastes. Here, as Qoheleth's final command, it is only fitting that this root comes through.

Additionally, this understanding of 12:1 as fearing God accounts well for the progression of Qoheleth's address as outlined in the previous chapter. Qoheleth sought wisdom and understanding (1:13, 16), but right from his initial summary of *hebel* (1:14) it was clear that something was awry. In his mid-point reflection, he confessed his failure. The wisdom he sought was beyond his grasp (7:23–24), and he found himself entrapped by lady folly (7:26). He was the sinner ensnared (7:26), the one who departed from created uprightness and sought many schemes (7:29). As

---

139. Fuhr, *Inter-Dependency*, 166–67.
140. Bartholomew, *Ecclesiastes*, 358; see 353–58 for his theological discussion.

Qoheleth increasingly moved from his failed quest to his present and primary goal of instruction, he regularly advocated for a proper understanding of humanity before God. And now, at the end of his address, conveying his final message, he calls his addressee to know that God will judge everything (11:9c), to remove evil (11:10), and to remember the Creator/fear God (12:1a). Proverbs encouraged the search for wisdom. And while the misguided quest of Qoheleth's younger self resulted in *hebel*, the message of the aged sage declares the proper foundation: the fear of the Lord.

In sum, it is clear that Qoheleth's final imperative reads "Remember your Creator." Moreover, this call is functionally equivalent to Israel's wisdom foundation: the fear of the Lord. This imperative, which calls to mind the rest of Qoheleth's teachings about God and is accompanied by calls for the recognition of divine judgment and moral conduct, serves as the foundation of Qoheleth's wisdom. Though the quest was laborious and the route circuitous, Qoheleth's message affirms orthodox wisdom.

4.3.8 Ecclesiastes 12:1b–7

The remaining verses of Qoheleth's final section comprise a marvelous poem. This poem is built on the main clause of Qoheleth's final imperative (12:1a), followed by a series of temporal clauses marked by עַד אֲשֶׁר לֹא ("before"; 12:1b, 2a, 6a). While, for the most part, it is clear what the words of the poem say, what they mean has long been debated. However, one thing is clear: death is coming.

There are many interpretations of Qoheleth's final poem. Ginsburg reads an approaching storm as a metaphor for approaching death.[141] Leahy sees a response to a thunderstorm, depicting the response of a household to death.[142] Loretz interprets a winter's day as a metaphor for old age.[143] Sawyer describes the poem as a parable of a house and its collapse, representing human achievement and failure.[144] In contrast to the many who see impending future events, Barbour looks backward and interprets a poem of urban decay, a city lament over the fall of Jerusalem

---

141. Ginsburg, *Coheleth*, 457.
142. Leahy, "The Meaning of Ecclesiastes," 297–300.
143. Loretz, *Qohelet und der alte Orient*, 192.
144. Sawyer, "The Ruined House in Ecclesiastes 12," 520.

at the hands of the Babylonians in 586 BC.[145] However, perhaps the most common interpretation is an allegorical reading of old age, with various images referring to the decrepitude of aged body parts.[146] Alternatively, readings of the eschatological are also prominent,[147] whether it refers to the end of the individual[148] or of all humanity and even of the cosmos itself.[149] What is to be made of this unwieldy array?

Many of these approaches have come under scrutiny, allegories in particular. The great difficulty with allegorical interpretations is their highly subjective nature and, as concerns Qoheleth's poem, their (in) consistent application.[150] What works in one place of the poem does not work well in another. And most scholars recognize that this approach cannot be applied consistently.[151] Whybray argues that "since the essence of an allegory is that it consists of a *coherent* series of metaphors forming a consistent whole, this is not an allegory."[152] Rather, Whybray suggests that the writer drew imagery from different sources.[153] Similarly, Krüger holds that the changing forms in the section make it more of a collage than a poem.[154] Some images may be figurative but as a whole, the poem is not an allegory.[155] While the common allegorical reading of aging body parts may be enticing, Fox argues that the text largely resists such a

---

145. Barbour, *Story of Israel*, 139. Additionally, Barbour sees this closing poem as forming a bracket with the opening account of Qoheleth's royal experiment (read Solomon's reign) such that the reader is invited to see the whole of Qoheleth's address as a meditation on Israel's demise from splendor (Barbour, *Story of Israel*, 164–65).

146. Whybray, *Ecclesiastes*, 163; Lohfink, *Qoheleth*, 140; Murphy, *Ecclesiastes*, 121; and Loader, *Polar Structures*, 110.

147. Perdue, *Wisdom and Creation*, 236; and Lee, *Vitality of Enjoyment*, 72. Provan sees an apocalyptic introduction (12:2), a community response to apocalyptic darkness as a description of advancing old age (12:3–4), and ecological disaster (12:5); see Provan, *Ecclesiastes*, 214–17.

148. Krüger, *Qoheleth*, 197–205; Lohfink, *Qoheleth*, 139; and Bundvad, *Time*, 64–65, 67.

149. Seow, *Ecclesiastes*, 53–54, 351–68, 372–82; Seow, "Qohelet's Eschatological Poem," 209–34; and Enns, *Ecclesiastes*, 108–09.

150. Longman, *Ecclesiastes*, 263.

151. Whybray, *Qoheleth*, 213.

152. Whybray, *Ecclesiastes*, 163; emphasis original.

153. Whybray, *Ecclesiastes*, 163–64.

154. Krüger, *Qoheleth*, 201.

155. Fox, "Aging and Death," 57.

reading.[156] Consequently, Fox seeks to draw attention to the literal, something many scholars too quickly abandon. He writes,

> The allegorical interpretation has invariably failed to recognize that the imagery, the surface of the poem, is what the author chooses to show us first and most clearly. Rather than thinking of imagery as an expendable outer garb, we should compare it to the visible surface of a painting. The imagery is the painting. We can discuss the painting's symbolism, emotive overtones, ideological message, and so on, but only as projections of the surface imagery, not as substitutes for it.[157]

Consequently, Fox argues for three levels of meaning: literal, symbolic, and figurative.[158] And these are not mutually exclusive—indeed, the latter two categories require a literal base. For Fox, the literal depicts a funeral scene; its description is not of aging but mourning.[159] At the symbolic level, as an extension of the literal, "eschatological symbolism is manifest but restrained" as images of grand disaster are used to depict the death of the individual.[160] And while the figurative (not properly an allegory) is not excluded by the other levels (contra Taylor), Fox argues that it is secondary in importance to them.[161]

For all of its varied interpretations, there is one (generally) unifying feature: the poem is about death.[162] The literal nature of 12:7 helps to make this clear. Fox writes, "This is a powerful poem, even if we don't quite know what it means. Actually, we do know what it means: enjoy life before you grow old and die. What we don't know is *how* it means

---

156. Fox, "Aging and Death," 56.

157. Fox, "Aging and Death," 57.

158. Fox, "Aging and Death," 59–71; Fox, *Time to Tear Down*, 333–49. See Krüger, *Qoheleth*, 202, who also opts for multiple levels. In contrast, Bartholomew considers such working with multiple levels of meaning unhelpful; see Bartholomew, *Ecclesiastes*, 346–47.

159. Fox, "Aging and Death," 59–63; Fox, *Time to Tear Down*, 320–32. Note the reading of Taylor, who argued against an allegorical-anatomical reading and in favor of a literal reading of 12:2–5 as a dirge of a household or community in mourning over a death; see Taylor, *The Dirge of Coheleth in Ecclesiastes XII*.

160. Fox, "Aging and Death," 67.

161. Fox, *Time to Tear Down*, 348–49.

162. For a recent study on death in Ecclesiastes and Wisdom, see Sitzler, *Der Tod in Den Weisheitsschriften Des Alten Testaments*.

it."[163] Further venture into the *how* does not serve the purposes of this chapter.[164] The larger picture is relatively clear.

But why this extended depiction of death? First of all, the theme is not new but has recurred throughout Qoheleth's address (see 2:15–16; 3:2, 19–21; 4:2–3; 5:14 [15]; 6:3–6; 7:15–17; 8:10; 9:3–6, 10–12). Death is a reality. It is, so to speak, part of the context that affects human life. But, one must remember, it is just that—context. Qoheleth describes death but his focus is on instruction for life![165] His aim is not to inform one of the end but to instruct one how to live in the present before that end is reached. And the elaborate and multitudinous imagery, coupled with the succession of temporal clauses, laden his advice with heavy urgency.[166] After all, no one knows his/her time (9:11–12). And so Qoheleth entreats, "Remember also your Creator" (12:1a). But this concluding urgency extends beyond his final imperative and speaks to all the advice of his concluding section, and even his address.[167]

In sum, much attention is often given to Qoheleth's extensive poetic descriptions. There is certainly a place for that, but one must not lose sight of Qoheleth's purpose. He seeks not simply to announce life's eventual end but to instruct the young on wise living in the present. And he does so with a great sense of urgency.

4.3.9 Conclusion

This section has examined Qoheleth's concluding unit to gain an understanding of his final advice and central message. Governed by a string of imperatives, Qoheleth instructs his addressee to remember, walk, know,

---

163. Fox, *Time to Tear Down*, 333; emphasis original.

164. For various overviews and treatments, see the following: Sawyer, "The Ruined House," 519–31; Fox, "Aging and Death," 55–77; Fox, *Time to Tear Down*, 319–49; Seow, *Ecclesiastes*, 351–68, 372–82; Seow, "Qohelet's Eschatological Poem," 209–34; Whybray, *Ecclesiastes*, 163–68; Krüger, *Qoheleth*, 197–205; Longman, *Ecclesiastes*, 262–73; and Bartholomew, *Ecclesiastes*, 346–53.

165. Qoheleth is, after all, addressing youth. Fox writes, "the poem's purpose is not to convey information; it is to create an attitude toward aging and, more importantly, death" (Fox, "Aging and Death," 71). Indeed, the mourners mourn for you—this is *your* fate! (Fox, "Aging and Death," 63).

166. A few scholars highlight the sense of urgency; see Ogden, *Qoheleth*, 215; and Fox, *Time to Tear Down*, 316.

167. The chapter division is particularly misleading here; however, the string of imperatives that drive 11:9—12:1 makes clear that the section should be held together.

remove, put away, and remember. Although *hebel* is pervasive and one cannot control nor know what might happen, one should still rejoice and pursue one's desires. However, lest Qoheleth be misunderstood, this enjoyment is qualified and guided by a recognition of future divine judgment. Therefore, one should remove/turn from evil and remember the Creator/fear God. Further, since life is fleeting and death looming, one should heed his instruction today.

Qoheleth's final instructions are similar to his teachings throughout his address. Yet, it is particularly in this final section that Qoheleth brings together the primary motifs of *hebel*, joy, and the fear of God, making clear the nature of their interrelation. *Hebel* represents the context from which Qoheleth instructs; life will have many days of darkness (11:8b). Joy represents a central part of Qoheleth's advice (11:9ab), but it is not the final word. The fear God motif represents the foundation as one should understand humanity's place before God, recognize future judgment, and conduct oneself accordingly (11:9c—12:1a). *Hebel* is the context. Joy is the advice. And fear God is the foundation.

4.4 THE INTERRELATION OF THE PRIMARY MOTIFS AND THE STATE OF SCHOLARSHIP

This section will consider and compare the work of this writer with the most similar scholarly positions, with the aim to bring clarity to the proposal of this project and highlight points of departure from others.

First, a significant portion of scholarship identifies *hebel* as Qoheleth's message. Whether it be "meaningless" (Longman), "futile" (Crenshaw), "absurd" (Fox), or a plethora of other propositions, *hebel* is elevated as *the* dominant motif and message of the address with the result that all other advice from the sage, including joy, becomes but a resignation. As demonstrated in the previous chapter, elevating *hebel* as Qoheleth's central message misses the narrative progression in Qoheleth's address from quest to instruction and the multifaceted advice that rises from his failure and findings.

Second, many scholars see *hebel* as the problem/context and joy as the message. Accordingly, interpretations of the joy motif range from a meaningless resignation (more common amongst those who elevate *hebel*) to a positive commendation to a divine command. This group of scholars rightly understands joy as a key part of Qoheleth's advice.

However, elevating this motif to first position misses and/or downplays other key aspects of Qoheleth's instruction.

There are, however, a handful of scholars who see the fear God motif as crucially important. In particular, the readings of Lee, Fuhr, and Bartholomew are noteworthy. While not the only ones, these three representatives each elevate the fear God motif but handle it differently and reach varied conclusions. These three will be addressed in turn.

For Lee, fearing God in Qoheleth has a meaning dissimilar to everywhere else in the OT—it means enjoyment. Lee does note that various aspects of piety may be included as part of fearing God but argues strongly that this is not what Qoheleth means nor focuses on and that for him, fear is most importantly, emphatically, and foundationally connected with enjoyment.[168] As such, joy and the fear of God are paired motifs; each comprises an integral part of the other.[169] The fear of God is demonstrated through enjoyment and enjoyment is a religious duty.[170] To enjoy is to do the will of God and failure results in judgment.[171] In the opinion of this writer, Lee makes too much of enjoyment and too little of the fear of God—the fear of God is not first and foremost presented by Qoheleth as a religious duty to enjoy. As argued, the fear God motif is routinely presented alongside notes of moral conduct and judgment and rests much closer to an understanding that is found in Job, Proverbs, Psalms, Deuteronomy, and indeed, much of the OT.

Fuhr takes up a position against Lee's.[172] He interprets 12:1 as meaning "fear God" and argues that throughout Qoheleth's address, the fear of God is presented as a conclusion.[173] While there are similarities with Lee's position, Fuhr ultimately disagrees with Lee's view of paired motifs that overlap in essence and fulfillment, opting instead for two conclusory motifs that correspond in equal balance to the other.[174] He writes,

> Although the "fear God" motif is not as clearly delineated or as common in reference as the "enjoy life" conclusions, it is equally

---

168. Lee, *Vitality of Enjoyment*, 85, 121–22.
169. Lee, *Vitality of Enjoyment*, 1–10.
170. Lee, *Vitality of Enjoyment*, 10, 85, 122.
171. Lee, *Vitality of Enjoyment*, 77, 80.
172. He writes, "The enjoyment of life is not an expression of the fear of God, nor is the enjoyment of life a mandated 'commandment' to which man is accountable" (Fuhr, *Inter-Dependency*, 179; see also 27, 185–86, 191).
173. Fuhr, *Inter-Dependency*, 166, 177.
174. Fuhr, *Inter-Dependency*, 27, 178–79, 185–86.

valid and functions as the essential balance to the 'enjoy life' motif. Thus, the fear of God drives the theological message of the book in such a way that it is completely compatible with other Hebrew canonical works, even to the extent that it contributes in such a way to heighten the piety of the people of God.[175]

Fuhr is right in his critique of Lee; however, his contribution does not go far enough. He is right that the joy and fear motifs are central to Qoheleth's message but, as argued above, the evidence suggests that the two are not presented as existing in equal balance to the other. Rather, the fear God motif is foundational. The fear of God, with its accompanying notes of God's sovereignty, humanity's place before him, future judgment, and encouragement to moral actions, qualifies and directs all of one's efforts in life, including enjoyment. The reverse cannot be said—enjoyment does not qualify fear. While both of these two motifs comprise a central part of Qoheleth's advice, it is clear that one is foundational.

Bartholomew views *hebel* and joy in tension and the fear of God as the answer. The juxtaposition of the *hebel* conclusions and carpe diem passages creates tension and opens a gap for the reader to consider its resolution.[176] This tension grows until it finally breaks in 11:7 and then, in his final section, Qoheleth offers his central message; namely, the exhortation to "Remember also your Creator" (12:1a), which Bartholomew interprets as equivalent to the call to "fear God."[177] This point of reorientation "undermines Qohelet's autonomous epistemology" and forms the proper foundation from which one can approach life with all its *hebel*.[178] Thus, Qoheleth's address leads to and culminates here.

While Bartholomew's reading of the fear God motif as the foundation and core of Qoheleth's message is, perhaps, the most similar to that of this writer, there are several points of departure, three of which will be noted. First, Bartholomew views a growing tension. He argues that *hebel* and joy are set in deliberate juxtaposition to create a tension that increases throughout the address, one that nears a breaking point in 9:7–10, and which is finally broken at 11:7.[179] Few would deny the pres-

---

175. Fuhr, *Inter-Dependency*, 26.
176. Bartholomew, *Ecclesiastes*, 81.
177. Bartholomew, *Ecclesiastes*, 345–46, 354, 356–58.
178. Bartholomew, *Ecclesiastes*, 354, 358. For a similar view, see Beldman, "Framed," 159–60.
179. Contrary to most, Bartholomew is adamant that joy is neither an answer nor response to *hebel* but that these two represent contradictory visions set in deliberate,

ence of various tensions in the address but that a tension builds to the end where it finally breaks seems odd. A closer look at the address reveals that while the joy motif does increase throughout the address, the *hebel* motif actually decreases—it is more prominent in the first half, particularly in connection with Qoheleth's quest. Yet, as Qoheleth confesses the failure of his quest (7:23–29) and moves into the second half, *hebel* fades and Qoheleth reveals a greater acceptance of the limitations of human wisdom and focuses more on his present concern of instruction. If the governing conceptual framework was a growing tension up to a breaking point with a final conclusion, one would expect *hebel* to increase with that tension rather than fade. The gradual diminishment of the *hebel* motif, coupled with the growing notes of joy and the narrative progression of the address from quest to instruction, suggests that *hebel* represents the conclusion of Qoheleth's quest and description of the world while the joy motif is closer to his instruction that rises from that context.

Second, Bartholomew speaks of joy as a shalomic vision that sits in tension with the way the world really is (that is, *hebel*). One by-product of this view is that it treats the many joy passages not as instruction but as reflection about an unrealized ideal—he holds that only the final joy passage breaks the tension and is able to offer joy in the right context. However, in the view of this writer, Qoheleth's various passages speak of joy as a gift from God, as one's portion, and as something good to be received and enjoyed in the *here and now*. They are not lamentations nor tension-producing enigmas, but *instruction*. And this leads to the final point.

Third, Bartholomew's position has the curious effect of creating a separation between the instruction of Qoheleth's final section (11:7–12:7) and the rest of his address. For example, consider joy. Of the final joy passage, Bartholomew writes, "for the first time in the carpe diem passages the enigma of life is set in the context of joy (and remembrance) rather than the other way around."[180] And so, the final passage contains the true message while the rest produce tension. However, a quick read of the joy passages reveals far greater continuity than discontinuity. Is the reader really to believe that only the final joy passage commends joy?

---

tension-producing juxtaposition (Bartholomew, *Ecclesiastes*, 152).

180. Bartholomew, *Ecclesiastes*, 353–54; so also, Beldmen, "Framed," 160. That is, 11:7 affirms life and then 11:8a affirms joy, after which 11:8b notes *hebel*. For a contrary explanation, see Loader, *Polar Structure*, 109, who, noting the *hebel*-joy inversion, attributes it to an intentional compositional effect of having Qoheleth's address end (ultimately at 12:8) as it started: with *hebel*.

Or consider Bartholomew's reading of 12:1a as functionally equivalent to the fear of God. He argues that this (finally) represents the conclusion, the point of reorientation that undermines Qoheleth's autonomous epistemology and provides the proper foundation for life. This implies that Qoheleth's ruminations up to this point belong to an inappropriate/incorrect context, which is only then corrected at the end. Should the reader not also take Qoheleth's prior exhortations to fear God as part of his instruction? Again, a curious separation between 11:7—12:7 and the rest of the address is created. This division is not only unnecessary but misleading as it has the effect of downplaying much of Qoheleth's wisdom. Rather than a linear progression of tension that increases until it is finally broken and the point of reorientation offered, this writer views that a general progression that moves from quest to instruction better reflects the narrative arc of the text. And this movement has a circular quality as Qoheleth oscillates between observation and advice, between one topic and another and back again. But as the circling continues, he gradually leaves behind the quest of his younger self and increasingly focuses on instruction, of which there is much—commendations of joy, calls to fear God, encouragement to proper moral conduct, swaths of sentence wisdom, acknowledgments of the limitations of human wisdom, etc. In the view of this writer, Qoheleth's final section is where he draws the matter to a close by emphasizing the main points in as direct a way as can be. But these concluding points are not new; their threads run throughout the whole. This is simply where he ties them together. After reading and rereading Qoheleth's address, 11:7 does not appear to produce the impression of a monumental shift in Qoheleth's mindset such that it can serve as *the* crucial shift of the entire address, the hinge between faulty and faithful wisdom.

In a field that has predominantly elevated *hebel* or joy as Qoheleth's central message, Lee, Fuhr, and Bartholomew have made significant contributions through the attention they have drawn to the crucial role of the fear God motif. Hopefully, this project will continue to highlight this motif and further an understanding of its place within Qoheleth's address.

4.5 THE VIEW FROM THE EPILOGUE

4.5.1 Introduction

Having reached the end of Qoheleth's address, its place within and relation to the rest of Ecclesiastes requires attention. As outlined in chapter 2, Qoheleth's address is situated within the context of a frame narrator who both introduces (1:1–11) and concludes (12:8–14). While this monograph has focused on the message of Qoheleth's address, the reading put forward here must account for this frame. Scholarship offers a remarkable breadth of interpretations on the epilogue, particularly in its relation to Qoheleth's address—this is matched, as expected, by the myriad of readings of Qoheleth as outlined in chapter 1.[181] If the reading of Qoheleth put forward here is correct, one should expect not only compatibility with the epilogue but support.

The purpose here is not to examine every difficulty and answer every question presented by the epilogue—that would be a project on its own. Rather, the purpose is to offer a brief analysis of the narrator's closing words to show that its assessment of Qoheleth and its own concluding remarks are not only compatible with but, in fact, support the interpretation of Qoheleth proposed in this project. And this compatibility is not garnered through creative coercion but rises most naturally from a plain-sense reading. This section argues that in the epilogue, the narrator affirms Qoheleth and his message, provides a warning to his son, and

---

181. The majority of scholarship holds the epilogue to be a later addition. For example, Murphy, while criticizing the obvious subjectivism of those who appeal to glosses and while pushing for a view of the book's unity, claims that the epilogue is "the obvious exception" and that it is certainly an editorial addition (Murphy, *Ecclesiastes*, xxxiv, 117). In fact, many scholars view multiple redactors at work, the implication of which is that the interpreter is freed to read some verses as affirming Qoheleth and others as completely antithetical—no unity of thought is required. The most common position here is to see two epilogists: the first (12:9–11) upholds and endorses Qoheleth, while the second (12:12–14) offers a warning and either corrects Qoheleth or provides an alternative (Crenshaw, *Ecclesiastes*, 48; and Whybray, *Ecclesiastes*, 169). Others divide the boundaries differently and see 12:13b–14 as a sort of postscript (Seow, *Ecclesiastes*, 47, 391–96; and Fox, *Time to Tear Down*, 360–61).

While possible, theories of later additions remain in the realm of speculation. There is no manuscript evidence in support. Moreover, such theories are primarily based on *perceived* contradictions between Qoheleth and the frame narrator—and these are spurred by various other presuppositions such as a developmental view of wisdom and a wisdom crisis. As per the stated methodology of this project, a canonical approach is employed, an approach that views the book as a whole and as received in its final form as Scripture.

echoes Qoheleth's conclusion. To this end, this section will first address each verse of the epilogue, noting the most prominent scholarly positions and points of disagreement. Subsequently, the message of Qoheleth and the narrator will be compared, both in terms of their respective conclusions as well as their use of the three primary motifs.

4.5.2 The Narrator's Closing Words: Ecclesiastes 12:9–14

The epilogue starts at 12:9.[182] Here, the narrator begins his assessment of Qoheleth and his activities: "Besides[183] being wise, [Qoheleth] also taught the people knowledge, weighing and studying and arranging many proverbs with great care" (12:9). More than simply "being wise," many understand חכם as suggesting the professional designation of a sage.[184] Further, Qoheleth is said to have taught (למד) the people knowledge (דעת), listened (אזן), studied (חקר), and arranged (תקן), all of which are activities commonly associated with the sages. The most straightforward (and majority) reading of this verse recognizes affirmation. Murphy holds that the verse places Qoheleth "firmly within the wisdom tradition."[185] Bartholomew reads clear evidence of the narrator's affirmation of both Qoheleth and his message.[186] The minority who read otherwise require more creativity. Longman, for example, sees an empty professional courtesy that merely acknowledges Qoheleth's industriousness and "lacks any honorifics or terms of respect."[187] The narrator "respectfully commends Qohelet, a professional wise man who worked hard and had good

---

182. As a structural marker and not part of the epilogue proper, 12:8 signals the end of Qoheleth's address and transitions the reader back to the voice of the narrator. In 12:8, the narrator reiterates the theme that Qoheleth wrestled with, that is, *hebel*, before providing an assessment of Qoheleth and finishing with his own conclusion. For discussion on 12:8, see section 3.3.2.

183. For discussion on שֶׁ-, וְיֹתֵר, see the following: *HALOT*, יֹתֵר, II:404; Shields, *End of Wisdom*, 55; Longman, *Ecclesiastes*, 277; Bartholomew, *Ecclesiastes*, 359; Holmstedt et al., *Qoheleth*, 304; Seow, *Ecclesiastes*, 383; and Fox, *Time to Tear Down*, 350. Whatever one concludes on the translation, the verse remains resolutely positive.

184. See Seow, *Ecclesiastes*, 384; Shields, *End of Wisdom*, 57–58; and Christianson, *Time to Tell*, 100.

185. Murphy, *Ecclesiastes*, 125; see also Seow, *Ecclesiastes*, 385; Wilson, "Words of the Wise," 176–78; Boda, "Speaking into the Silence," 264–65; and Shields, *End of Wisdom*, 59.

186. Bartholomew, *Ecclesiastes*, 363.

187. Longman, *Ecclesiastes*, 277.

intentions."[188] Such efforts are ultimately unconvincing in their attempt to escape the verse's positive tenor.

In 12:10, the narrator's evaluation continues: "[Qoheleth] sought to find words of delight, and uprightly he wrote[189] words of truth." Building on the positive assessment of 12:9, the narrator continues the praise, describing Qoheleth's instruction as "words of delight" (דִּבְרֵי־חֵפֶץ), "upright" (יֹשֶׁר), and "words of truth" (דִּבְרֵי אֱמֶת). The most common view reads this verse as positively describing both the form and content of Qoheleth's instruction.[190] Seow argues that the verse points to the "legitimacy and correctness of Qohelet's words" and serves as "an endorsement of Qohelet's aptitude as a sage."[191] In contrast, a few argue for a neutral position. Murphy holds that the verse merely presents factual data in line with some ANE colophonic practices.[192] For Fox, the epilogist is "subtly non-committal" about the success of Qoheleth's efforts and the truth of his words.[193] And, strangely, some read veiled criticism. Although Longman takes the descriptors in 12:10 as clearly positive, he asserts that the contrast between "words of delight" and Qoheleth's chaotic and problematic presentation is proof of the epilogist's rejection of Qoheleth.[194] Furthermore, Longman argues that Qoheleth "sought" but failed; that is,

---

188. Longman, *Ecclesiastes*, 284.

189. The verb וְכָתוּב presents, perhaps, the largest challenge in the verse. This difficulty, however, remains primarily with the grammar and does not much affect interpretation. For discussions, see the following: Holmstedt et al., *Qoheleth*, 305; Fredericks, and Estes, *Ecclesiastes & the Song of Songs*, 244; Shields, *End of Wisdom*, 67–68; Bartholomew, *Ecclesiastes*, 364; and Seow, *Ecclesiastes*, 385.

190. Boda, "Speaking into the Silence," 265, sees these as identifying Qoheleth's message as normative. See also Enns, *Ecclesiastes*, 112; Bartholomew, *Ecclesiastes*, 364–65; and Christianson, *Time to Tell*, 103.

191. Seow, *Ecclesiastes*, 386. Drawing from similarities with the epilogue of the Egyptian *Instruction of Anii*, Seow argues that in Ecclesiastes, the narrator's words here serve "as an apology for the efficacy and sufficiency of the sage's words" (Seow, *Ecclesiastes*, 392; see *AEL*, II: 144). Note also Childs, *Introduction*, 585, who holds that the term "pleasing" is "not an aesthetic description, but rather portrays his writings as 'fitting' and 'appropriate.'"

192. Murphy, *Ecclesiastes*, 127.

193. Fox, "Frame-Narrative," 101. Note also Boda, "Speaking into the Silence," 267–68, who rejects both positive and negative readings of this verse, arguing that they depend on external evidence and that the verse itself is ambiguous in its evaluation—in the end, he refrains from taking a position.

194. Longman, *Ecclesiastes*, 278. However, describing Qoheleth's words as chaotic and void of delight or unartful is highly subjective.

he did not find these words of truth.[195] Qoheleth is thus branded as a "double-failure" and the verse as a whole constitutes strong criticism and rejection.[196] This negative reading fails on two fronts. First, it does not recognize the narrative progression of Qoheleth's address. While the quest of the younger Qoheleth failed, from that context the older Qoheleth imparts much instruction. Second, there is no indication to suggest an ironic interpretation. Yes, Qoheleth often failed to find what he sought; however, he was clear in his reporting of such matters and did not use irony to do so.[197] In short, there is nothing in 12:10 nor its immediate context to suggest irony, failure, or criticism. Such attempted feats of interpretive ingenuity are unnecessary. The plain sense, with the support of the majority, reads commendation.

In 12:11, the narrator writes, "The words of the wise are like goads, and like nails firmly fixed are the collected sayings; they are given by one Shepherd."[198] Now with an expanded scope, evidenced by the plural חֲכָמִים, the narrator brings the larger tradition into view.[199] The words of the wise are likened to a shepherd's goad/implanted nail, with which one would prod the flock. While the basic imagery is more or less clear, the main point of contention is whether this association is positive or negative, that is, whether it represents an indictment against Qoheleth's words as dangerous and hurtful or an affirmation of their ultimate value in leading and guiding. For example, Longman sees the verse as wholly negative and argues that the narrator is emphasizing "the dangerous and painful

---

195. Longman, *Ecclesiastes*, 278.

196. Longman, *Ecclesiastes*, 278.

197. Bartholomew, *Ecclesiastes*, 162–63, 365. Longman acknowledges the subjectivity of his ironic interpretation, but he still holds that it is securely grounded by the rest of the epilogue (Longman, *Ecclesiastes*, 278).

198. Translations and interpretations of מַרְעֶה אֶחָד: vary. Some translate with an indefinite article and emphasize the continuation of the wisdom saying; that is, the shepherd is a wisdom teacher (see Fox, *Time to Tear Down*, 355–56; Longman, *Ecclesiastes*, 279). Others argue that the "one Shepherd" is a strong reference to God. For example, Bartholomew argues for such a connection and identifies an echo of the "One" of Deut 6:4 (Bartholomew, *Ecclesiastes*, 367–68). Childs sees here a statement that all wisdom is from God and holds that "This characterization thus legitimates Ecclesiastes as divine wisdom" (Childs, *Introduction*, 586). Still, others translate "one" but not as a reference to God. Holmstedt et al., *Qoheleth*, 307, argue that one should translate the MT as it stands, that is, "one shepherd," and that this "one" draws attention to and is a "not-so-subtle" allusion to the one shepherd who particularly goads: Qoheleth. For an overview of various positions, see Shields, *End of Wisdom*, 76–84.

199. See Fox, *Time to Tear Down*, 353. But to be sure, Qoheleth is numbered among the referents.

aspects of wisdom teaching, a very appropriate image after presenting the skeptical and pessimistic teaching of the wise man Qohelet."[200] Conversely, Murphy writes that "wisdom sayings are conceived as stimulating and directing those who would hear them" and that "the intention of the entire verse is to exalt the wisdom tradition."[201] Should a positive or negative reading be preferred? In 7:5, Qoheleth writes, "It is better for a man to hear the rebuke of the wise than to hear the song of fools," a sentiment common to the tradition (see Prov 3:11–12; 6:23–24; 9:8–9; 12:1; 13:1; 15:10; 17:10; 27:6). However, Proverbs also warns of the uselessness and harm of a proverb in the mouth of fools (Prov 26:7, 9). While both ideas represent wisdom themes, the narrator makes it clear which should be applied here. First, the narrator identifies the subject of 12:11 not as fools but as דִּבְרֵי חֲכָמִים ("The words of the wise"; 12:11); that is, the narrator is specifically speaking about the wise. Second, Qoheleth is identified with this category. The narrator opens the epilogue by saying וְיֹתֵר שֶׁהָיָה קֹהֶלֶת חָכָם (12:9). And this is followed by a description of Qoheleth as one who taught the people knowledge, arranged many proverbs with great care, and uprightly wrote words of truth (12:9–10). A negative view of this verse requires the similes to *only* communicate the danger and pain of the prodding. A positive interpretation is much fuller as it acknowledges the painful but also points to the larger purpose of guidance and given the evidence of the epilogue thus far, this reading is to be preferred. The narrator does not buffer or suppress Qoheleth's message—he was given ample room to speak—nor does the narrator alleviate all of the tensions nor solve all of the mysteries. Rather, while acknowledging their difficulty, the narrator affirms their value, assuring that the one who heeds this goad will find guidance.

200. Longman, *Ecclesiastes*, 280. Note also the view of Shields, who, based on his reading of 12:11b as "a lone shepherd," writes, "As a lone shepherd must employ painful goads to direct his flock, so the wise use their words to manipulate and coerce their students" (Shields, "Wisdom and Prophecy," 879). Shields has a more unique view in that while recognizing that a shepherd can guide the flock, he identifies the path as that of the mistaken wise men who will lead you astray (Shields, *End of Wisdom*, 83). Thus, while Shields reads the prior verses of 12:9–10 as affirmation, it was for the purpose of recognizing Qoheleth as the preeminent sage and true representative of the tradition so that the narrator can reject and warn against the entire movement (Shields, *End of Wisdom*, 106, 235).

201. Murphy, *Ecclesiastes*, 125. See also Boda, "Speaking into the Silence," 270; and Bartholomew, *Ecclesiastes*, 366–67, who favors the traditional interpretation that affirms the "value of the words of the wise, with the two similes developing slightly different aspects of that value: prodding in the right direction, on the one hand, and providing stability, on the other."

The next verse brings a warning: "My son,[202] beware of anything beyond these. Of making many books there is no end, and much study is a weariness of the flesh" (12:12). There is general agreement that this verse presents an important warning to the son; however, there is great disagreement about what the warning entails. There are three primary views.[203] 1) The verse is a warning *against* Qoheleth/the wise.[204] 2) The verse warns about *going beyond* Qoheleth/the wise and thus, comprises a positive evaluation. Seow argues that the warning is "formulaic: it is an affirmation of the completeness and sufficiency of the text."[205] And Wilson sees "a canonical statement of limitation."[206] 3) The warning concerns the second half of the verse and speaks against endless study and bookwork.[207] That is, rather than trying to answer all of life's questions and solve every mystery, one should recognize the limitations of human wisdom as encouraged by Qoheleth. He sought an understanding and an account of all that is done (1:13; 7:25), but through his failure (7:23–29), came to accept the limits of what one cannot find and cannot know and encouraged humble submission to God (see 3:9–15; 8:17; 11:5;

---

202. In a similar way to Qoheleth's address (11:9), after general discussion, the addressee is brought to the fore and entreated directly as the writer moves to communicate his central message through a series of final imperatives.

203. That is, ignoring a few outlying interpretations, such as that by Ogden, who sees a warning that being a sage is hard work and calls for great commitment, as demonstrated by Qoheleth (Ogden, *Qoheleth*, 229), and Lohfink, who takes the verse in a different direction and sees it as a possible warning "against the overburdening of students through ever more extensive textbooks" (Lohfink, *Qoheleth*, 143).

204. See Longman, *Ecclesiastes*, 280, who sees the narrator as informing that the words of the wise (12:11) are dangerous and should thus be avoided; and Fox, *Time to Tear Down*, 356–57.

205. Seow, *Ecclesiastes*, 393. He draws attention to a similar warning at the end of the *Instruction to Kagemni*: "All that is written in this book, heed it as I said it. Do not go beyond what has been set down" (Seow, *Ecclesiastes*, 393; *AEL*, I:60). And similar to "The end of the matter" (12:13a), its colophon reads, "It is finished" (*AEL*, I:60). Seow also points to similar formulae in Deut 4:2; 12:32; and Rev 22:18–19.

206. Wilson, "Words of the Wise," 178. He writes, "The implication is that in 12:12 limits are being set on a body of knowledge and a warning issued to those who might exceed them" (Wilson, "Words of the Wise," 177; see also Bartholomew, *Ecclesiastes*, 369; Murphy, *Ecclesiastes*, 126; and Crenshaw, *Ecclesiastes*, 191). Additionally, the second part of verse 12 is a further warning (Wilson, "Words of the Wise," 177).

207. Boda interprets וְיֹתֵר מֵהֵמָּה as a discourse marker introducing a new section, dividing the epilogue into two halves (12:9–11 and 12:12–14), leaving the warning then to relate to the second half of 12:12 (Boda, "Speaking into the Silence," 271–73). See also Shields, *End of Wisdom*, 84–92; and Shields, "Re-Examining the Warning of Eccl. XII 12," 123–27.

11:9—12:1). Those who fail to heed his wisdom are doomed to repeat his folly.[208] To be sure, there is a significant measure of compatibility between the interpretations of the second and third views; these find far greater substantiation and are to be preferred over the antithesis of the first.[209]

The final words of the narrator, and the book, come in 12:13–14: "The end of the matter; all has been heard. Fear God and keep his commandments, for this is the whole duty of man. For God will bring every deed into judgment, with every secret thing, whether good or evil." It is clear that the final two verses of the book encapsulate the narrator's concluding message. And there is widespread consensus that the narrator's words here reveal an orthodox position, aligning with Israel's covenantal faith and expressly connecting wisdom with Torah obedience. This is where the question of the relationship between Qoheleth and the narrator becomes most pronounced. What does the juxtaposition of their respective concluding messages reveal? Is the narrator attempting to echo and affirm or reject and correct? Or is the narrator taking a more intermediate approach and aiming to temper, nuance, emphasize, clarify, or redirect? Scholarly positions vary widely and are largely reflective of one's interpretation of Qoheleth's address. The most prevalent positions are outlined below.[210]

The first common view is that the narrator's concluding message is incompatible with Qoheleth's; accordingly, the narrator is rejecting and correcting the wayward sage. Crenshaw views the epilogist's exhortation as a corrective and "alien to anything Qohelet has said thus far."[211] Christianson sees this addition by the narrator as unfortunate and misrepresenting and concludes, "There seems to be no other viable reason for this conservatism than that the frame narrator is again overriding

---

208. This is an adaptation of a popular phrase accredited to the Spanish philosopher George Santayana, who wrote, "Those who cannot remember the past are condemned to repeat it" (Santayana, *The Life of Reason*, 172).

209. For further discussions, note the various references to scholars above.

210. And of course, the field resists rigid categorization; scholarly interpretations differ not just in kind but in matters of degree. As such, it may be more appropriate to speak of the positions as comprising a spectrum from affirmation to antithesis. See Boda, "Speaking into the Silence," 260, who has formulated a chart showing such a spectrum. While some represent extremes, many take mediating positions that see affirmation and antithesis in varying degrees on various points.

211. Crenshaw, *Ecclesiastes*, 192; Crenshaw, *Ironic Wink*, 116. See also Shields, *End of Wisdom*, 6, who paraphrases, "Beware of the sages, for they can lead you astray. Rather, choose the path of true wisdom: fear of God and obedience to his commands."

Qoheleth's more radical message with his own more tacit priorities."[212] And for Longman, Qoheleth's entire address is merely a foil for the true message of 12:13–14.[213]

However, many scholars consider positions of antithesis too strong and seek subtler alternatives such as that of redirection or emphasis. Enns argues that the epilogue does not try to correct or sanitize Qoheleth but offers a "mild corrective," for Qoheleth did not go far enough; thus, the narrator provides the added duty of 12:13–14.[214] Murphy holds that "The epilogue is obviously putting forth an ideal which has been developed elsewhere and which is not a concern of Ecclesiastes."[215] Seow argues that the second epilogist adds the dimensions of obedience and eschatological judgment and while this is not contradictory to Qoheleth, it puts a different spin on his words.[216] And Boda argues that while the narrator ignores many of the significant themes of Qoheleth's message, the narrator's strategy was to emphasize an implicit theme, that of keeping God's commands.[217]

Others see the narrator serving as a buffer between Qoheleth and the reader. Fox argues that the narrator works to ease acceptance by creating a "protective distance."[218] It allows room for Qoheleth's message but blunts its thorns and sets boundaries on wisdom.[219] The narrator does not contradict Qoheleth but by adding a new dimension of obedience (12:13–14), it "relegates all the words of the wise, Qohelet's in particular, to a place of secondary importance."[220] Ogden sees Qoheleth as a revolutionary pushing the bounds—an editor was required to vouch for him to ensure circulation.[221] While Whybray sees the first epilogue as prais-

---

212. Christianson, *Time to Tell*, 114.

213. Longman, *Ecclesiastes*, 38.

214. Enns, *Ecclesiastes*, 13.

215. Murphy, *Ecclesiastes*, 126. See also, Sheppard, "Epilogue," 182–89, who notes that while 12:13–14 has similarities with Qoheleth, only Sirach has the same ideology.

216. Seow, *Ecclesiastes*, 394–95.

217. Boda, "Speaking into the Silence," 278–79.

218. Fox, "Frame-Narrative," 103; Fox, *Time to Tear Down*, 371–72. See also Lohfink, *Qoheleth*, 12–13.

219. Fox, *Time to Tear Down*, 95–96.

220. Fox, "Frame-Narrative," 103.

221. Ogden, *Qoheleth*, 20.

ing, he views the second as attempting to soften Qoheleth's teaching by emphasizing its more edifying features.[222]

Lastly, some see the narrator as affirming and/or echoing Qoheleth. Bartholomew argues that the epilogue affirms not all of Qoheleth's words but his concluding viewpoint and 12:13b can thus, be understood as a summary of Qoheleth's message.[223] Shead speaks specifically against those who view the epilogue as a canonizing addition (Wilson, Shephard), who think the epilogue gets the book wrong (Murphy), or who consider that the epilogist is protecting/buffering Qoheleth in some way (Fox).[224] Shead argues for lexical and thematic contiguity between the epilogue and Qoheleth and that the epilogue/frame encapsulates Qoheleth's words and serves as a guide for reading and interpreting.[225]

How should such positions be adjudicated? While the narrator has been remarkably clear up to this point concerning his assessment of Qoheleth and his message, further clarity can be gained by comparing their respective conclusions. The juxtaposition of the final message of Qoheleth (11:7—12:7) and the narrator (12:13-14) reveals striking similarities. First, there is a similar addressee in "O young man" (11:9) and "My son" (12:12), with both making use of this common wisdom trope. And in both, the only explicit mention of the addressee comes here, at the end of their respective addresses. Second, after revealing the addressee, both speakers transition to communicate their final message, and both do so primarily through emphatic imperatives. Third, and more significantly, there is substantial overlap in their final imperatives. The narrator concludes with three notes: fear God; keep his commandments; and God will judge. These same three points appear in Qoheleth's conclusion. Fear God (12:13) is equivalent to the call to remember your Creator (12:1a). Keeping God's commands (12:13) corresponds to Qoheleth's two imperatives about the removal and avoidance of evil (11:10). And the narrator's declaration of divine judgment (12:14) parallels Qoheleth's note of judgment (11:9c). Further, this judgment was to guide all of one's actions ("all these"; 11:9c), including one's enjoyment and walking in the ways/sight of one's heart/eyes (11:9ab); this is similar to 12:14 and its emphasis on "every secret thing, whether good or evil."[226] The correspondence

---

222. Whybray, *Ecclesiastes*, 169.
223. Bartholomew, *Ecclesiastes*, 370–71.
224. Shead, "Reading Ecclesiastes 'Epilogically,'" 86–91.
225. Shead, "Reading Ecclesiastes, 'Epilogically,'" 67–86.
226. Lee notes that 11:9 and 12:14 have "remarkable similarity in phraseology" and

is not strict in the number of imperatives; nevertheless, the thematic similarities are striking and cannot be dismissed as coincidental.[227] This overlap strongly supports this book's thesis that Qoheleth's final section comprises his central, and orthodox, message. Further, its similarity with 12:13-14 supports the view of narratorial affirmation. It is in this way that the narrator can rightly be said to echo Qoheleth.

In sum, the narrator does nothing to reject, correct, or redirect away from Qoheleth's message. Interpretations of antithesis are largely rooted in perceived contradictions between the conclusion of Qoheleth and the message of the narrator, with the assumption that the former is obviously unorthodox. But, a closer look has revealed that the narrator's conclusion is not only compatible with Qoheleth's message but strikingly similar. In conjunction with the narrator's affirmation of Qoheleth, the similar concluding messages suggest as a preferred reading that the narrator echoes Qoheleth.

4.5.3 The Primary Motifs and the Narrator

This project identified three primary motifs in Qoheleth's address; namely, *hebel*, joy, and the fear of God. It argued that *hebel* represents the context out of which Qoheleth gives his instruction, which centered around joy and the fear of God, with the latter being the foundational principle. If these motifs are central to Qoheleth, and if the narrator is thought to echo Qoheleth, one would expect the narrator to pick them up, so to speak. And if the narrator does so, his use of them should correspond with their use in Qoheleth's address. This would certainly lend support to the reading of Qoheleth put forward here. However, many scholars view the narrator as ignoring much of Qoheleth's address—even among those who see the two sages as largely compatible. For example, Boda writes concerning 12:13-14, "The epilogist, however, does ignore

---

that "the language in the postscript is so reminiscent of Qohelet's imperative of enjoyment in 11:9, it can hardly be incidental" (Lee, *Vitality of Enjoyment*, 115–16; cf. Fuhr, *Inter-Dependency*, 175–76; and Seow, *Ecclesiastes*, 395, who views similar phraseology but differing contents). In fact, 11:9 and 12:14 are so similar that some have thought them both to be glosses by the same hand (Lohfink, *Qoheleth*, 139; see also Crenshaw, *Ecclesiastes*, 48, 184, 192).

227. What may be coincidental is how the narrator's final notes mirror Qoheleth's in reverse order: fear God (12:13a) and remember your Creator (12:1a); keep his commands (12:13b) and turn from evil (11:10); judgment (12:14a) and judgment (11:9c); and every secret thing (12:14b) and rejoicing, walking, and "all these" (11:9).

many of the darker and more pessimistic elements in Qohelet's testimony as well as Qohelet's focus on enjoying creation's delights. In their place, the epilogist makes explicit what is only a minor element in Qohelet's testimony: obedience to Torah."[228] Does the narrator ignore the darker side of Qoheleth's address as well as that of joy and instead, highlight a third area (obedience/fear God) that is only minor to Qoheleth? Each of these three motifs will be considered in connection with the narrator.

The darker side of Qoheleth's address can be summed up with the *hebel* motif. And the narrator by no means ignores this theme but rather, through the emphatic inclusion of 1:2 and 12:8, presents it with a force that exceeds even that of Qoheleth.[229] In addition to these verses, the narrator recognizes the difficulty of Qoheleth's words by likening them to goads (12:11). Further, the warning about endless study (12:12) and the phrase "with every secret thing" (12:14) draw attention to all the unanswered questions and unsolved mysteries that Qoheleth wrestled with. However, the narrator also appears to recognize that *hebel* represents the theme/context and not the final message, for the narrator moves on to provide his own instruction in response. Just as it does for Qoheleth, *hebel* represents the context, not the message. Life's darker side is by no means ignored by the narrator; it is put in its place.

The fear of God is memorably declared in 12:13–14 as the pinnacle of the narrator's words and his central message. The previous chapter outlined Qoheleth's use of this motif and noted how it was commonly accompanied by notes of judgment and encouragement of moral conduct. This chapter has shown the dominance of this motif in Qoheleth's final section as the foundation of his instruction as well as its similarities with 12:13–14. One could speak of Torah obedience as a muted theme for Qoheleth if one means that Torah obedience is not explicitly mentioned. However, the fear God motif, which includes a call to turn from evil (read Torah Obedience), is central to Qoheleth's wisdom and is thus, certainly not minor. It may not occur with the same frequency as *hebel*, but it is elevated as the very heart of his message.

For being such a prominent motif in Qoheleth's address, joy is noticeably subdued in the narrator's words. It is possible that the narrator makes a passing reference when he says, "[Qoheleth] sought to find

---

228. Boda, "Speaking into the Silence," 278–79; see also Murphy, *Ecclesiastes*, 126.

229. The concentration of the word הבל (five out of the eight words in 1:2 and three out of the six words in 12:8) is far greater than anywhere in Qoheleth's address and the only three uses of the superlative (הבל הבלים) occur in 1:2 (x2) and 12:8.

words of delight, and uprightly he wrote words of truth" (12:10; emphasis added).[230] Additionally, the joy motif finds an implicit reference in 12:14, as the narrator notes that God will bring "every deed" and "every secret thing" into judgment. As noted above, this verse particularly echoes 11:9c and its note of judgment on "all these," which encompasses the enjoyment of 11:9ab as its most proximate referent. As such, the joy motif may lie in the background but is not forgotten. It is also worth noting that the narrator says nothing to contradict nor reject Qoheleth's commendations of joy. Still, this motif is quite restrained in comparison to its prevalence in Qoheleth's address. This suggests that the joy motif is not the final word. And it would appear that the narrator focuses on reiterating the foundation that is to guide all of one's enjoyment and life; namely, the fear of God. After all, the narrator only offers a brief response and does not have the length to address Qoheleth's breadth; thus, focusing on what is most foundational would not be inappropriate nor a misrepresentation. In this way, the narrator's understanding of the relationship between the primary motifs corresponds to Qoheleth's.

In sum, the narrator gives clear recognition to the difficult side of Qoheleth's address. And the fear God motif, with all that it entails, is certainly not a minor theme for Qoheleth. While joy is, perhaps, only implicitly mentioned by the narrator, it would seem that the narrator focuses on the foundation that is to guide all of one's actions, revealing that joy is not the final message. In this way, the narrator puts forward a view of the interrelation of these primary motifs that is fully compatible with Qoheleth's. And ultimately, this supports this project's reading of Qoheleth's message.

4.5.4 Conclusion

This section has considered Qoheleth's address from the view of the narrator, particularly as represented in the book's epilogue. The opening verses of the epilogue (12:9–10) provide clear affirmation of Qoheleth and his teachings. While acknowledging the difficulty of his words, the narrator upholds their guiding value (12:11). Moving past assessment and toward instruction, the narrator warns his son (12:12). One should learn from Qoheleth's failures and successes, heeding his hard-earned wisdom and

---

230. Though "words of delight" is commonly thought to refer to the form of Qoheleth's writing (that is, well written, carefully crafted proverbs, etc.), it may be that this phrase gives recognition to Qoheleth's pronounced calls for enjoyment.

accepting human limitations. The narrator then concludes with his final and emphatic instruction (12:13–14), echoing Qoheleth's central teaching and displaying a similar understanding of the interrelation of the primary motifs. Every verse of the epilogue comprises an affirmation of Qoheleth/his message. While this affirmation is more implicit at times, it at no point reaches anything near antithesis. The most natural reading of the text finds affirmation.

4.6 CONCLUSION

After considering the context and shape of Qoheleth's address in the previous chapters, this chapter has focused on Qoheleth's central message. Qoheleth's final section has been identified as 11:7—12:7, a unit that is particularly governed by a string of imperatives as Qoheleth emphatically delivers his final instruction. Qoheleth begins by commending joy and that one pursues one's desires, but this is shortly qualified and grounded by a recognition of future divine judgment. In light of this coming judgment, Qoheleth exhorts one to live properly before God by turning from evil. Lastly, Qoheleth commands that one remembers the Creator, a call functionally equivalent to the fear of God. And this call is followed by a poem depicting one's death, adding a strong sense of urgency to the message. Qoheleth's final instructions are not new; they have risen at various points throughout his address. It is here, however, that Qoheleth particularly brings these various threads together and in so doing, makes clear their interrelation. *Hebel* represents the context from which Qoheleth puts forward his instruction of enjoyment of life and the fear of God, with the latter being foundational to the former.

And turning to the epilogue, this chapter considered the most common interpretations and points of scholarly disagreement and revealed that the most natural reading is one of affirmation as the narrator upholds Qoheleth and echoes his message. In this way, the epilogue supports this chapter's reading of the message of Qoheleth's address.

Conclusion

Taking a canonical approach, this project looked at the book of Ecclesiastes as a whole and pursued a theological interpretation of Qoheleth's message within its more immediate and broader canonical context. This project argued that the narrative of Qoheleth's address progressed to a conclusion in 11:7—12:7, in which Qoheleth brought together the primary motifs of *hebel*, joy, and the fear of God, made clear their interrelation, and conveyed his central message. While this instruction, rising from the context of *hebel*, commended joy, it was the fear of God that constituted the foundation of Qoheleth's wisdom.

First, chapter one considered the state of scholarship and revealed how most scholars identify Qoheleth's central message with one or more of Qoheleth's key motifs; that is, *hebel*, joy, and the fear of God. Those who elevate *hebel* tend to read joy as a resignation. Those who read joy as the core tenet typically read *hebel* not as a conclusion but as the situation to which Qoheleth offers his counsel. A minority of scholars ascribe more weight to the fear of God motif, reading it in connection with joy as Qoheleth's advice or on its own as Qoheleth's foundational instruction.

Chapter two examined the context of Qoheleth and argued for three contextual levels. First, Qoheleth's address comes in the context of a hermeneutically significant narrative frame. Second, Qoheleth comes in the context of Israel's wisdom tradition and has a particular connection with Proverbs. Moreover, this connection is complementary and not indicative of a wisdom crisis. Third, this chapter argued for a close, complementary relationship between Israel's wisdom books and the rest of the OT. It argued that Israel's wisdom was not universal nor rooted in creation but in a covenantal relationship with the Lord.

Chapter three analyzed the design of Qoheleth. It argued that the address should be read as a narrative, providing cohesion to the whole as it unites all of his investigations and counsels. It also recognized a general progression from quest to instruction, one that purposefully culminates in Qoheleth's concluding section. Further, this chapter examined Qoheleth's key motifs. First, *hebel* was seen to represent the conclusion of the search of Qoheleth's younger self; moreover, this became the context for his subsequent instruction. Accordingly, *hebel* was not the message of the aged Qoheleth. Second, the joy motif increased throughout his address as it led to Qoheleth's final section and comprised a key part of his counsel. Third, the fear of God motif represented a recurrent part of Qoheleth's instruction. Thus, these motifs complement the narrative reading.

Lastly, chapter four examined Qoheleth's final section (11:7—12:7) in an effort to discern his central message. In that final unit, it was found that Qoheleth brought together his primary motifs, solidifying for the reader his understanding of their interrelation. Rising from the context of *hebel*, Qoheleth commended enjoyment and the pursuit of one's desires. However, this advice was tempered and guided by a recognition of future divine judgment. Accordingly, Qoheleth commanded that one turn from evil and remember one's Creator, a call functionally equivalent to the tradition's foundational dictum, the fear of the Lord. This chapter also brought the narrator's evaluation to bear on the matter. The epilogue was revealed to express strong affirmation of both Qoheleth and his message. Moreover, the narrator's own conclusion was shown to echo Qoheleth's.

As with any project, there are limitations; accordingly, a few concessions are in order. First, in discussing Qoheleth's canonical context, this monograph has focused on similarities both between Ecclesiastes and Proverbs and between these wisdom books and the OT. This emphasis was necessary to display their complementary relationship and to push back against long-held views of antithesis. There is much room here for further study, not only to articulate differences and unique contributions but also to further an understanding of the various relationships between these compatible, complementary witnesses. Second, this project required selectivity in its discussion of Qoheleth's testimony, leaving parts unaddressed. While those areas judged most crucial were covered, additional investigation into the many corners of Qoheleth's address would serve to further reveal the richness of his wisdom and, in the opinion of this writer, support the proposed thesis. And third, while the aim was to present a canonical reading, it does not claim to represent the only one.

That being said, the thesis argued here offers a defensible reading of the whole that accounts for its most significant and difficult parts in an appealing and compelling way.

Qoheleth is honest about life's difficulties, evils, and mysteries, but his response is not one of skepticism, cynicism, or hedonism. Rather, Qoheleth encourages humble submission before God, the one who is sovereign over all and who will, in the end, reveal all and judge all. Qoheleth stands in the canon as a faithful witness, offering counsel for navigating all that life brings. And like many who came before him, he proclaims: the fear of the Lord, that is wisdom.

Bibliography

Ansberry, Christopher B. "Wisdom and Biblical Theology." In *Interpreting Old Testament Wisdom Literature*, edited by David G. Firth and Lindsay Wilson, 174–93. Downers Grove, IL: InterVarsity, 2017.

Antic, Radisa. "Cain, Abel, Seth, and the Meaning of Human Life as Portrayed in the Books of Genesis and Ecclesiastes." *AUSS* 44 (2006) 203–11.

Ballard Jr., Harold Wayne, and Dennis Tucker Jr. eds. *An Introduction to Wisdom Literature and the Psalms*. Macon, GA: Mercer University Press, 2000.

Baltzer, Klaus. "Women and War in Qohelet 7:23–8:1a." *HTR* 80 (1987) 127–32.

Barbour, Jennie. *The Story of Israel in the Book of Qohelet: Ecclesiastes as Cultural Memory*. Oxford: Oxford University Press, 2012.

Bartholomew, Craig G. *Ecclesiastes*. BCOTWP. Grand Rapids: Baker Academic, 2009.

———. "Old Testament Wisdom Today." In *Interpreting Old Testament Wisdom Literature*, edited by David G. Firth and Lindsay Wilson, 3–33. Downers Grove, IL: InterVarsity, 2017.

———. *Reading Ecclesiastes: Old Testament Exegesis and Hermeneutical Theory*. AnBib 139. Rome: Pontifical Biblical Institute, 1998.

———. "The Theology of Ecclesiastes." In *The Words of the Wise Are Like Goads: Engaging Qohelet in the 21st Century*, edited by Mark J. Boda et al., 367–86. Winona Lake, IN: Eisenbrauns, 2013.

Bartholomew, Craig G., and Ryan P. O'Dowd. *Old Testament Wisdom Literature: A Theological Introduction*. Downers Grove, IL: IVP Academic, 2011.

Belcher Richard P., Jr. *Finding Favor in the Sight of God: A Theology of Wisdom Literature*. Downers Grove, IL: InterVarsity, 2018.

Beldman, David J. H. "Framed! Structures in Ecclesiastes." In *The Words of the Wise Are Like Goads: Engaging Qohelet in the 21st Century*, edited by Mark J. Boda et al., 137–61. Winona Lake, IN: Eisenbrauns, 2013.

Boda, Mark J. *Return to Me: A Biblical Theology of Repentance*. NSBT. Downers Grove, IL: InterVarsity, 2015.

———. "Speaking into the Silence: The Epilogue of Ecclesiastes." In *The Words of the Wise Are Like Goads: Engaging Qohelet in the 21st Century*, edited by Mark J. Boda, 257–79. Winona Lake, IN: Eisenbrauns, 2013.

Boda, Mark J., Kevin Chau, and Beth LaNeel Tanner eds. *Inner-Biblical Allusion in the Poetry of Wisdom and Psalms*. LHBOTS 659. London: T. & T. Clark, 2018.

Boda, Mark J. et al., eds. *The Words of the Wise Are Like Goads: Engaging Qohelet in the 21st Century*. Winona Lake, IN: Eisenbrauns, 2013.

Bolin, Thomas M. *Ecclesiastes and the Riddle of Authorship*. BibleWorld. New York: Routledge, 2017.

Bollhagen, James G. *Ecclesiastes*. ConcC. Saint Louis: Concordia, 2011.

Bonaventure, St. *Commentary on Ecclesiastes*. Edited and translated by R. J. Karris and C. Murray. Works of St. Bonaventure 7. St. Bonaventure, NY: Franciscan Institute, 2005.

Boström, Lennart. "Retribution and Wisdom Literature." In *Interpreting Old Testament Wisdom Literature*, edited by David G. Firth and Lindsay Wilson, 134–54. Downers Grove, IL: InterVarsity, 2017.

Breitkopf, Alexander W. *Job: From Lament to Penitence*. Hebrew Bible Monographs 92. Sheffield: Sheffield Phoenix, 2020.

Brown, Stephen G. "Structure in Ecclesiastes." *ERT* 14 (1990) 195–208.

Brueggemann, Walter A. *In Man We Trust: The Neglected Side of Biblical Faith*. Richmond, VA: John Knox, 1972.

———. "The Social Significance of Solomon as a Patron of Wisdom." In *The Sage in Israel and the Ancient Near East*, edited by John G. Gammie and Leo G. Perdue, 117–32. Winona Lake, IN: Eisenbrauns, 1990.

Brown, William P. *Wisdom's Wonder: Character, Creation, and Crisis in the Bible's Wisdom Literature*. Grand Rapids: Eerdmans, 2014.

Bundvad, Mette. *Time in the Book of Ecclesiastes*. Oxford: Oxford University Press, 2015.

Castellino, George. "Qohelet and His Wisdom." *CBQ* 30 (1968) 15–28.

Childs, Brevard S. *Biblical Theology of the Old and New Testaments: Theological Reflection on the Christian Bible*. Minneapolis: Fortress, 1993.

———. *Introduction to the Old Testament as Scripture*. Philadelphia: Fortress, 1979.

Christianson, Eric S. *Ecclesiastes Through the Centuries*. BBC. Malden, MA: Blackwell, 2007.

———. *A Time to Tell: Narrative Strategies in Ecclesiastes*. JSOTSup 280. Sheffield: Sheffield Academic, 1998.

Clines, David J. A. *Job 1–20*. WBC 17. Waco, TX: Word, 1989.

Collins, John J. *Jewish Wisdom in the Hellenistic Age*. Louisville: Westminster John Knox, 1997.

Craigie, Peter C. *The Book of Deuteronomy*. NICOT. Grand Rapids: Eerdmans, 1976.

Crenshaw, James L. *Ecclesiastes: A Commentary*. OTL. London: SCM, 1988.

———. *Old Testament Wisdom: An Introduction*. 3rd ed. Louisville: Westminster John Knox, 2010.

———. *Qoheleth: The Ironic Wink*. Studies on Personalities of the Old Testament. Columbia: University of South Carolina Press, 2013.

Crüsemann, Frank. "The Unchangeable World: The 'Crisis of Wisdom' in Koheleth." In *God of the Lowly: Socio-Historical Interpretations of the Bible*, edited by Willy Schottroff and Wolfgang Stegemann, 57–77. Translated by Matthew J. O'Connell. Maryknoll, NY: Orbis, 1984.

Dahood, M. J. "Qoheleth and Recent Discoveries." *Bib* 39 (1958) 302–18.

Davis, Ellen F. *Proverbs, Ecclesiastes, and the Song of Songs*. Westminster Bible Companion. Louisville: Westminster John Knox, 2000.

deClaissé-Walford, Nancy L., ed. *The Shape and Shaping of the Book of Psalms: The Current State of Scholarship*. AIL 20. Atlanta: SBL Press, 2014.

deClaissé-Walford, Nancy L., Rolf A. Jacobson, and Beth LaNeel Tanner. *The Book of Psalms*. NICOT. Grand Rapids: Eerdmans, 2014.
Delitzsch, Franz. *Commentary on the Song of Songs and Ecclesiastes*. Translated by M. G. Easton. Grand Rapids: Eerdmans, 1950.
Dell, Katharine J. "Ecclesiastes as Wisdom: Consulting Early Interpreters." *VT* 45 (1994) 301–29.
―――. "Exploring Intertextual Links Between Ecclesiastes and Genesis 1–11." In *Reading Ecclesiastes Intertextually*, edited by Katherine Dell and Will Kynes, 3–14. LHBOTS 587. London: T. & T. Clark, 2014.
―――. *Interpreting Ecclesiastes: Readers Old and New*. Winona Lake, IN: Eisenbrauns, 2013.
―――. "Reading Ecclesiastes with the Scholars." In *Interpreting Old Testament Wisdom Literature*, edited by David G. Firth and Lindsay Wilson, 81–99. Downers Grove, IL: InterVarsity, 2017.
Dell, Katharine J., and Will Kynes. *Reading Ecclesiastes Intertextually*. LHBOTS 587. London: T. & T. Clark, 2014.
Eichrodt, Walther. *Theology of the Old Testament*. Vol. 2. Translated by J. A. Baker. OTL. Philadelphia: Westminster, 1967.
Enns, Peter. *Ecclesiastes*. THOTC. Grand Rapids: Eerdmans, 2011.
Estes, Daniel J. *Handbook on the Wisdom Books and Psalms*. Grand Rapids: Baker Academic, 2005.
―――. "Wisdom and Biblical Theology." In *Dictionary of the Old Testament Wisdom, Poetry, and Writings*, edited by Tremper Longman III and Peter Enns, 853–58. Downers Grove, IL: InterVarsity, 2008.
Fidler, Ruth. "Qoheleth in the 'House of God': Text and Intertext in Qoh 4:17–5:6 (Eng 5:1–7)." *HS* 47 (2006) 7–21.
Firth, David G. "Worrying about the wise: Wisdom in Old Testament Narrative." In *Interpreting Old Testament Wisdom Literature*, edited by David G. Firth and Lindsay Wilson, 155–73. Downers Grove, IL: InterVarsity, 2017.
Firth, David G., and Lindsay Wilson, eds. *Interpreting Old Testament Wisdom Literature*. Downers Grove, IL: InterVarsity, 2017.
Firth, David G., and Philip S. Johnston, eds. *Interpreting the Psalms: Issues and Approaches*. Downers Grove, IL: InterVarsity, 2005.
Fitschen, Florian. *"Eine Gabe Gottes ist es": Schöpfungstheologie im Koheletbuch*. Kieler Theologische Reihe 17. Münster: LIT, 2020.
Forti, Tova. "*Gattung* and *Sitz im Leben*: Methodological Vagueness in Defining Wisdom Psalms." In *Was There a Wisdom Tradition? New Prospects in Israelite Wisdom Studies*, edited by Mark R. Sneed, 205–20. AIL 23. Atlanta: SBL Press, 2015.
Fox, Michael V. "Aging and Death in Qoheleth 12." *JSOT* 42 (1988) 55–77.
―――. *Ecclesiastes* קהלת: *The Traditional Hebrew Text with the New JPS Translation*. JPS Bible Commentary. Philadelphia: Jewish Publication Society, 2004.
―――. "Frame Narrative and Composition in the Book of Qohelet." *HUCA* 48 (1977) 83–106.
―――. *Proverbs 1–9: A New Translation with Introduction and commentary*. AB 18A. New York: Doubleday, 2000.
―――. *Proverbs 10–31: A New Translation with Introduction and commentary*. AB 18B. New York, NY: Doubleday, 2009.
―――. *Qohelet and his Contradictions*. JSOTSup 71. Decatur, GA: Almond, 1989.

―――. *A Time to Tear Down and A Time to Build Up: A Rereading of Ecclesiastes*. 1999. Reprint, Eugene, OR: Wipf & Stock, 2010.

―――. "Wisdom in Qoheleth." In *In Search of Wisdom: Essays in Memory of John G. Gammie*, edited by Leo G. Perdue, Bernard Brandon Scott, and William Johnston Wiseman, 115–31. Louisville: Westminster John Knox, 1993.

Fredericks, Daniel C. *Coping with Transience: Ecclesiastes on Brevity in Life*. BibSem 18. Sheffield: JSOT Press, 1993.

Fredericks, Daniel C., and Daniel J. Estes. *Ecclesiastes and the Song of Songs*. ApOTC. Nottingham, England: Apollos, 2010.

Frydrych, Tomáš. *Living Under the Sun: Examination of Proverbs and Qoheleth*. VTSup 90. Leiden: Brill, 2002.

Fuhr, Richard Alan. *An Analysis of the Inter-Dependency of the Prominent Motifs Within the Book of Qohelet*. SBL 151. New York, NY: Peter Lang, 2013.

Ginsburg, Christian D. *Coheleth, commonly called the Book of Ecclesiastes*. London: Longman, 1861.

Gordis, Robert. *Koheleth—the Man and His World: A Study of Ecclesiastes*. 3rd augmented ed. New York, NY: Schocken, 1985.

Grant, J.A. "Wisdom and Covenant." In *Dictionary of the Old Testament Wisdom, Poetry, and Writings*, edited by Tremper Longman III and Peter Enns, 858–63. Downers Grove, IL: InterVarsity, 2008.

Greidanus, Sidney. *Preaching Christ From Ecclesiastes: Foundations for Expository Sermons*. Grand Rapids: Eerdmans, 2010.

Gunkel, Hermann. "The Literature of Ancient Israel." In *Relating to the Text: Interdisciplinary and Form-Critical Insights on the Bible*, edited by Timothy J. Sandoval and Carleen Mandolfo, translated by Armin Siedlecki, 26–83. JSOTSup 384. London: T. & T. Clark, 2003.

Hartermann, Viktoria. "Auch dies erkannte ich, dass es von Gottes Hand kommt (Koh 2,24a) die Theologie des Buches Kohelet." PhD, Carl von Ossietzky Universität, 2017.

Hartley, John E. *The Book of Job*. NICOT. Grand Rapids: Eerdmans, 1988.

Hatton, Peter T. H. *Contradiction in the Book of Proverbs: The Deep Waters of Counsel*. SOTSMS. 2008. Reprint, New York, NY: Routledge, 2016.

Heiser, Michael S. *The Unseen Realm: Recovering the Supernatural Worldview of the Bible*. Bellingham, WA: Lexham, 2015.

Hengel, Martin. *Judaism and Hellenism: Studies in Their Encounter in Palestine During the Early Hellenistic Period*. 2 vols. Translated by John Bowden. 1974. Reprint, Eugene, OR: Wipf & Stock, 2003.

Hobbins, John F. "The Poetry of Qohelet." In *The Words of the Wise Are Like Goads: Engaging Qohelet in the 21st Century*, edited by Mark J. Boda et al., 163–92. Winona Lake, IN: Eisenbrauns, 2013.

Holmstedt, Robert D. "אֲנִי וְלִבִּי: The Syntactical Encoding of the Collaborative Nature of Qohelet's Experiment." *JHebS* 9 (2009) 1–26.

―――. "Hebrew Poetry and the Appositive Style: Parallelism; *Requiescat in pace*." *VT* 69 (2019) 617–48.

Holmstedt, Robert D., John A. Cook, and Phillip S. Marshall. *Qoheleth: A Handbook on the Hebrew Text*. Waco: Baylor University Press, 2017.

Jackson, D. R. "Solomon." In *Dictionary of the Old Testament Wisdom, Poetry, and Writings*, edited by Tremper Longman III and Peter Enns, 733–37. Downers Grove, IL: InterVarsity, 2008.

Jacobson, Diane. "Wisdom Language in the Psalms." In *The Oxford Handbook of the Psalms*, edited by William P. Brown, 147–57. New York, NY: Oxford University Press, 2014.

Jarick, John, ed. *Perspectives on Israelite Wisdom: Proceedings of the Oxford Old Testament Seminar*. LHBOTS 618. London: Bloomsbury T. & T. Clark, 2016.

Jong, Stephan de. "A Book on Labour: The Structuring Principles and the Main Theme of the Book of Qohelet." *JSOT* 54 (1992) 107–16.

———. "God in the Book of Qohelet: A Reappraisal of Qohelet's Place in the Old Testament." *VT* 47 (1997) 154–67.

Ingram, Doug. "The Riddle of Qohelet and Qohelet the Riddler." *JSOT* 37 (2013) 485–509.

Jacobson, Diane. "Wisdom Language in the Psalms." In *The Oxford Handbook of the Psalms*, edited by William P. Brown, 147–57. New York: Oxford University Press, 2014.

Johnston, Robert K. "Confessions of a Workaholic: A Reappraisal of Qoheleth." *CBQ* 38 (1976) 14–28.

Kidner, Derek. *The Wisdom of Proverbs, Job, and Ecclesiastes: An Introduction to Wisdom Literature*. Downers Grove, IL: InterVarsity, 1985.

Klingbeil, G. A. "Wisdom and History." In *Dictionary of the Old Testament Wisdom, Poetry, and Writings*, edited by Tremper Longman III and Peter Enns, 863–76. Downers Grove, IL: InterVarsity, 2008.

Kline, Meredith G. *The Structure of Biblical Authority*. Grand Rapids: Eerdmans, 1972.

Koh, Y. V. *Royal Autobiography in the Book of Qoheleth*. BZAW 369. Berlin: de Gruyter, 2006.

Koch, Klaus. "Gibt es ein Verbeltungsdogma im Alten Testament." *ZTK* 52 (1955) 1–42.

———. "Is There a Doctrine of Retribution in the Old Testament?" In *Theodicy in the Old Testament*, edited by James L. Crenshaw, 42–56. Issures in Religion and Theology. Philadelphia: Fortress, 1983.

Krüger, Thomas. *Qoheleth: A Commentary*. Hermeneia. Edited by Klaus Baltzer. Translated by O. C. Dean Jr. Minneapolis: Fortress, 2004.

Kynes, Will. "The Modern Scholarly Wisdom Tradition and the Threat of Pan-Sapientialism: A Case Report." In *Was There a Wisdom Tradition?: New Prospects in Israelite Wisdom Studies*, edited by Mark R. Sneed, 11–38. AIL 23. Atlanta: SBL Press, 2015.

———. *An Obituary for "Wisdom Literature": The Birth, Death, and Intertextual Reintegration of a Biblical Corpus*. Oxford: Oxford University Press, 2019.

Lauha, Aarre. *Kohelet*. BKAT 19. Neukirchen-Vluyn: Neukirchener Verlag, 1978.

Leahy, Michael. "The Meaning of Ecclesiastes." *ITQ* 19 (1952) 297–300.

Lee, Eunny P. *The Vitality of Enjoyment in Qohelet's Theological Rhetoric*. BZAW 353. Berlin: de Gruyter, 2005.

Levinson, Bernard M. "'Better That You Should Not Vow Than That You Vow and Not Fulfill': Qoheleth's Use of Textual Allusion and the Transformation of Deuteronomy's Law of Vows." In *Reading Ecclesiastes Intertextually*, edited by Katherine Dell and Will Kynes, 28–41. LHBOTS 587. London: T. & T. Clark, 2014.

Lo, Alison. *Job 28 as Rhetoric: An Analysis of Job 28 in the Context of Job 22–31*. VTSup 97. Atlanta: SBL Press, 2003.

Loader, J. A. *Polar Structures in the Book of Qohelet*. BZAW 152. Berlin: de Gruyter, 1979.

Lohfink, Norbert. *Qoheleth*. Translated by Sean McEvenue. Continental Commentaries. Minneapolis: Fortress, 2003.
Longman, Tremper III. *The Book of Ecclesiastes*. NICOT. Grand Rapids: Eerdmans, 1998.
———. *The Fear of the Lord Is Wisdom: A Theological Introduction to Wisdom in Israel*. Grand Rapids: Baker Academic, 2017.
———. *Fictional Akkadian Autobiography*. Winona Lake, IN: Eisenbrauns, 1991.
———. "Inclusio." In *Dictionary of the Old Testament Wisdom, Poetry, and Writings*, edited by Tremper Longman III and Peter Enns, 323–35. Downers Grove, IL: InterVarsity, 2008.
———. *Job*. BCOTWP. Grand Rapids: Baker Academic, 2012.
———. *Proverbs*. BCOTWP. Grand Rapids: Baker Academic, 2006.
Longman, Tremper III, and Peter Enns, eds. *Dictionary of the Old Testament Wisdom, Poetry, and Writings*. Downers Grove, IL: InterVarsity, 2008.
Loretz, Oswald. *Qohelet und der alte Orient: Untersuchungen zu Stil und theologischer Thematik des Buches Qohelet*. Freiburg: Herder, 1964.
Lucas, Ernest C. "The Book of Proverbs: Some Current Issues." In *Interpreting Old Testament Wisdom Literature*, edited by David G. Firth and Lindsay Wilson, 37–59. Downers Grove, IL: InterVarsity, 2017.
———. *Proverbs*. THOTC. Grand Rapids: Eerdmans, 2015.
Luther, Martin. "Notes on Ecclesiastes." In *Luther's Works*, Vol. 15, edited and translated by J. Pelikan and H. C. Oswalt, 3–193. St. Louis: Concordia, 1972.
Matthews, Victor H., and Don C. Benjamin eds. *Old Testament Parallels: Laws and Stories from the Ancient Near East*. 4th ed. New York: Paulist, 2016.
McLaughlin, John L. *An Introduction to Israel's Wisdom Traditions*. Grand Rapids: Eerdmans, 2018.
Meek, Russell L. "The Meaning of הבל in Qohelet: An Intertextual Suggestion." In *The Words of the Wise Are Like Goads: Engaging Qohelet in the 21st Century*, edited by Mark J. Boda et al., 241–56. Winona Lake, IN: Eisenbrauns, 2013.
———. "Twentieth- and Twenty-First Century Readings of *Hebel* (הֶבֶל) in Ecclesiastes." *CBR* 14 (2016) 279–97.
Miller, Douglas B. *Symbol and Rhetoric in Ecclesiastes: The Place of* Hebel *in Qohelet's Work*. Academia Biblica 2. Atlanta: SBL Press, 2002.
Mills, Mary E. *Reading Ecclesiastes: A Literary and Cultural Exegesis*. 2003. Reprint, New York: Routledge, 2016.
Murphy, Roland E. *Ecclesiastes*. WBC 23A. Dallas: Word, 1992.
———. *Proverbs*. WBC 22. Nashville: Nelson, 1998.
———. *The Tree of Life: An Exploration of Biblical Wisdom Literature*. 3rd ed. Grand Rapids: Eerdmans, 2002.
———. "Wisdom—Theses and Hypotheses" In *Israelite Wisdom: Theological and Literary Essays in Honor of Samuel Terrien*, edited by John G. Gammie, 35–42. Missoula, MT: Scholars, 1978.
Najman, Hindy, Jean-Sébastien Rey, and Eibert J. C. Tigchelaar, eds. *Tracing Sapiential Traditions in Ancient Judaism*. JSJSup 174. Leiden: Brill, 2016.
Ogden, Graham S. *Qoheleth*. 2nd ed. Sheffield: Sheffield Phoenix, 2007.
Oswalt, J. N. "God." In *Dictionary of the Old Testament Wisdom, Poetry, and Writings*, edited by Tremper Longman III and Peter Enns, 246–59. Downers Grove, IL: InterVarsity, 2008.

Overland, Paul. "Did the Sage Draw from the Shema? A Study of Proverbs 3:1–12." *CBQ* 62 (2000) 424–40.
Parker, Kim Ian. "Solomon as Philosopher King? The Nexus of Law and Wisdom in 1 Kings 1–11." *JSOT* 53 (1992) 75–91.
Perdue, Leo G. *Wisdom and Creation: The Theology of Wisdom Literature*. Nashville: Abingdon, 1994.
———. *Wisdom Literature: A Theological History*. Louisville: Westminster John Knox, 2007.
Perry, Theodore Anthon. *Dialogues with Kohelet: The Book of Ecclesiastes: Translation and Commentary*. University Park: Pennsylvania State University Press, 1993.
Pritchard, James B., ed. *The Ancient Near East: An Anthology of Texts and Pictures*. Princeton: Princeton University Press, 2011.
Provan, Iain. *Ecclesiastes, Song of Songs*. NIVAC. Grand Rapids: Zondervan, 2001.
Rad, Gerhard von. *Old Testament Theology*. 2 vols. Translated by D. M. G. Stalker. New York: Harper & Row, 1962–65.
———. *Wisdom in Israel*. Translated by James D. Martin. London: SCM, 1972.
Rousseau, François. "Structure de Qohelet 1:4–11 et Plan du Livre." *VT* 31 (1981) 200–17.
Salyer, Gary D. *Vain Rhetoric: Private Insight and Public Debate in Ecclesiastes*. JSOTSup 327. Sheffield: Sheffield Academic, 2001.
Santayana, George. *The Life of Reason: Introduction and Reason in Common Sense*. Crit. ed. Edited by Marianne S. Wokeck and Martin A. Coleman. Introduction by James Gouinlock. Cambridge: MIT Press, 2011.
Sawyer, John F. A. "The Ruined House in Ecclesiastes 12: A Reconstruction of the Original Parable." *JBL* 94 (1975) 519–31.
Schipper, Bernard U., and David Andrew Teeter, eds. *Wisdom and Torah: The Reception of "Torah" in the Wisdom Literature of the Second Temple Period*. JSJSup 163. Leiden: Brill, 2013.
Schoors, Antoon. *Ecclesiastes*. HCOT. Leuven: Peeters, 2013.
Schultz, Richard L. "The Reuse of Deuteronomy's 'Law of the Vow' in Ecclesiastes 5.3–5 [4–6] as an Exemplar of Intertextuality and Reinterpretation in Ecclesiastes 4.17–5.6 [5.1–5.7]." In *Inner-Biblical Allusion in the Poetry of Wisdom and Psalms*, edited by Mark J. Boda et al., 120–32. LHBOTS 659. London: T. & T. Clark, 2018.
———. "Unity or Diversity in Wisdom Theology? A Canonical and Covenantal Perspective." *TynBul* 48 (1997) 271–306.
Schwáb, Zoltán S. *Toward an Interpretation of the Book of Proverbs: Selfishness and Secularity Reconsidered*. JTISup 7. Winona Lake, IN: Eisenbrauns, 2013.
Seitz, Christopher R. "A Canonical Reading of Ecclesiastes." In *Acts of Interpretation: Scripture, Theology, and Culture*, edited by S. A. Cummins and Jens Zimmermann, 100–115. Grand Rapids: Eerdmans, 2018.
———. *The Elder Testament: Canon, Theology, Trinity*. Waco: Baylor University Press, 2018.
Seow, C. L. *Ecclesiastes: A New Translation with Introduction and Commentary*. AB 18C. New York: Doubleday, 1997.
———. *Job 1–21: Interpretation and Commentary*. Illuminations. Grand Rapids: Eerdmans, 2013.
———. "Qohelet's Eschatological Poem." *JBL* 119 (1999) 209–34.
Shead, Andrew G. "Ecclesiastes from the Outside In." *RTR* 55 (1996) 24–37.
———. "Reading Ecclesiastes 'Epilogically.'" *TynBul* 48 (1997) 67–91.

Sheppard, Gerald T. "The Epilogue to Qohelet as Theological Commentary." *CBQ* 39 (1977) 182–89.

———. "The Role of the Canonical Context in the Interpretation of the Solomonic Books." In *Solomon's Divine Arts: Joseph Hall's Representation of Proverbs, Ecclesiastes, and Song of Songs (1609), with Introductory Essays*, edited by Gerald T. Sheppard, 67–107. Cleveland, OH: Pilgrim, 1991.

———. *Wisdom as a Hermeneutical Construct: A Study in the Sapientializing of the Old Testament*. BZAW 151. Berlin: de Gruyter, 1980.

Shields, Martin A. *The End of Wisdom: A Reappraisal of the Historical and Canonical Function of Ecclesiastes*. Winona Lake, IN: Eisenbrauns, 2006.

———. "Qohelet and Royal Autobiography." In *The Words of the Wise Are Like Goads: Engaging Qohelet in the 21st Century*, edited by Mark J. Boda et al., 117–36. Winona Lake, IN: Eisenbrauns, 2013.

———. "Re-examining the Warning of Eccl XII 12." *VT* 50 (2000) 123–27.

———. "Wisdom and Prophecy." In *Dictionary of the Old Testament Wisdom, Poetry, and Writings*, edited by Tremper Longman III and Peter Enns, 876–84. Downers Grove, IL: InterVarsity, 2008.

Sitzler, Jean-Pierre. *Der Tod in Den Weisheitsschriften Des Alten Testaments: Eine Untersuchung Zu Den Büchern Kohelet Und Weisheit*. Arbeiten zu Text und Sprache im Alten Testament 104. Sankt Ottilien: Eos, 2019.

Sneed, Mark R. "הבל as 'Worthless' in Qoheleth: A Critique of Michael V. Fox's 'Absurd' Thesis." *JBL* 136 (2017) 879–94.

———. "'Grasping After the Wind': The Elusive Attempt to Define and Delimit Wisdom." In *Was There a Wisdom Tradition?: New Prospects in Israelite Wisdom Studies*, edited by Mark R. Sneed, 39–67. AIL 23. Atlanta: SBL Press, 2015.

———. "Is the 'Wisdom Tradition' a Tradition?" *CBQ* 73 (2011) 50–71.

———. *The Politics of Pessimism in Ecclesiastes: A Social-Science Perspective*. AIL 12. Atlanta: SBL Press, 2012.

Sneed, Mark R. et al., eds. *Was There a Wisdom Tradition?: New Prospects in Israelite Wisdom Studies*. AIL 23. Atlanta: SBL Press, 2015.

Soulen, Richard N., and R. Kendal Soulen. *Handbook of Biblical Criticism*. 4th ed. Louisville: Westminster John Knox, 2011.

Spears, A. D. "The Theological Hermeneutics of Homiletical Application and Ecclesiastes 7:23–29." PhD diss., University of Liverpool, 2006.

Steinberg, Julius. "The Place of Wisdom Literature in an Old Testament Theology: A Thematic and Structural-Canonical Approach." In *The Shape of the Writings*, edited by Julius Steinberg and Timothy Stone, 147–73. Siphrut 16. Winona Lake, IN: Eisenbrauns, 2015.

Taylor, C. *The Dirge of Coheleth in Ecclesiastes XII: Discussed and Literally Interpreted*. Edinburgh: Williams & Norgate, 1874.

Treier, Daniel J. *Proverbs & Ecclesiastes*. Brazos Theological Commentary on the Bible. Grand Rapids: Brazos, 2011.

Van der Toorn, Karel et al., eds. *Dictionary of Deities and Demons in the Bible*. 2nd ed. Grand Rapids: Eerdmans, 1999.

Van Leeuwen, Raymond. "Wealth and Poverty: System and Contradiction in Proverbs." *HS* 33 (1992) 25–36.

Verheij, Arian. "Paradise Retried: On Qohelet 2:4–6." *JSOT* 50 (1991) 113–15.

Walsh, Carey. "Theological Trace in Qoheleth." *BTB* 42 (2012) 12–17.

Waltke, Bruce K. *The Book of Proverbs: Chapters 1-15*. NICOT. Grand Rapids: Eerdmans, 2004.

———. *The Book of Proverbs: Chapters 15-31*. NICOT. Grand Rapids: Eerdmans, 2005.

Waltke, Bruce K., and David Diewert. "Wisdom Literature." In *The Face of Old Testament Studies: A Survey of Contemporary Approaches*, edited by David W. Baker and Bill T. Arnolds, 295-328. Grand Rapids: Baker, 1999.

Walton, John H., and J. Harvey Walton. *The Lost World of the Torah: Law as Covenant and Wisdom in Ancient Context*. Downers Grove, IL: InterVarsity, 2019.

Walton, Timothy L. *Experimenting with Qohelet: A Text-Linguistic Approach to Reading Qohelet as Discourse*. Amsterdamse Cahiers voor Exegese van de Bijbel en zijn Tradities Supplement 5. Maastricht: Shaker, 2006.

Weeks, Stuart. *Ecclesiastes and Scepticism*. LHBOTS 541. New York: T. & T. Clark, 2012.

———. *Instruction and Imagery in Proverbs 1-9*. Oxford: Oxford University Press, 2007.

———. "Solomon and Qoheleth." In *Megilloth Studies: The Shape of Contemporary Scholarship*, edited by Brad Embry, 80-95. Hebrew Bible Monographs 78. Sheffield: Sheffield Phoenix, 2016.

———. "Wisdom, Form and Genre." In *Was There a Wisdom Tradition? New Prospects in Israelite Wisdom Studies*, edited by Mark R. Sneed, 161-77. AIL 23. Atlanta: SBL Press, 2015.

Weinfeld, Moshe. *Deuteronomy 1-11*. AB 5. New York: Doubleday, 1991.

Whybray, R. N. *Ecclesiastes*. NCBC. Grand Rapids: Eerdmans, 1989.

———. "The Identification and Use of Quotations in Ecclesiastes." In *Congress Volume: Vienna*, edited by J. A. Emerton, 435-51. VTSup 32. Leiden: Brill, 1981.

———. "Qoheleth, Preacher of Joy." *JSOT* 23 (1982) 87-98.

———. "Qoheleth the Immoralist? (Qoh 7:16-17)." In *Israelite Wisdom: Theological and Literary Essays in Honor of Samuel Terrien*, edited by John G. Gammie et al., 191-204. Missoula, MT: Scholars Press for Union Theological Seminary, 1978.

Williams, Ronald J. *Williams' Hebrew Syntax*. 3rd ed. Revised and expanded by John C. Bechman. Toronto: University of Toronto Press, 2007.

Wilson, Gerald H. *The Editing of the Hebrew Psalter*. SBLDS 76. Chico, CA: Scholars, 1985.

———. *Job*. NIBCOT. Peabody, MA: Hendrickson, 2007.

———. "'The Words of the Wise': The Intent and Significance of Qohelet 12:9-14." *JBL* 103 (1984) 175-92.

Wilson, Lindsay. *Job*. THOTC. Grand Rapids; Eerdmans, 2015.

———. *Joseph Wise and Otherwise: The Intersection of Wisdom and Covenant in Genesis 37-50*. Waynesboro, GA: Paternoster, 2004.

Wright, Addison G. "Additional Numerical Patterns in Qoheleth." *CBQ* 45 (1983) 32-43.

———. "The Riddle of the Sphinx Revisited: Numerical Patterns in the Book of Qoheleth." *CBQ* 42 (1980) 38-51.

———. "The Riddle of the Sphinx: The Structure of the Book of Qoheleth." *CBQ* 30 (1968) 313-34.

Wright, G. Ernest. *God Who Acts: Biblical Theology as Recital*. SBT 8. London: SCM, 1952.

Zimmerli, Walther. "The Place and Limit of the Wisdom in the Framework of the Old Testament Theology." *SJT* 17 (1964) 146-58.

Author Index

Antic, Radisa, 67

Baltzer, Klaus, 92
Barbour, Jennie, 21–22, 32, 55, 145–46
Bartholomew, Craig, 18–20, 24, 25,
    28–29, 31–32, 37–38, 43–44,
    48, 52, 55, 59–65, 70, 74–79,
    85–86, 88–94, 100, 102–4,
    108, 110–14, 119–20, 122–23,
    125, 132–34, 142, 144, 147–48,
    150–59, 162
Barton, George, 78
Belcher, Richard, 59
Beldman, David, 20, 28–29, 74, 76–77,
    86, 88–90, 92–93, 95, 104, 114,
    119, 151
Benjamin, Don, 62
Boda, Mark, 81–82, 136, 155–56, 158–
    61, 163–64
Bonaventure, St., 98
Boström, Lennart, 38, 40
Breitkopf, Alexander, 66
Brown, Stephen, 76
Brown, William, 46, 61
Brueggemann, Walter, 39, 61
Bundvad, Mette, 21–23, 32, 55, 67, 99,
    143, 146

Castellino, George, 84
Childs, Brevard, xv, 33–34, 59, 156–57
Christianson, Eric, 13, 24, 27–29, 81–
    85, 89–90, 93–96, 99–101, 103,
    107, 112, 119, 125, 127, 143,
    155–56, 160–61
Clines, David, 39
Collins, John, 61
Craigie, Peter, 50
Crenshaw, James L., 2–5, 29, 31, 39, 47,
    62, 74, 76, 78, 91–92, 99, 102–3,
    109, 114, 119–20, 122–25,
    128–29, 133–35, 138–41, 149,
    154, 159–60, 163

Dahood, Mitchell J., 91
Davis, Ellen, 91
deClaissé-Walford, Nancy, 56
Delitzsch, Franz, 74
Dell, Katharine, 29, 41, 66, 67

Eichrodt, Walther, 61
Enns, Peter, 6, 25, 29, 31, 88, 91, 93, 99,
    103, 109–12, 120, 122, 129, 132–
    34, 138–39, 143, 146, 156, 161
Estes, Daniel, 57, 100, 156

Firth, David, 53–54, 56
Fitschen, Florian, 67
Forti, Tova, 55
Fox, Michael, 6–9, 12–13, 18, 24,
    28–30, 64, 70, 76–81, 85, 88–91,
    93, 97, 99–103, 105, 109–10,
    112, 114, 119–20, 122–24, 126,
    128, 133–35, 138–40, 142–43,
    146–49, 154–57, 159, 161–62

Fredericks, Daniel, 99–101, 156
Fuhr, Richard, 20, 24, 78, 96–97, 99–100, 107, 114, 125, 129–30, 132, 144, 150–51, 153, 163

Galling, Kurt, 78
Ginsburg, Christian, 145
Gordis, Robert, 5, 78, 126, 129, 141–42
Grant, J. A., 5, 52, 58–60, 114–15
Gunkel, Hermann, 29, 37

Hartermann, Viktoria, 132
Hartley, John, 60
Hatton, Peter, 45
Heiser, Michael, 63
Hengel, Martin, 61
Hertzberg, H. W., 78
Hobbins, John, 120
Holmstedt, Robert, 88, 90, 120, 130–31, 136, 155–57

Ibn Ezra, Abraham, 78
Ingram, Doug, 91

Jackson, D. R., 32, 55
Jacobson, Diane, 55
Jacobson, Rolf, 55
Jong, Stephan de, 84
Johnston, Philip, 56
Johnston, Robert, 13–15, 18, 76

Kidner, Derek, 62, 115
Klingbeil, G. A., 53, 55
Kline, Meredith, 53
Koh, Y. V., 28, 85
Koch, Klaus, 37–40, 45–46
Krüger, Thomas, 11–12, 16, 25, 99, 120, 122, 140, 143, 146–48
Kynes, Will, 29, 57, 66

Lauha, Aarre, 76, 128, 140
Leahy, Michael, 145
Lee, Eunny, 15–16, 20, 24, 107–9, 111, 119–20, 122, 127, 130, 132, 134, 140, 143, 146, 150–51, 153, 162–63
Levinson, Bernard, 52, 112
Levy, Ludwig, 78

Lo, Alison, 60
Loader, J. A., 12, 18, 61, 75, 78, 119–20, 122, 146, 152
Lohfink, Norbert, 16–20, 32, 75, 91, 100, 114, 119–20, 122–24, 128, 140–41, 146, 159, 161, 163
Longman, Tremper III, 2–3, 5, 25, 27–29, 31–32, 35, 44, 48–50, 54–55, 58–59, 62–63, 65–66, 69, 77, 79, 85, 88–89, 92–94, 97, 99, 102–3, 109, 111–14, 119–20, 122, 124–26, 128–29, 132–34, 138–43, 146, 148–49, 155–59, 161
Loretz, Oswald, 76, 145
Lucas, Ernest, 37, 42, 59
Luther, Martin, 98

Matthews, Victor, 62
McLaughlin, John, 31, 53, 62–64
McNeile, Alan, 78
Meek, Russell, 67, 99, 100, 108
Michel, Diethelm, 78
Miller, Douglas, 78, 84–85, 99–100, 119, 139
Murphy, Roland E., 5, 8, 31, 34, 37, 40–41, 48, 56, 62–64, 74, 76, 78, 89–92, 98, 102, 107, 109–10, 114, 119–20, 122, 127, 133–34, 138–39, 141, 143, 146, 154–56, 158–59, 161–62, 164

O'Dowd, Ryan, 38, 43–44, 52, 59–60, 62–65, 70
Ogden, Graham, 5, 10–11, 28, 88, 91, 93, 100, 104, 107, 111, 113–14, 119–20, 122–23, 125, 131–32, 135, 139–42, 148, 159, 161
Oswalt, J. N., 51
Overland, Paul, 52

Perdue, Leo G., 146
Perry, Theodore, 76, 78
Podechard, Emmanuel, 78
Pritchard, James B., 62
Provan, Iain, 29, 32, 44, 100, 111–14, 119–20, 127, 131, 133–34, 138, 146

Rousseau, François, 75

Salyer, Gary, 74, 76, 79, 81, 84, 90, 93, 99
Santayana, George, 160
Sawyer, John, 145, 148
Schoors, Antoon, 126, 142
Schultz, Richard, 32, 38, 44–45, 48–52, 59, 61, 67–68, 70, 112
Schwáb, Zoltán, 70
Seitz, Christopher, 32, 55, 57, 67, 83
Seow, C. L., 14–15, 25, 28, 31–32, 55, 76, 79, 88–94, 98, 100–102, 114, 119–20, 122–24, 126–29, 132–34, 138, 140–42, 146, 148, 154–56, 159, 161, 163
Shead, Andrew, 137, 162
Sheppard, Gerald T., 34–36, 161
Shields, Martin, 6–7, 28–29, 39–40, 85, 91–93, 99, 101–3, 112, 114, 119, 122, 129, 133, 135, 139–40, 143, 155–60
Siegfried, Carl, 78
Sitzler, Jean-Pierre, 147
Sneed, Mark, 29, 54–55, 99
Soulen, R. Kendall, xv
Soulen, Richard N., xv
Spears, A. D., 89–93
Steinberg, Julius, 36

Taylor, C., 147
Toorn, Karel van der, 63
Treier, Daniel, 119, 142

Van Leeuwen, Raymond, 38, 42–43
Verheij, Arian, 67

Waltke, Bruce, 31, 35, 56, 58–59, 63–65
Walton, J. Harvey, 50
Walton, John H., 50
Walton, Timothy, 75, 90
Weeks, Stuart, 12–13, 28–29
Weinfeld, Moshe, 50
Whybray, R. N., 5, 9–11, 13, 15, 19, 40, 78, 93, 98, 105–8, 111–12, 120, 122–23, 126–27, 129–30, 133–35, 139, 141–43, 146, 148, 154, 161–62
Williams, Ronald J., 129
Wilson, Gerald H., 31–36, 49–52, 56, 155, 159, 162
Wilson, Lindsay, 54
Wright, Addison G., 14, 74–76, 88–89, 140
Wright, G. Ernest, 47

Zimmerli, Walther, 37, 47, 65–66

Scripture Index

OLD TESTAMENT

Genesis
1–11	66–67
1–4	68
1–2	67n172
1	57n133
2	19
2:7	141
2:17	67
3:19	67, 141
4	67, 99

Exodus
1:10	54
1:17	54
20:12–17	49
20:16	49n100
23:1–3	49n102
23:1	49n100
23:8	49n99
23:16	47
34:26	47

Leviticus
2:14	47
19:35–36	49n98
27:2–29	47

Numbers
15:39	126
18:12	47
30:3	47

Deuteronomy
1:1–5	50
1:9—3:27	50
1:16–17	49n102
4–26	50
4:1	51
4:2	159n205
4:6	50, 52
4:19	56
4:29–31	56
4:31	56
4:32	56
4:40	51
5:16	49
5:20	49n100
5:28–29	51
5:32–33	50
6:1–2	51
6:2	51, 59
6:4–9	52
6:4	157n198
6:6–9	51
6:10–11	19, 108
8:1–2	51
8:2–6	52
8:5	56
8:6	51
8:18	142
10:12–13	58–59
10:14	56

Deuteronomy (continued)

10:17	49n99, 56
11:13–17	56
11:18–19	51n109
11:26–28	49
13:5	51
15:7–11	49n103
16:18–20	49n99
17:19	51
19:14	49n97
19:15–21	49n100
21:18	49n101
21:21	49n101
22:4–11	56
22:13–19	49n100
23:10–14	56
23:14	56
23:22–24	48, 52, 112n194
24:11–12	49n103
25:13–16	49n98
26:1–11	47
27–28	50
27:16	49n101
27:17	49n97
27:19	49n103
27:25	49n99, 49n102
29:4	56
29:26	56
30:9	19, 108
30:15–18	49
30:19–20	50
32:35	56
32:40–41	56
34:9	54

1 Samuel

12:24	112n195
25	54

2 Samuel

13:3	54, 110
13:13	54
20:14–22	55
20:16	54
20:19	55

1 Kings

2–13	57n133
3–11	55
3:9	113n195
8	32n18
10	63n153

Esther

8:3	136

Job

1:1	35n30, 60, 69, 136
1:5	47, 69
1:8	35n30, 60, 69, 136
1:9	69
1:22	69
2:3	35n30, 60, 69, 136
2:9	69
2:10	69
3:16	122n15
4:17	51n109
6:10	50n109
28	51, 60, 66, 69, 90
28:1–11	69
28:12	60, 69
28:13	69
28:14	69
28:19	60
28:21	69
28:22	69
28:28	51, 60, 69, 136
31:16–23	56
32:22	51n109
33:17	136
33:28	122n15
33:30	122n15
35:10	51n109, 142n122
36:3	51n109
37:2	35n32
38–41	66, 69
42:8	47

Psalms

1	55, 56n128
19	57n133
37	55

39	55	3:11–13	52
49	55	3:11–12	56, 158
56:14	122n15	3:18	66
73	55	3:19–20	56, 66
73:16–17	113n195	3:30	49
104	57n133	3:32	56
112	55	3:33–35	49
119	55	4:1	49, 51, 124
149:2	142n122	4:4	51
		4:5	40, 88

Proverbs

		4:6	40
1–9	35n30, 49n106, 51, 59, 60n143, 68, 70, 91n93	4:10–19	49
		4:10	49
1:1–7	68	4:20	113n195
1:1	31	4:27	136
1:2–7	33	5:1–6	91n93
1:2	35	5:1	51, 113n195, 124
1:3	34, 35	5:1–23	49
1:4	35	5:15–18	140
1:5	35	5:20	91n93
1:6	31n14, 33, 34, 35	5:21–22	56
1:7	34, 35, 52, 58, 59, 68, 112n195	5:21	56
		6:1	51
1:8	49, 51, 124	6:6	66
1:10–12	49	6:16–19	56
1:13–14	49	6:17	49
1:29	58n134	6:18	49
2:1–8	52	6:19	49
2:1	51, 124	6:20–35	49
2:2	113n195	6:20–23	51
2:4	88	6:20	51, 124, 125n31
2:5	58n134	6:23–24	158
2:9	48	6:23	51
2:14	40	6:24–35	91n93
2:16–19	49, 91n93	7:1–27	49
2:16–17	48	7:1–3	51
2:20–22	50	7:1–2	51
3:1–12	52	7:1	51, 124
3:1–2	51	7:5–27	91n93
3:1	51, 124	7:5	40
3:3	48	7:6	40
3:5–7	52	7:14	47
3:5	70	8	39n51
3:7–10	40	8:8	48
3:7–8	112n195	8:13	48, 58n134
3:7	58n135, 137	8:20	48
3:9–10	47, 56	8:22–31	66
		8:25	88

Proverbs (continued)

8:32–36	49
9:1–6	125n31
9:8–9	158
9:9	48
9:10	48, 50n109, 52, 58n134, 59
9:13–18	91n93, 92
9:17	40
10–29	40
10–15	50n106
10–12	45
10:1	31, 49
10:2	40
10:12	40
10:18	49
10:21	48
10:23	48
10:27	58n134
11	45
11:1	49, 56
11:8	40
11:14	35n32
11:16	42, 43
11:20	56
11:30	66
12:1	158
12:5	35n32
12:7	49
12:17	49n100
12:19	49
13:1	49, 158
13:12	66
13:19	137
13:23	42, 43
13:25	42
14:2	58n135
14:5	49n100
14:9	47
14:12	42
14:16	137
14:20–21	49n103
14:21	56
14:22	48
14:25	49n100
14:26	58n134
14:27	58n134
14:31	49n103, 51n109, 56, 66
15:3	56
15:4	66
15:5	49n101
15:8	56
15:9	56
15:10	158
15:16–17	43
15:16	44, 58n134
15:25	49n103
15:27	49n99
15:29	56
15:31	113n195
15:33	58n134
16:1–9	56
16:6	48, 58n134, 137
16:8	42, 43
16:11	49n98
16:16	42, 43
16:17	137
16:19	43
16:33	56
17:1	43
17:5	49n103, 51n109, 66
17:8	49n99
17:10	158
17:15	49n102, 56
17:23	49n99
17:26	49n102
18:5	49n102
18:15	113n195
19:1	44
19:5	49n100
19:6	49n99
19:9	49n100
19:10	42, 43
19:17	49n103
19:21	42, 56
19:23	58n134
19:26	49n101
19:28	49n100
20:10	49n98
20:12	66
20:18	35n32
20:20	42, 49n101
20:23	49n97
20:24	56
20:28	48

21:13	43n69, 49n103, 113n195
21:14	49n99
21:30	42
22:2	51n109, 66
22:4	58n134
22:7	49n103
22:9	49n103
22:14	91n93
22:16	43n69, 49n103
22:17–24:22	63
22:17–18	64
22:17	31, 33, 113n195
22:19	64, 65
22:21	64
22:28	49n97
22:20	63
23:10–11	49n103
23:10	49n97
23:12	113n195
23:17–18	43n69
23:17	58n134
23:24	48
23:27–28	91n93
24:6	35n32
24:20	43n69
24:21–22	65
24:21	58n135
24:23–25	49n102
24:23	31
25:1	31
25:12	113n195
26:4–5	42
26:7	158
26:9	158
26:27	42
27:1	42
27:6	158
28:6	43
28:9	49, 112n195
28:13	56
28:15–16	43
28:20	43n69
28:24	49n101
29:13	56, 66
29:18	49
30:1	31
30:3	50n109
30:14	43
31	60n143
31:1–2	125n31
31:1	31
31:10–31	125n31
31:26	125n31
31:30	58n135, 59

Ecclesiastes

1:1—6:9	89n86
1:1–11	86, 154
1:1	26, 27, 31, 32, 84n64
1:2—12:14	80
1:2–11	27
1:2	3, 6n37, 26, 27, 32, 84n64, 89, 93n96, 97, 98n113, 99, 101, 103, 104, 119, 123, 164
1:3—12:7	27
1:3—4:16	84n64
1:3–11	27
1:3	10, 11, 12, 28n6, 97n111, 107, 111
1:4—4:16	84
1:4–11	17, 22, 69n180
1:9	97n111
1:10	83n59
1:12—12:7	27, 28n5, 29, 33, 93n96, 110n192
1:12—6:9	75
1:12—3:15	17
1:12—2:26	10n59, 106n159
1:12—2:20	22
1:12–18	86, 88
1:12–13	81–82
1:12	26, 27, 28, 31, 32, 80, 85, 88, 102
1:13—6:9	85
1:13	23, 26, 67, 80, 81, 82n51, 88, 89, 90, 102, 134n81, 144, 159
1:14	26, 75, 81, 88, 89, 94, 97n111, 98n113, 102, 123
1:15	88, 95, 102, 111
1:16–17	88
1:16	32, 88, 144

Ecclesiastes (continued)

1:17	75, 88n82, 89, 90, 94, 97n111, 102
1:18	88, 133
2	21
2:1	15n107, 82n51, 83n59, 86, 89n88, 98n113, 101, 104n152, 105, 107, 111, 130
2:2	104n152, 105
2:3	82n51, 97n111, 111
2:4–6	32
2:4	83
2:7–8	32
2:9	26, 32
2:10	97n111, 104
2:11	67, 75, 82n51, 88, 94, 97n111, 98n113, 101, 123n24
2:12	82n51
2:13	97n111
2:15–16	77, 148
2:15	97n111, 98n113
2:17–20	83
2:17	10n59, 75, 88, 94, 97n111, 98n113, 101, 122, 123n24, 134n81
2:18	26, 67, 97n111, 122
2:19	97n111, 98n113
2:20	82n51, 97n111, 122
2:21	97n111, 98n113, 134n81
2:22	97n111
2:23	98n113, 133
2:24–26	10n59, 105, 125, 127
2:24–25	107, 111
2:24	9n57, 15n107, 67, 97n111, 104, 105, 107, 129
2:26	48, 75, 88, 92n93, 97n111, 98n113, 104n152
3:1–15	10n59, 106n159
3:1–8	111
3:1	97n111, 104n152
3:2	148
3:9–15	159
3:9	97n111, 111
3:10–11	111
3:11	66, 110, 111, 141, 143n135
3:12–13	107, 111, 125, 127
3:12	9n57, 15n107, 104n152, 105, 106, 107, 111
3:13	6, 97n111, 104, 105, 111, 129
3:14–15	143n135
3:14	111, 114, 141
3:16—6:10	17
3:16–22	10n59, 106n159
3:16–17	114, 130n65
3:16	97n111
3:17–18	128
3:17	4n24, 48, 104n152, 114, 130n65
3:19–21	148
3:19	98n113, 101, 123n24
3:20	67, 141
3:21	123
3:22	9n57, 104, 105, 106, 107, 125
4:1–3	56
4:1	26, 82n51, 97n111
4:2–3	148
4:2	77
4:3	77, 97n111, 122, 134n81
4:4–6	75
4:4	88, 94, 97n111, 98n113
4:6	88n82, 97n111
4:7	82n51, 97n111, 98n113
4:8	97n111, 98n113, 134n81
4:9	97n111
4:13–16	21, 22
4:15	97n111
4:16	88, 94, 97n111, 98n113, 104n152
4:17—12:12	84
4:17—5:8	84n64
4:17—5:6	17, 21, 47, 52, 87n79, 111, 114, 115

SCRIPTURE INDEX

4:17	83, 84, 87n79, 111, 112n194, 112n195, 115, 130n65, 134n81	6:11—9:6	17
		6:11	97n111, 98n113
		6:12	95, 97n111, 98n113, 103
5:1	97n111, 111, 112n195	7	89
5:3–5	112n194	7:1—8:17	75
5:3	104n152, 111	7:1–13	127
5:5	48, 111, 112n194, 115, 128, 130n65	7:2–4	105, 130
		7:2	6, 133
5:6	98n113, 112, 114, 115	7:3	133
5:7–8	56	7:4	104n152, 133
5:7	104n152	7:5	158
5:8	97n111	7:6	98n113
5:9—6:9	84n64	7:9	133, 134
5:9–19	10n59, 106n159	7:11	97n111, 122n15
5:9	98n113	7:12–14	113
5:12–16	21	7:12	97n111
5:12	134n81	7:13–14	103, 111, 141
5:13	97n111, 134n81	7:13	95, 113, 143n135
5:14	97n111, 148	7:14	15n107, 95, 107, 113, 125, 134n81
5:15	97n111, 134n81		
5:16	122, 133	7:15–17	113, 148
5:17–19	125	7:15	26, 98n113, 113, 115, 131, 134n81, 135
5:17–18	130		
5:17	9n57, 66, 97n111, 104, 105, 110, 141	7:16–17	77
		7:16	97n111, 113
5:18–20	107	7:17	113
5:18–19	129	7:18	113, 115
5:18	6, 97n111, 104, 105, 111, 127	7:20	67, 91n93, 97n111, 113, 114
5:19	104n152, 127n50	7:23–29	19n128, 84n64, 85, 86, 89–94, 103, 152, 159
6:1–6	21		
6:1	97n111, 134n81		
6:2	98n113, 101, 134n81	7:23–24	90, 91n93, 144
6:3–6	148	7:23	89, 90
6:3	77	7:24	90
6:4	98n113	7:25	48, 82n51, 89, 90, 91n93, 93, 94, 102, 159
6:5	122n15		
6:7	97n111, 127n50		
6:8	97n111	7:26	48, 90, 91n93, 92n95, 110, 144
6:9	75, 88, 89n86, 94, 97n111, 98n113, 127		
		7:27–29	92
6:10—12:14	89n86	7:27	26, 27, 32, 86, 92, 93, 94
6:10—12:7	85		
6:10—11:6	75	7:28	92, 94
6:10—7:22	84n64	7:29	66, 67, 91n93, 92, 93, 94, 110, 144
6:10–12	75		
6:10	89n86	8:1–8	84n64

Ecclesiastes (continued)

8:3	104n152, 134n81
8:5	134n81
8:6	104n152, 134n81
8:9—9:12	84n64
8:9	97n111, 134n81
8:10-15	10n59, 106n159
8:10-13	115
8:10-11	113
8:10	26, 48, 98n113, 114, 148
8:11-12	135
8:11	134n81
8:12-13	4n24, 113, 114, 115, 128, 130n65
8:12	48, 115, 134n81
8:14	77, 97n111, 98n113, 101, 114, 131
8:15	9n57, 97n111, 104n152, 105, 107, 110, 141
8:16-17	95, 103, 114
8:16	97n111
8:17	97n111, 111, 131, 143n135, 159
8:33-34	142
9:1—11:6	75
9:1-10	10n59, 106n159
9:1	26
9:2	48
9:3-6	148
9:3	97n111, 134n81
9:4	77, 122
9:6	97n111
9:7—12:8	120n9
9:7—12:7	17
9:7-10	105, 107, 108, 127, 151
9:7-9	9n57, 120n9, 125
9:7	104, 120, 127, 129
9:9	15n107, 97n111, 98n113, 104, 107, 110, 123, 127, 130, 141
9:10-12	148
9:10	127
9:11-12	148
9:11-18	21
9:11	82n51, 97n111
9:12	134n81
9:13—12:7	84n64
9:13-15	22
9:13	97n111
9:17-10:20	127
9:17	33
10:5	97n111, 134n81
10:7	26
10:10	97n111
10:11	97n111
10:13	134n81
10:14	123
10:15	97n111
10:16-17	127
10:17	130
10:19	104n152
11:1-6	120n8, 126, 127
11:1	120
11:2	97n111, 134n81
11:5	66, 103, 110, 111, 141, 143n135, 159
11:7—12:8	120n9
11:7—12:7	xv, xvi, 10n59, 79, 86, 95, 106n159, 107, 116, 117, 119-49, 152, 153, 162, 166-68
11:7—12:1	9n57
11:7-8	120-24, 138n97
11:7	19, 24, 108, 120-24, 151, 152n180, 153
11:8—12:7	19n133, 108
11:8	98n113, 104n152, 120-25, 149, 152n180
11:9—12:7	120
11:9—12:1	83-84, 106, 121-45, 148n167, 149, 159-60
11:9-10	120
11:9	4n24, 15, 23n157, 48, 86, 95, 104n152, 105, 107, 115, 120, 124-32, 137-39, 149, 159, 162-63, 165
11:10	98n113, 101, 115, 133-40, 144-45, 162-63
12:1-7	21, 22, 69n180, 120, 138-45

12:1	10n61, 20n134, 51n109, 66, 104n152, 111, 114, 115, 120, 122, 125, 138–45, 148, 150–51, 153, 162
12:2–5	147n159
12:2	120, 145–46
12:3–4	146n147
12:5	123n23, 132, 146n147
12:6	120, 145
12:7	28, 66, 67, 111, 119, 120, 141, 143, 147
12:8–14	27, 68, 84n64, 86, 154–66
12:8	3, 6n37, 26, 27, 32, 84n64, 93n96, 97, 98n113, 101, 103, 104, 119, 123, 152n180, 155n182, 164
12:9–14	35n30, 154–66
12:9–11	154n181, 159n207
12:9–10	33, 34, 158, 165
12:9	26, 32, 35, 97n111, 155–56, 158
12:10	27, 32, 35, 104n152, 156–58
12:11	33, 34, 35, 57n133, 157–59, 164, 165
12:12–14	154n181, 159n207
12:12	33, 35, 51, 87n78, 97n111, 159–60, 162, 164, 165
12:13–14	7n40, 18n123, 20n134, 34n30, 51, 111, 115n203, 116, 128, 137, 144, 154n181, 160–66
12:13	34, 35, 60, 159n205, 160–66
12:14	34, 35, 132n71, 134n81, 160–66

Isaiah

1	56
1:4–6	56
1:16–17	56
1:16	136
5:21	53n121
17:10	142
19:11	53n121
22:13	124
29:13–14	54n121
31:2	54n121
33:5–6	54n121
42:5	56
44:24–25	53n121
45:1–13	56
48:1	142
54:5	142n122
56:7	56
63:7	56

Jeremiah

7	56
8:8–9	53n121
9:23	54n121
16:17	56
32:35	56
49:7	53n121
50:35	53n121
51:50	142

Ezekiel

45:9	136

Obadiah

8	53n121

Nahum

1:2	56

Haggai

1:10–11	56

Malachi

3	56

NEW TESTAMENT

Revelation

22:18–19	159n205

www.ingramcontent.com/pod-product-compliance
Lightning Source LLC
Chambersburg PA
CBHW070328230426
43663CB00011B/2248